CAMBRIAN WAY

The Mountain Co[illegible] Walk

A PR[illegible] BOOK

CONTENTS

ISBN 0 9509580 4 2

Whilst every care has been taken to ensure the accuracy of the information provided, the author does not accept any responsibility for errors or omissions. Reports would be welcome from readers who walk the Cambrian Way as to where they have stayed or camped and of any difficulties encountered. Write to 2 Beech Lodge, 67 The Park, Cheltenham, GL50 2RX. Tel/Fax 01242 232131.

PREFACE TO THE FIFTH EDITION

Yet again I have failed to get a new edition ready before the previous edition has run out. This unfortunately meant that many would be Cambrian Way walkers were frustrated in 1999 but will hopefully sally forth with this new edition in 2000. The Cambrian Way is clearly catching on as *the* mountain walk but just how many walk it is very difficult to gauge. 5300 copies of the book were sold between 1984 and 1999, but this gives little indication of actual usage.

Cambrian Way continues to be just a walk in a book, with no official recognition. Wales Tourist Board has, however, realised its potential and gave it a good boost with the help of Janet Street-Porter's TV series in autumn 1998, but alas the Countryside Council for Wales disapproved and told the board not to promote it any more. It was considered too dangerous for inexperienced walkers who might be attracted by tourist promotional material. Before promotion the CCW would require assurances from the local authorities concerned that the route was safe, that there were no serious conflicts between landowners and users (none are known of) and that the authorities would maintain those parts that were public rights of way to a standard consistent with its use. We live, it seems, in a nanny state, where authorities are fearful of litigation. How does one define what is safe? Thank goodness there is still some scope for adventure at one's own risk.

The most significant change affecting navigation on the Cambrian Way is the introduction by the Ordnance Survey of the Explorer series of maps at 1:25,000 scale to replace the Pathfinder series. Using the same conventions and sheet size as the Outdoor Leisure maps the whole route is now on 11 maps (2 only marginally) at the ideal scale for navigation.

Shortly before this edition goes to press the Queen's Speech in November 1999 announced the promised legislation to give the public a right of access, with several safeguards, to open country, This will undoubtedly make access legal to many parts of the Welsh hills but is not likely to have a dramatic effect on the Cambrian Way. It will, however, legalise some of the de facto access sections that have been used without let or hindrance for many years.

Keeping the accommodation section as up to date as possible has continued to be a major time consumer. I have stayed at well over half the bed and breakfast houses at some time or other and found some real gems amongst the providers. Sadly five Youth Hostels have closed since the last edition, mainly due to higher standards required and lack of bednights, but an excellent hostel was opened at Conwy.

As the acting, unpaid, self appointed warden of the Cambrian Way your author has secured some modest improvements to the route. In particular after years of pressure Ceredigion Council made a splendid job of raising the path alongside the stream at Strata Florida so that it is no longer necessary to wade through. A landslide and toxic mine water in the Rheidol valley has necessitated a longer though attractive alternative between Pontbren Plwca and Ystumtuen. Whilst vast sums, in path terms, are being spent in Central Wales on Glyndwr's Way as a future national trail, Cambrian Way is already in being, costs the authorities virtually nothing, brings considerable income to the Welsh tourist economy and is without doubt a more scenic and stimulating walk.

The author is increasingly conscious of anno domini and the need for others to take on inspection of the route and update of the acccommodation list. Offers of assistance are invited.

Tony Drake December 1999

THE MOUNTAIN CONNOISSEUR'S WALK

The Cambrian Way is a mountain walking route from Cardiff to Conwy traversing much of the highest, wildest and most scenically beautiful parts of Wales. It was originally conceived as a long distance path to be created under the National Parks & Access to the Countryside Act 1949, but following much opposition the Countryside Commission abandoned the scheme for its creation in 1982. The Way described in this guidebook is basically the route originally proposed by the Cambrian Way Committee in 1971, with some modifications to make greater use of existing public rights of way. Where the public does not have a legal or permissive right to go the Way is across mountain and moorland on routes where there has been de facto access for many years.

The Cambrian Way is designed for the connoisseur of mountain walking. It is not intended to appeal to the "beeliner" and those of the John o' Groats to Land's End by road mentality. It is for those who like to follow a well tried route, where the quality of the scenery has been the first consideration in planning. The Cambrian Way should be walked only for the pleasure and achievement it brings to the individual. It is not for the masochists who need to be spurred on by sponsorship.

At 275 miles (440Km) the length of the Cambrian Way is 25 miles more than the Pennine Way. A possible schedule using seven Youth Hostels would be 284 miles. The ascent involved is 61,540 feet (18,742 metres) which is nearly double that of the Pennine Way. This greater ascent must be very seriously taken into account not only as to the length of time required, but also as to whether the Way should be attempted at all, especially if backpacking. With the average time taken for the Pennine Way being about nineteen days, the Cambrian Way is likely to need at least three days more. It is much more of a mountaineering expedition than the Pennine Way and is more of a high level route than the West Highland Way. 64% of the route is at over 800 feet (240 metres) above sea level. 20% is over 2,000 feet (610m) and 2% is over 3,000 feet (915m).

A Countryside Commission survey identified two factors above all others as to why people walked the Pennine Way. These were the scenery and the challenge. The Cambrian Way has both scenery and challenge in abundance.

Almost all of Wales can be said to be attractive but those parts designated as national parks have been selected because they are extensive tracts of country where their natural beauty calls for preservation and enhancement for the purpose of promoting their enjoyment by the public. 60% of the Cambrian Way is through the national parks of Snowdonia and the Brecon Beacons. A further 20% in central Wales is through what the Countryside Commission considered worthy of national park status but which the Secretary of State for Wales rejected as such in 1973. Even the remaining 20% is mostly through pleasant rolling country. Little industrialisation is seen and only one motorway is crossed. The biggest eyesore is probably Trawsfynydd nuclear power station.

The challenge is to find the physical and mental stamina to walk the continuous route. The Cambrian Way should not be the first long distance walk to be undertaken. Shorter, less arduous, ways should be tried first. Additional attributes are required on the Cambrian Way. Wind and rain at higher altitudes can be quite destructive and demoralising. Waterproof clothing is absolutely essential and walkers should be warned of the really lethal effect of hypothermia. caused by the combination of a wet body and the cold conditions frequently experienced in mountains. Although much of the Way is on popular routes, most of it is unfrequented and where the way is undefined on the ground and is unwaymarked. The additional height means that much of the time will be in cloud where navigation is bound to be difficult. Ability to use a compass is essential but more important is being able to read maps and particularly to interpret contours. The maps in this guidebook are designed so that they provide complete navigation requirements together with the 1:25,000 and/or 1:50,000 maps of the Ordnance Survey. The size of the guide is just less than the folded size of the Ordnance Survey maps to facilitate either carrying in a long hip pocket or mounted in the open position, back to back with two side by side segments of the OS. map in a map case or transparent plastic bag .

The routes described are not the result of just walking over the ground once and writing it up. Much surveying of possible routes was carried out by members of the Cambrian Way Committee, and the author must have spent several hundred days in surveys. The legal status of the route traversed has been carefully checked and visits have been made to all the county councils involved to view public path definitive maps, road records and commons registers. A few obstruction problems have been reported to the highway authorities. The original proposals assumed that some new rights of way would be created following approval of the route by the Secretary of State for Wales. Surprisingly the greater use of rights of way has only resulted in an increase of six miles (2%) over the length proposed in 1971. As will be seen in the analysis on a later page, 87½% of the Way is where the public either has a right to go or where there is permissive use. 10% is over rural commons and the remaining 2½% is over mountain, moorland and paths where de facto access has been enjoyed for many years.

It must be stressed that there is no official recognition to the Cambrian Way, either by the Countryside Council for Wales (successors to the Countryside Commission) or any of the authorities. Whilst the Commission strongly supported the project until 1978, most of the county and district councils along the route and the two national park authorities were opposed to the concept. The farming unions were vociferous in their opposition. Hopefully the use of the Way resulting from this guide will prove that the opposition was unjustified and that it will become accepted as has Wainwright's popular Coast to Coast walk across northern England, though without some of the problems caused by lack of adequate research into rights of way and access land status, and failure to update, that characterised that particular walk.

Most of the well known summits of Wales are included, with Snowdon the highest point in England and Wales as a fitting climax. Some lesser known summits are visited but some of the well known ones are omitted. Notable amongst these are the Arans, not omitted because of the access problems that arose there but because a route over the Arans does not fit in conveniently with the more interesting traverse of Cader Idris and the Rhinogs. The route is not always on the tops and sometimes deliberately follows a valley where the valley is particularly attractive. Thus the wild Doethie valley is followed for several miles and descent is made at Devil's Bridge to the gorge of the Rheiddol. Wales has many attractive woodlands of traditional hardwoods and several of these are visited.

Planning overnight accommodation is the biggest headache for most who walk long distance paths. The backpacker has fewer problems but must still find a site where his or her night's stay will not cause offence. Those prepared to hostel will find the Youth Hostel chain is already more complete than it was on the Pennine Way when that path was opened, even though several have closed since the Cambrian Way project was mooted. Those wanting a little more luxury will find the bed and breakfast houses provide the traditonal Welsh "welcome in the hillside" and that there is an adequate selection in the comprehensive list in this guide

THE HISTORY OF THE CAMBRIAN WAY

My first involvement in long distance path planning was in the early 1950s when the Ramblers Association in Gloucestershire did the initial planning for the Cotswold Way. About the same time I was involved in negotiations for amendments to the designated route for the Offa's Dyke path in the Wye Valley. Between 1957 and 1960 I was involved in the planning of a serial walk along the Dyke path for the three Gloucestershire rambling clubs. These were very popular and when it was over the cry was "What can we do next? " I did some preliminary planning for a route from Gloucester to Snowdon via the Black Mountains, Brecon Beacons and Plynlimon. The enormous attraction of this mostly mountain route was apparent, but the Gloucestershire ramblers did not take it up. It was not until 1967 that it occurred to me to wonder why no one had proposed a long distance route over the principal mountains of Wales. Soundings in the Ramblers Association and the Youth Hostels Association circles in Wales brought an immediate and enthusiastic response. Both the RA and YHA passed motions at their respective national council meetings in March 1968 calling for the creation of a Cambrian Way Long Distance Footpath.

The Cambrian Way Committee . Roger Brickell, the South Wales R.A. secretary at that time, convened a meeting at Kington Youth Hostel on June 23rd 1968, at which a Cambrian Way Committee was formed with myself as chairman and Roger as secretary. A predominantly high level mountain route was to be surveyed and various organisations undertook sections by counties. The south part was divided between the R.A., Y.H.A., the Brecon Beacons Voluntary Wardens Association and Pontypool Group of the R.A. In the north the British Mountaineering Council was to be offered the Caernarvonshire section but turned out to be hostile to the whole concept . Subsequently the R.A. and Y.H.A., based on Liverpool, joined forces, led by Bill Hall and Brian Steventon respectively, and surveyed all the northern half.

The survey methods varied considerably. In the south some of the committee, notably Bob Rowson and Keith Mascetti were already knowledgeable of their area. Denis Veasey, David Robinson and Don Sutor made surveys in the lesser known Elenydd and concluded that the western side of that wild area had fewer forestry problems. The Liverpool ramblers and hostellers had different methods and descended on their allotted area by coach and dispersed into several survey groups. Although I had visited much of Wales, particularly on meets of the Gloucestershire Mountaineering Club, my roving commission on all sections took me to many delightful parts of Wales I might never have gone to.

My first proposal was for a route from Capel-y-ffin to Snowdon but this soon got extended in both directions. Capel-y-ffin was clearly no equivalent of Edale on the Pennine Way but proposals to start a little further south at Abergavenny did not satisfy the South Wales members of the committee, who devised a route from Cardiff skirting the coalfield. At the north end the natural extension was to the North Wales coast and soon the attraction of the long ridge of the Carneddau and the idea of a castle to castle route clinched Conwy as the northern terminus.

At the subsequent three meetings of the committee the difficulty of arriving at a consensus view increased and there was a temptation to suggest alternatives because of disagreement. However, certain alternatives were agreed upon for safety reasons, such as a lower level alternative to the Rhinog ridgeline, and the Pyg Track or Crib Goch on Snowdon .

One alternative never properly resolved was whether to go north from Plynlimon to Cader Idris via Machynlleth or the longer way via Dylife, Dinas Mawddwy and Maesglase. (See later in the guide for the main arguments.) There was considerable discussion over the Black Mountains, partly as to whether to include them, and, if so, where to cross over to the Brecon Beacons. I never liked the variation proposed via Mynydd Llangorse and Talybont, because it omitted the very fine Pen Allt Mawr ridge, and the Llangattock cave area. The Brecon Park wardens advocated use of the Brecon and Usk canal towpath from Llangattock and Talybont but I could never see keen mountain walkers wanting to walk nine miles of towpath, however attractive.

The 1971 Proposals. On July 10th 1971, after the ceremony at Knighton declaring the Offa's Dyke Path officially open, I handed John Cripps, chairman of the Countryside Commission, a set of maps giving the Cambrian Way Committee's proposed route for Cambrian Way. In November that year I produced what I called the **Interim Report** and this lamentably was the only information on the Cambrian Way that I found time to produce until the first edition of this guidebook in 1984. Many hundreds of a scruffy 34 page duplicated report were sold to would be walkers until most of the stencils wore out.

The Countryside Commission had the responsibility for making recommendations to the Secretaries of State for the Environment or for Wales for the creation of long distance paths, under provisions of the National Parks & Access to the Countryside Act 1949.(Since 1991 these duties have been taken over by the **Countryside Council for Wales)** Routes approved by the Secretary of State become the responsibility of the local authorities to create with 100% grant from national funds. New rights of way can be created by agreement or compulsorily by creation order. The Commission from the beginning made encouraging noises and first mentioned the Cambrian Way in its annual report for 1968. The Interim Report was well received but it was made clear that restricted resources would dictate only limited commitment to the proposals. This proved to be a considerable understatement, such that the Commission's next four annual reports only indicated that the route was " under consideration". It sought to get reactions from the likely user organisations before approaching local authority and landowning interests. The Committee for Wales of the Countryside Commission was enthusiastic both under the chairmanship of Dr. Margaret Davies and later of Trevor Lewis and James Kegie.

In April 1976 the Commission approved the Cambrian Way project in principle and in September 1977 started official consultations on the basis of a map showing both the Cambrian Way Committee's route and the Commission's **Preferred Route** which differed in many respects . All the principal summits in Snowdonia were omitted. The route was to go over the Arans and the Arenigs instead of the Rhinogs and Cader Idris. The crossover from Black Mountains to Brecon Beacons was to be via Mynydd Llangorse.

Following opposition from many quarters, the Commission issued another line in January 1980 called a **Consultation Route.** This time the Cambrian Way Committee's route was not shown on the map, though the new route was closer to it than the 1977 line. Snowdon was included but still not the ridge of the Carneddau. Cader Idris was included and a route to the seaward side of the Rhinogs instead of a route over the Arans, where in the meantime an access row had blown up. The Black Mountains were omitted altogether following pressure from the national park - authority .

There had been much criticism of lack of consultation by the Commission, so to meet this it had decided to appoint **field officers** to meet landowners and other authorities. The first field officer, John Tetlow, a lecturer of the Department of Town Planning at the University of Wales, was appointed for a year and asked to report on the southern section up to Llandovery. He started off full of enthusiasm and the right ideas but when confronted with the opposition of commoners' committees and the national park authority, came up with some extraordinary compromises. Neither Pen y Fan nor the Carmarthen Van summits were to be part of the route, Pen y Fan because of erosion problems on the obvious route, and the Vans because the commoners would only agree to a route creeping round the base of the common and through conifer woods. The Cnewr Estate would not agree to any access during its lambing period (April 15th to May 10th) and the Countryside Commission was not prepared to have a long distance path with such a limitation.

The second field officer to be appointed, Donald Hoare, of Cwmystwyth, a former principal of an outdoor pursuits centre in Wales, fared better than John Tetlow and found general acceptance of the Cambrian Way proposals in the central section.

After years of support for the project and considerable determination to see the Cambrian Way designated, the Countryside Commission suddenly caved in and, with regret, abandoned it in January 1982. It concluded that there was continuing and widespread opposition to the proposed route, even when alternatives were considered. It was one of the earliest major decisions of the Commission following the appointment of Derek (later Sir Derek) Barber as its new chairman and who was advised to abandon the project by Martin Fitton, then the Principal Welsh Officer of the Commission, and currently National Park Officer for the Brecon Beacons. The decision was seen as an act of appeasement to the Welsh farmers in the hope of more cooperation on other countryside issues.

Donald Hoare's contract was terminated and the Commission never got round to appointing a field officer for the northern section. Who knows what ghastly compromises he or she might have been forced into in the Snowdonia National Park?

The Recreational Organisations

The Ramblers Association has consistently supported the Cambrian Way concept. Its National Executive Committee approved the principle of a Cambrian Way following a meeting, which I attended, in July 1972 but agreed that any guide on the subject should stress that it was a mountain route . It was proposed that the title should be "The Cambrian Mountain Way". In the late 80s support for the Cambrian Way was confirmed as the RA's preferred additional national trail in Wales.

The Youth Hostels Association likewise consistently supported the idea of a high level route with low level alternatives. It looked forward to an exciting new outlet for the energies of young travellers.

The British Mountaineering Council's North Wales Committee was bitterly opposed to the idea of a Cambrian Way and in particular to it going over the Rhinogs. At a meeting in February 1972, at which I was representing the Gloucestershire Mountaineering Club, only the London Mountaineering Club representative gave support. The B.M.C.'s South-west and Southern Committee, covering South Wales, decided in favour so that the matter was called in nationally. I attended a meeting of the Committee of Management in October 1972 and after an hour and a half's debate Cambrian Way was approved by II votes to 4 . Subsequently however the B.M.C. Safety Committee secured a reversal of the decision on safety grounds, and thought that designation would "encourage peak baggers and merit badge enthusiasts into difficult and remote areas". The North Wales Committee was asked to work out an alternative to the Rhinogs and it was their route over the relatively dull Arenig Fawr and moorland to the south-east of Ffestiniog that appeared as part of the Countryside Commission's preferred route in 1977.

The County Councils and the National Parks

Numerically the county councils were equally divided as to the merits of a Cambrian Way, Gwent, South Glamorgan and Mid Glamorgan being in favour with Dyfed, Gwynedd and Powys against. Those against however controlled 87% of the proposed route.

Both the national park authorities opposed the Cambrian Way. **Brecon Beacons National Park** claimed that the route proposed was neither logical nor in keeping with the policies of the national park plan. That plan defined the Carmarthen Vans as a remote and vulnerable area where additional recreation activity would not be encouraged by the provision of further facilities. The use of two further ridges of the Black Mountains for a long distance path was said to be difficult to accept and support. Despite the 100% grants available for long distance paths it was argued that concentration of limited resources on long distance paths reduced the amount of work carried out on the path network generally. It was pointed out that the cost of erosion work in the Brecon Beacons was falling entirely on the national park and the National Trust, but no mention was made that 100% grant could be available if the erosion was on an official long distance route.

The opposition continued and the national park committee even went to the length of passing a resolution in 1986 to ban the sales of this book from its Mountain Centre near Brecon.

Snowdonia National Park in its national park plan (1977) said "The National Park Authority is not convinced of the desirability of the proposed Cambrian Way long distance footpath. In particular they are opposed to the suggested route linking most of the principal summits of Snowdonia. The Authority will therefore seek further discussions on the topic with the Countryside Commission and other interested bodies. " They certainly had discussions with the Commission but not with the R.A. or Y.H.A.

The Farming Interests

Both the **National Farmers Union** and the **Farmers Union of Wales** were vociferous in their opposition to Cambrian Way and used their powerful lobby to influence the local authorities and park committees. The **Country Landowners Association** was apparently not opposed to the project.

THE INSTANT CAMBRIAN WAY

The arguments raged furiously from 1968 to 1982 as to whether a Cambrian Way was desirable and if so where it should go. If the project had not been abandoned, the arguments would probably have gone on for decades and the end result, if any, would at best have been a set of miserable compromises.

It was becoming apparent, even before abandonment, that if the compromises being considered were adopted, there would have arisen the anomalous situation of Cambrian Way walkers watching others go the obvious well established ways while they were plodding round the edges of commons and missing the tops. Guidebooks would have appeared advocating different routes to the official line and the whole concept of national trails would have fallen into disrepute.

Following abandonment there was a freedom to choose any way over which the public has a right of way or access, or where there is permissive use. On commons and other open country it is reasonable to describe well used routes - there would have been no books on mountain walks in Wales if rights of way only had to be followed.

With hindsight it is perhaps a pity I did not produce a guidebook during the mid 70s but the need not to prejudice possible new rights of way was felt to be paramount. After abandonment much further survey was carried out to make more use of existing rights of way. In the event I was "pipped at the post" by Richard Sale, whose "A Cambrian Way" was published in February 1984. Constables had commissioned Richard to write a book which was not to be published until the route became official. After abandonment they decided to go ahead but to avoid certain controversial areas . Subtitled " A personal guide to an unofficial route", the book was not a practical guide and handbook as this book sets out to be, but has 270 pages packed with fascinating reading, mostly historical, and which makes excellent reading after a day on the Cambrian Way. Richard and I had several meetings to coordinate routes but we agreed to differ on some. Richard's book was published too early to take advantage of the purchase of part of Fforest Fawr by Brecon Beacons National Park and the permissive arrangements for the Cnewr estate had not been announced. Although Richard used the Machynlleth variant from Plynlimon, he did write up the Dinas Mawddwy route as an alternative, but Constables thought the book was long enough. A second edition is expected early in 2000,(see page 18) Hopefully others will write books on other aspects of the Cambrian Way such as the industrial archaeology, geology and bird life.

How can it be that the Cambrian Way, officially abandoned after much opposition, suddenly came into existence at the behest of Messrs. Drake and Sale? Is it irresponsible to take advantage of the right of any citizen to suggest to others where they may walk? Some books have undoubtedly caused embarrassment where insufficient research has been carried out as to rights of way and as to possible impacts on wildlife and erosion problems. The public status of the routes in this guidebook has been the subject of all reasonable checks and has been made by one who has a background of 50 years experience in handling rights of way problems. The sections of the route over de facto access land on rural commons (10%) and other mountain and moorland (2½%) have been carefully chosen to be along well established routes where even the most law abiding walker would not feel it necessary to try to ascertain who the owner was and to ask permission to use.

The following pages detail how the aspects that caused opposition have been considered and taken into account in evolving the routes in this guide. Meanwhile it is pertinent to ask how different the walker will find the route compared with the official long distance paths.

Some sections are already popular routes and are maintained to a reasonable standard, but many sections, including some in the national parks, are poorly maintained or not at all, so walkers must take things as they find them. One of the joys of Cambrian Way is that on many of the higher level sections the way is undefined on the ground. Some of these sections may develop a defined path in time but much will still be wild and give that sense of remoteness that so many seek and do not find on our long distance paths.

The main difference that long distance path addicts will find is that there is little signposting and even less waymarking than one may be accustomed to. Stiles and gates are generally of a low standard. These aspects are elaborated on below. Several obstructions have been found and reported to the county councils, with varying results. Enforcement procedures are none existent or painfully slow and weak in most parts of Wales. Some of the problems reported have taken years to resolve and are difficult to follow up adequately at a distance. In some instances diversions are desirable to provide a better route, but take a long time to process, as notably the diversion at Dinas Mawddwy which took 11 years. Two diversions in Forestry Enterprise land, stimulated by the author, have legalised obstructions made in the 1960s.

There are about 90 stiles and 165 gates on the main route - a fair number but compared to the Offa's Dyke Path, with its 450 stiles and 125 gates (in only 176 miles), Cambrian Way is clearly less of a steeplechase. The difference reflects how different the terrain and land use is, with so much more open country. However, that said, be warned about the gates. Very few Welsh gates are properly hung. The majority are held up at one or both ends with binder twine and sometimes with barbed wire. Getting over these gates can be a greater hazard than many more expected dangers. Maintenance of stiles and gates is the responsibility of whoever maintains the fence, wall or hedge. A grant of at least 25% of the cost is available but seldom claimed as it is just not worth the bother. One might expect gates in regular use to be reasonably well maintained but little used gates, and more particularly stiles, are way down most farmers' priority list for attention. There is little incentive to improve stiles and gates for the benefit of the public and often a distinct inclination to discourage passage by those whose dogs may chase sheep.The bonanza of schemes in the late 80s, using unemployed labour, that got so much work done on footpaths in England never got going in the remoter Welsh counties. Voluntary work is relatively undeveloped but is increasing.

As with maintenance, so also the extent of signposting and waymarking is patchy. More waymarking is desirable to avoid trespass in the lower sections, in the interests of both walker and farmer. I have waymarked several sections, mostly in Forestry Enterprise land, using the Countryside Commission system of yellow painted arrows for footpaths and blue for bridleways. (plus usually the Welsh hat logo at beginning of each section) I am willing to waymark other stretches by agreement with the farmer concerned. On the open mountains waymarking is much less acceptable and appropriate. Cairns are the natural and traditional method, though less efficient than arrows, but should be used sparingly, such as at particular descent points such as the top of the Zig Zags on Snowdon.

MEETING THE OPPOSITION

This section reviews the main reasons for opposition to the designation of the Cambrian Way as an official long distance path and shows how these aspects have been taken into account in planning the routes in this guide.

Erosion

It is only in the last thirty years that erosion has been taken seriously. The enormous increase in mountain walking since the second world war caused the breaking up of the surface of many popular routes. While natural erosion is accepted as a fact of life erosion that is man made offends. Attitudes to erosion are now less hysterical than they were when Cambrian Way was first advocated and research and experiment has shown that much erosion can be coped with or prevented, though at considerable cost. Other more difficult problems remain and seem insoluble. One is inclined to feel that if we can land men on the moon then surely something can be done about erosion. It should not be necessary to discourage access to mountains because what amounts to a very small area is wearing away offensively and because some of such problems defy solution. Like the Cambrian Way itself, erosion is a challenge to be tackled and not something that is used as an excuse to discourage whorthwhile activities.

A sense of proportion is necessary in considering erosion. A few thousand extra walkers going up Snowdon will make little difference when the numbers using the paths there run into millions over the years. Where excessive numbers have caused erosion remedial action appropriate to the situation is a justifiable expense. The public had the Snowdon paths on the cheap in the past, but under the management scheme of recent years sterling work has been done by both volunteers and paid staff and the problem is now under control.

Much consideration has been given to erosion problems in planning the Cambrian Way route in this guide. As the Cambrian Way is envisaged as a south to north route and since most erosion is caused in descent, (and more particularly by those who run down), many eroded spots which are taken in ascent are not likely to be further eroded by Cambrian Way traffic. Where the eroded ascent is itself a hazard, such as Penyrole-wen, an alternative, albeit longer, ascent has been recommended. Some eroded descents have been avoided such as the north face of Blorenge and the descent from Glyder Fawr to Llyn Cwn and Cwm Idwal .

One type of erosion which is never likely to be a serious problem on the Cambrian Way, but which has often been quoted against it, is the traverse of peat bogs of the kind which cause such problems on the Pennine Way. The dropping of enormous slabs by helicopter, which is the latest attempt to solve the Pennine Way peatbog problem, will not be necessary on the Cambrian Way.

Horse riding has been the main cause of erosion on the Black Mountains but it would be most unfair to deny walkers the superb mountain walking there because horse riding had not been adequately brought under control.

Many sections are on broad ridges where, if use had been spread evenly, no breaking up of the grass cover would have occurred. Inevitably however people tend to follow where a path becomes visible, and if used to excess erosion occurs. Our Mountain Connoisseur must use discretion and decide whether to walk well away from the worn path or whether using the path will cause no more erosion. Generally one can serve the cause better by keeping to one side, but not immediately on the edge of the path - that's the next bit to go.

The relative contribution of Cambrian Way walkers to erosion at already eroded sites will be small but care has had to be taken in planning to avoid routes where only a relatively little usage could cause a nasty gash in the mountainside. For this reason steep descents have been avoided such as the new permissive way off Fan Gihirych on the Cnewr Estate.

The ghastly upper section of the Watkin Path was included in the Countryside Commission's 1980 consultative route yet this part of the Snowdon Horseshoe is quite unnecessary if approaching Snowdon from the south-east. The much nicer Allt Maenderyn ridge leading to Bwlch Main is also showing some signs of having appeared in guide books, but it is a wide stony ridge which is unlikely to provide serious problems and will not wear away for a few million years yet.

An unsolved problem is the south-east ridge of Pen y Fan which is a much softer slope. Any solution is likely to look artificial. Probably large stone steps are the answer but unfortunately they are not so readily available as they were for repair of the Snowdon paths.

At the time of editing the 4th edition a newly formed body,the *British Uplands Footpaths Trust,* supported by mountaineering and rambling interests together with camping and outdoor leisure trade interests had been formed to raise money for sensitive repair of eroded popular upland footpaths. Hopefully some of the money raised will ensure remedial action on some of Cambrian Way's intractable erosion problems

The Farmers

I am sure the farmers were needlessly alarmed about the Cambrian Way. They tend to see any proposals for more public access as meaning more sheep worried and killed by dogs, more gates left open, more walls and fences climbed over and more vandalism generally. Each farmer you meet has some horrific tale to tell. One bad incident is inclined to sour a farmer for ever against the public.

Some farmers are very possessive, while others have a greater sense of holding the land in trust and are willing to share use with those who get a pleasure from walking the mountains. Most Welsh farmers are friendly and enjoy a chat if they are not too busy. In all my walks planning the Cambrian Way I have only once been challenged by a farmer and that was on a right of way.

The farmers are a very powerful lobby in the rural counties of Wales. They can attend daytime meetings of county and district councils and national park committees, and used their muscle to oppose Cambrian Way. One wonders if those opposing the project had any idea of the satisfaction that many people derive from following a long continuous route on foot. For certain few, if any, had walked a long distance path - and that goes for most other opponents.

Other long distance paths were said to give farmers trouble, including Offa's Dyke, yet Offa's Dyke Association seldom hears of any problems. It hears much more from farmers wanting to be put on the bed and breakfast list. There are said to be 1250 farms providing accommodation and meals in Wales. Farm tourism means a lot to the economy of the uplands, and with farm subsidies now very much being questioned a second form of income, from path walkers, should be more than welcome .

I am sure that Cambrian Way walkers will be better behaved than the average tourist and holiday maker, if only because there will be little time to get up to mischief as there is an objective to be reached each day. In any case, those who have the strength of character to embark on an expedition such as the Cambrian Way are most unlikely to come from the strata of to-day's society that is involved in petty crime and vandalism. There are however "black sheep in every family" and some of the problems farmers suffer from are due to sheer ignorance or incompetence, so the following particular aspects of countryside behaviour are mentioned specifically.

Dogs. Whatever you do don't take a dog with you on the Cambrian Way. Dogs are the cause of more antagonism from farmers than any other cause. It is now an offence to walk with a dog in a field of sheep unless the dog is on a lead or "under close control" A farmer can shoot a dog worrying, or about to worry, livestock. Even the most placid of dogs can go berserk on seeing sheep and it is claimed that thousands of sheep are killed by dogs every year. Cattle dislike dogs and both bulls and cows with calves will chase them. Even if your dog is well behaved, you will be regarded with great suspicion by farmers. As far as I am concerned, no one who has had a dog with them will qualify for having walked the Cambrian Way.

Gates. A gate left open can cause the most awful problems. I heard of one farmer who brought several hundred sheep down to the valley the day before a contractors van was due to collect them. Someone left a gate open and not only did the van leave empty but the sheep got onto another farm and it took days to sort out the chaos. Remember farmers should not lock gates on a bridleway, so locking may not be the answer. Sometimes you find gates open. I do not entirely subscribe to the Country Code which tells you to shut all gates. You may be depriving animals of access to water. It is better to leave them as you find them, but if in doubt - shut. Leaders of parties should ask someone with them at the front to stay with the gate until the party is through, whether it has to be closed or not.

Rights of Way. Make certain that your map reading is impeccable so that you keep to the rights of way across farmland. Use both the Ordnance Survey maps and the maps in this guide and consult them frequently. Good map reading will be much more required than on, say, the Pennine Way. Avoid getting into the situation where you have to trespass to get back on course. Ensure that all members of a party have the necessary maps and can map read. Contour map reading is important, particularly at higher levels, and experience with this aspect may prove vital in cloud conditions.

Many farmers do not know where their rights of way are or may try to persuade you to go another way. If your right of passage is denied on what you believe to be a public right of way, use due discretion as to insisting on your rights. It is important to report such incidents to the county council and the Ramblers Association.

Nature Conservation

It speaks well for the defences built up by the nature conservation movement that the routing for the Cambrian Way was questioned in several places on conservation grounds. One had, however, to resist the almost automatic reaction of "You can't go that way - that's a nature reserve". One had to ask (a) what was it that was being conserved at that site, (b) what effect would Cambrian Way usage have on it, and (c) would that effect really matter? Generally the more knowledgeable the conservationist the more reasonable the answers received, and frequently it was clear that there was no real problem. One also concluded that the nature conservationists were often their own worst enemies in that they cannot keep secrets as to locations of rare species. Just as we were being told that a certain national nature reserve should be avoided, a radio broadcast was saying that this was the only place in the world that a certain tree grew. Walkers on the Cambrian Way are highly unlikely to be interested in identifying rare trees and digging them up. Nevertheless, I am not saying in this guide where that tree grows .

The red kite is not the only rare bird in Wales but was the only one mentioned as likely to be affected by the Cambrian Way, particularly in the Towy valley. This matter is covered more fully in the main text under "Rhandirmwyn". The effect in the nesting season of a few more walkers going up the Doethie valley will surely be very minimal.

Early in 1972 the Nature Conservancy offices at Bangor and Aberystwyth requested copies of the Cambrian Way Interim Report, which were sent with an offer to discuss any problems likely to arise on the routes concerned. In the autumn of that year, having heard nothing, I wrote to the Director of the Nature Conservancy asking for informal discussions. The reply, from the assistant director for Wales, was that discussions would be premature, so my attempts to become better informed were thwarted. No one can say I didn't try.

The Danger Aspects

It might be thought that one was proposing a walk over the highest peaks in the Alps to judge from some of the remarks passed about the dangers of the Cambrian Way. None of the summits traversed are technically difficult by the routes suggested for any normally healthy person, but of course any mountain can be a hazard in bad weather conditions, and the higher and steeper it is, the more the danger. Surely there is still scope for a spice of adventure in life. The critics point to the people who have to be rescued from the mountains because of ignorance of the basic requirements of equipment or because of foolhardiness in just not appreciating the hazards of venturing in the mountains. As with road safety, one can only go on plugging the need for care, rather than banning the pastime.

The attitude of many of the climbing fraternity was condescending to walkers to say the least. One statement made that particularly stuck in the gullet was that "paths should be laid out in areas of no interest to mountaineers". The attitude over use of the Rhinogs was near hysterical and akin to the sort of opposition Tom Stephenson had to his proposals to take the Pennine Way over Kinderscout. That wild moor was then forbidden territory. The northern Rhinogs provide a fantastic walk over rough and rocky ground, but in this case there is a public right of access to it, as it is Crown common. The national park authority would have the Rhinogs put in a glass case, labelled "Wilderness". Granted that such an area should not be developed for general tourist use but the one recreational use it is suitable for is a tough high level walk. If wilderness areas must be found, there are plenty of other parts of Wales that few want to go to which could qualify.

There was much pressure to work out a lower level alternative route, but really those who want such routes should follow other long distance paths and not try adulterating a natural high level route. The sort of compromises which were being proposed in the Brecon Beacons area just before abandonment were completely debasing the concept of a high level route. As a concession to mountain safety and as official long distance routes have to have specific routes designated, the Cambrian Way Committee put forward additional alternative routes for the Rhinogs, and for the Snowdon and Glyder areas, based on the precedent of official alternatives on the Pennine Way and Offa's Dyke. These have not been specified so precisely in this guide because there is much greater flexibility anyway with an unofficial route. Many alternatives are mentioned or are apparent from the Ordnance Survey maps

RIGHTS OF WAY AND ACCESS

It is important that walkers on the Cambrian Way should be conscious both of their right to proceed and of their obligations to those who live and work on the land they traverse. Whatever their rights, as detailed in the paragraphs below, they should always regard their travel over the land as a privilege given and accepted by persons mostly long since departed, and only occasionally due to recent negotiations.

A high proportion (161 miles = 59%) of the recommended routes are over public rights of way (also known as "highways"). There are varying degrees of public right of passage according to the status of the highway. If the way is a public footpath there is a right of way on foot. A bridleway has the additional right of riding or leading a horse or of riding a pedal cycle. "Roads used as public paths" may have vehicular rights of passage and "Byways open to all traffic" certainly have. These categories of highway are marked on the Ordnance Survey maps by different symbols, in red for the 1:50,000 scale and in green for the 1:25,000 Leisure, Explorer and former Pathfinder series . The O.S. gets its information from definitive maps of rights of way prepared by county councils and the existence of a path on the definitive map is conclusive evidence that it was a right of way at the relevant date of the definitive map. Legal orders changing rights of way have to be notified to the O.S. and should be taken account of at the next edition of the maps.

Public roads are mostly shown in various colours on the O.S. maps according to classification but there are many public roads that are uncoloured. These so called "white" roads are mostly untarred stony roads or green lanes and were until recently indistinguishable on the maps from private roads. The author was particularly involved in a campaign by the RA and other organisations to get all public roads marked as such on OS maps. At last there has been a breakthrough. The Explorer maps at 1:25,000, and the Landranger maps at 1:50,000 as they are revised, have the white roads marked at intervals with green or red spots respectively and are referred to in the map legend as "Other routes with public access". This is somewhat vague as to exact status because the authorities' records of maintainable highways do not specify if they are only, for instance, alleyways in towns. An example of an ORPA on the Cambrian Way is the eastern approach to Mallwyd on OS Leisure map 23 (See Page 59).

Rights of way have become established by prolonged usage with the acquiescence of the owner of the land, and must be on a defined route. Although many public paths exist over open country it is common for the way to be less defined. When the survey of rights of way was being conducted from which the definitive maps were derived uncertainty as to the line of paths across open land often led to them being marked only to the edge of the open country. This was not thought to matter as the facility to roam at large was never disputed. This can however present problems if right of access is disputed. In English and Welsh law one cannot establish a right to roam at large by continued usage with acquiescence of the owner, as one can with defined rights of way. Regardless of what right of access may be obtained in forthcoming legislation there are some categories of open country where the public already has a legal right of access and this has considerable relevance to the Cambrian Way.

Urban Commons

Under the Law of Property Act 1925 the public acquired a right of access for "air and exercise" to commons that at the time were administered by borough or urban district councils. At the south end of Cambrian Way this includes Mynydd Machen and a long line of commons from Twmbarlwm, near Newport, to the Blorenge near Abergavenny. At the north end Tal y Fan, Conwy Mountain and the exciting traverse path leading to the Sychnant Pass are on commons in former urban districts. 11½ miles of the Way are over non-definitive routes on urban commons.

Crown commons

Under the same act owners of common land were able to make a deed of declaration which gave the public the same rights of access over commons in former rural districts. In 1932 this procedure was adopted by the Crown Commissioners for its extensive commons in the rural districts of Wales (though not for England). Thus sections of the Cambrian Way, amounting to 11 miles, run over public access Crown commons, including the northern parts of the Carneddau, Plynlimon, the northern Rhinogs, Moelwyn Mawr, Domen Milwyn and Teifi Pools.

Difference between Rights of Way and Access

A right of way is a greater right over its width than a right of access. With a right of way the highway authority has a duty to maintain and to keep it free from obstruction. No such duty applies over the area of land to which the public may have access so that one cannot, for instance, expect bridges everywhere over streams or the clearing of gorse and bracken.

The Birmingham Clauses

The route passes over the fringe of the gathering grounds of the Elan Valley reservoirs which were built to supply Birmingham with water. The whole area is covered by the famous " Birmingham Clauses" which give "the public a privilege at all times to enjoy air, exercise and recreation".

National Trust Land

Several sections of Cambrian Way traverse National Trust land which is open to the public. The longest stretch of non-definitive route on National Trust land is the high parts of the Carneddau from Ogwen to Drum. Other sections are on Sugar Loaf, Pen y Fan, the Glyders and recently acquired Cnicht - total 11½ miles.

National Park Authority Land

It cannot be too often stressed that land in national parks is generally privately owned and that national park status does not give the public any additional right of access. In recent years however the Brecon Beacons National Park Authority has itself acquired certain large tracts of common land in order to ensure public access. This applies to the eastern section of Fforest Fawr (Great Forest) (see page 35) and the west side of the Black Mountain (see page 43). In 1989 it entered into a management agreement with Welsh Water for the western part of Forest Fawr (the east side of the Black Mountain.) This will safeguard public access on foot. These sections cover 12 miles (4½%) of the main Cambrian Way route.

Forestry Commission (for a recent period called Forest Enterprise)

Forestry Commission allows general access on foot to its land subject to certain restrictions. Two sections of the Cambrian Way are on non definitive paths through such land. The OS has resumed marking of FC freehold land after a lapse of several years

Cardiff

Cardiff City has no definitive map as yet but the route follows publically maintained paths and roads or is through public parks or council owned former canal towpath open to the public.

Access under Tir Cymen and Tir Gofal Schemes

Tir Cymen, roughly translated means "a well crafted landscape", and was an experimental scheme started in 1995 in three parts of Wales under which farmers have been paid in return for positive management of their land for the benefit of wildlife, landscape, archaeology and geology, and for providing better opportunities for quiet enjoyment of the countryside. If moorland or improved upland grassland is involved then public access must be allowed on foot for quiet enjoyment. It is similar to the Countryside Stewardship scheme in England but there is no direct payment for access. Four sections of Cambrian Way have such permissive access, under 10 year agreements, - from Bwlch Siglen to Cribin Fawr (page 60), part of the east approach to Cader Idris (62), and at Llethr, Clip and Moel y Gyrafolen in the Rhinogs (64 &66), a total of 5½ miles.

Tir Gofal, ("land care") is a similar scheme, but for all Wales, starting in 1999. It comprises four elements, including voluntary agreements for linear and area access,

Countryside Council for Wales (as successors to the Nature Conservancy)

The CCW owns Cader Idris and the Rhinogs, Fawr and Fach, and allows general access to those very important mountains, with an emphasis on conservation.

Rural Commons

Commons in areas administered before 1974 by rural district councils do not provide a legal right of access for the public, unless there is a Law of Property Act deed. In practice the facility to roam is virtually never disputed. A legal right of access is likely to be the least controversial part of the forthcoming access bill. The areas concerned are already documented following the survey made under the Commons Registration Act 1965.

The longest stretch of rural common on the Cambrian Way is the Black Mountains section from Bal Mawr via the Tumpa, Waun Fach and Pen Allt Mawr to Table Mountain near Crickhowell. All this is very well known as a mountain walk. Another such section is Mynydd Llangynidr. On these commons there is "de facto" access and no one would dream of trying to find out who the owner was and asking permission to walk over them. Other large stretches of rural commons include Fforest Fawr and the Black Mountain, as referred to above.

Open Country Access Land

There remain five miles in four sections on high ground that do not fall into any of the above categories but which are open mountain country with de facto access, that is to say that so far as is known walkers are not denied access as long as they act in a reasonable manner. Since 1949 legal access could have been made under the National Parks and Access to the Countryside Act 1949, either by agreement or compulsorily by order. Whatever definition is made of access land under the forthcoming legislation these sections will certainly qualify as mountain or moor..

Other Non-Definitive Sections

New routes. In three instances waymarked paths are followed which have been negotiated by the National Park authorities. These may or may not be dedicated as rights of way.

Uncertain status routes. In two cases paths are followed which appear to be public but are not on the definitive maps or road plans. It may be that applications should be made for modification orders to add them to the definitive maps.

Courtesy Paths - this phrase, coined in Snowdonia, applies to certain negotiated routes such as the way from Pen-y-Pass to Glyder Fawr over open country in ownership of Mrs. Esme Kirby.

Unofficial Diversions. Frequently the route on the ground is different from the definitive route. A legal diversion should take place if it is a better route than the definitive line or the original route must be opened up if obstructed. A new right of way may have come about by twenty years use but the old way is still a right of way.

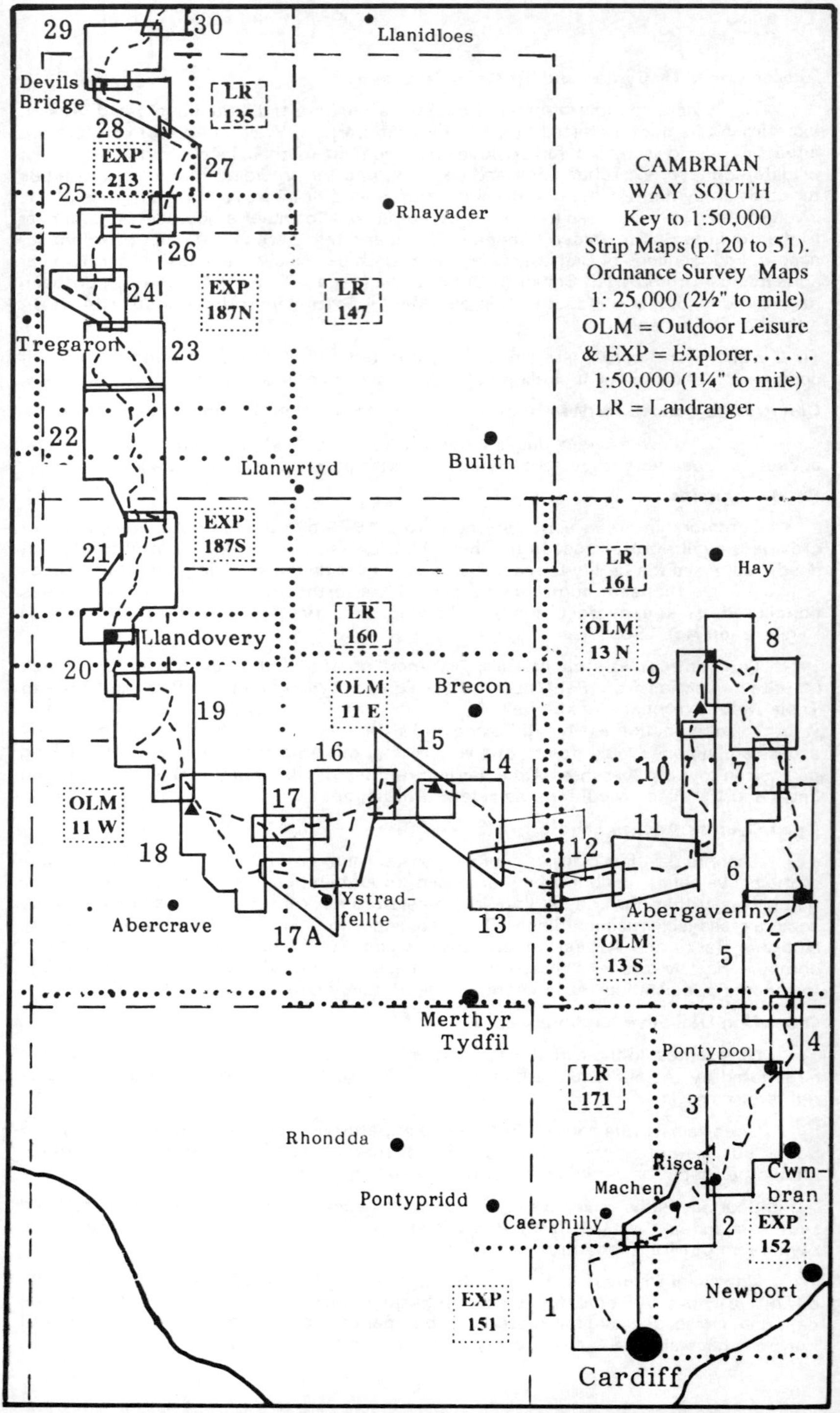
CAMBRIAN
WAY SOUTH
Key to 1:50,000
Strip Maps (p. 20 to 51).
Ordnance Survey Maps
1: 25,000 (2½" to mile)
OLM = Outdoor Leisure
& EXP = Explorer, ...
1:50,000 (1¼" to mile)
LR = Landranger —
Llanidloes
Devils Bridge
Rhayader
Tregaron
Builth
Llanwrtyd
Hay
Llandovery
Brecon
Abercrave
Ystradfellte
Abergavenny
Merthyr Tydfil
Pontypool
Rhondda
Risca
Machen
Cwmbran
Pontypridd
Caerphilly
Newport
Cardiff
LR 135
EXP 213
EXP 187N
LR 147
EXP 187S
LR 161
LR 160
OLM 13 N
OLM 11 E
OLM 11 W
OLM 13 S
LR 171
EXP 152
EXP 151
1
2
3
4
5
6
7
8
9
10
11
12
13
14
15
16
17
17A
18
19
20
21
22
23
24
25
26
27
28
29
30

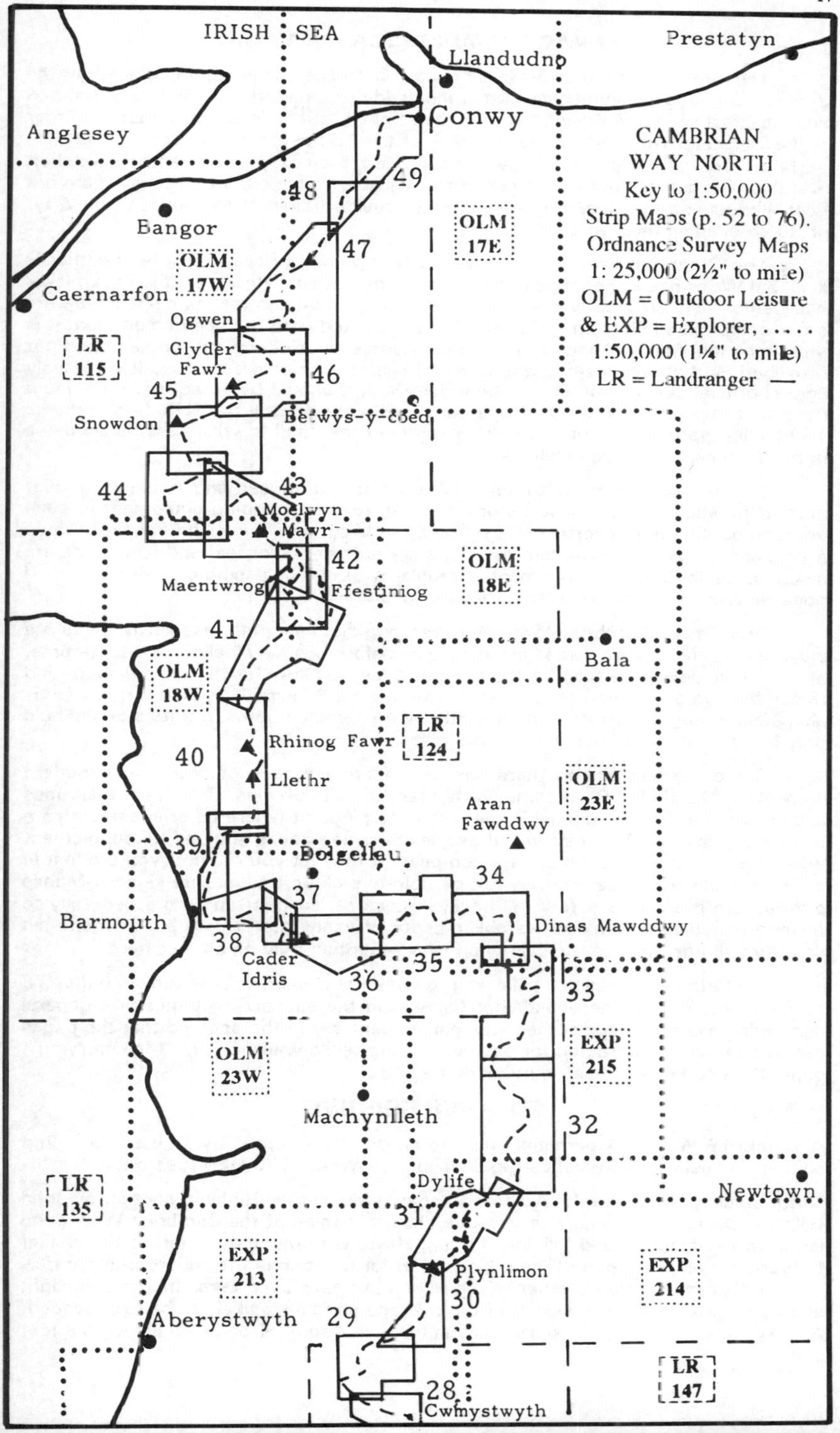
IRISH SEA
Prestatyn
Llandudno
Conwy
Anglesey
CAMBRIAN
WAY NORTH
Key to 1:50,000
Strip Maps (p. 52 to 76).
Ordnance Survey Maps
1: 25,000 (2½" to mile)
OLM = Outdoor Leisure
& EXP = Explorer, ...
1:50,000 (1¼" to mile)
LR = Landranger —
49
48
OLM 17E
Bangor
47
OLM 17W
Caernarfon
Ogwen
LR 115
Glyder Fawr
46
45
Snowdon
Betwys-y-coed
44
43
Moelwyn Mawr
42
OLM 18E
Maentwrog
Ffestiniog
41
Bala
OLM 18W
LR 124
Rhinog Fawr
40
Llethr
OLM 23E
Aran Fawddwy
39
Dolgellau
34
37
Barmouth
Dinas Mawddwy
38
Cader Idris
35
36
33
OLM 23W
EXP 215
Machynlleth
32
LR 135
Dylife
Newtown
31
EXP 213
Plynlimon
EXP 214
30
29
Aberystwyth
LR 147
28
Cwmystwyth

PLANNING TO WALK THE CAMBRIAN WAY

The main decision to be made is how one is to spend the nights in between the daily walking. The accommodation list in this guide gives addresses mostly of the bed and breakfast variety. Although Youth Hostels appear briefly in the geographical order of the list, a separate section gives details of the 17 hostels on or near the Way, In parts of Central Wales and Snowdonia hostels provide the only accommodation available. The quantity of bed and breakfast available varies but increasingly there are B&B operators off the route who are willing to provide transport to and from the Way, or to an evening meal at a pub.

The Cambrian Way is superb backpacking country provided the weather is kind, but Wales has an enormous rainfall in the mountains. However, the backpacker has greater freedom as to where to decide to stop and camp for the night. There are a few official camp sites en route and these are listed with the accommodation. It is most important that backpackers should get permission to camp on farmland and not take liberties that will upset relations with farmers who as a body fought vigorously against official designation of the Cambrian Way. It should be noted that there is no right to camp on common land and camping is specifically prohibited on National Trust land, water gathering grounds, and most other land to which the public has a right of access for air and exercise.

Those who are used to fell walking but not to carrying a big load over mountains should think twice before deciding to take camping equipment in case accommodation is not forthcoming. Cambrian Way has double the Pennine Way's ascent and can be wet under foot even in a dry summer. Wet feet and high loads are a sure recipe for blisters, not to mention problems of overbalancing on wet rocks, and possible ankle sprains miles from roads or habitation.

Don't make Cambrian Way your first long distance path, especially if you are backpacking and haven't carried camping gear before. Above all allow adequate time, at least three days more than for the Pennine Way, to allow for the extra ascent and remember there is a high dropout rate even on the Pennine Way. Cambrian Way is altogether a tougher proposition than other long distance paths in Britain and should only be tackled during the summer months.

Since the last edition there has been increasing use of two of the modern wonders, - the Global Positioning System and mobile phones. Both have their uses and limitations. GPS units enable the walker to pinpoint where he or she is within a hundred yards or so. The main use of this can be when one is in cloud, to supplement what one can glean from map and compass. It may let you down if you are lost in a forest because the device may not be able to pick up the satellite signals. Mobile phones are more of a satefy fall back, in case of accident and more generally to forewarn bed and breakfast establishments of likely late arrival, but in mountain country such as most of the Cambrian Way reception may be non existent.

For further information on planning to walk the Cambrian Way turn to pages 78 to 96 at the end of the book.What follows on the succeeding pages is a general description and strip maps of the route, placed centrally in the book so that the pages can, if desired, be extracted for ease of reading while walking (see "Map carrying", page 81, also key to the strip maps on page 96)

FURTHER READING

A Cambrian Way - "A personal guide to an unofficial route" by Richard Sale. 2nd edition. Published by Gwasgcarreg Gwalch, Llanwrst, LL26 OEH (See page 8)

"Snowdonia to the Gower". "A coast to coast walk across Highest Wales". by John Gillham. Diadem Books, London. A much shorter version of the Cambrian Way, done in the wrong direction, and split into 11 long days, with much more left to the walker to work out on the ground. The main reason for mention is the superb photographs by John Gillham and Van Greaves which all seem to have been taken in sharp sunlight and which give a false impression of the average conditions likely to be experienced. A bulky book, not for the rucksack, though there is also a 24 page version of the text only.

ROUTE DESCRIPTION AND STRIP MAPS

SOUTHERN SECTION
Cardiff to Llandovery
Via the Black Mountains & Brecon Beacons

Distance 107.5 miles(173km) Ascent 21,163 feet (6455met)

The southern section of the Cambrian Way is the longer of the three sections into which the route naturally divides. Most of it is within the Brecon Beacons National Park which is entered just north of Pontypool, at 26 miles from the start. These non-national park miles are through the areas of local authorities which were the only ones to support the concept of the Cambrian Way t

Although a large city may sound like an unpromising start for a mountain walk Cardiff is increaingly important, not only as the seat of the Welsh Assembly, but, with the exciting cultural and leisure developments at Cardiff Bay. The start of the Cambrian Way could well be moved to the Bay, for the next edition, and hopefully a flagship Youth Hostel will have been established there. Curently the start is at Cardiff Castle and steps straight into parkland and follows a green belt between the built up area and the River Taff The M4 interchange crossing is horrific or fascinating according to taste but then the towers of Castell Coch beckon and one follows pleasant woodland and pastureland on the ridge between Cardiff and Caerphilly before crossing the ends of the famous mining valleys of Rhymney and Ebbw.The coalfield itself is by-passed to the south and east. The scenery in general is acceptable for a long distance path but in terms of the Cambrian Way is only a foretaste of better things to come.

Although the walk is rewarding it is not through a tourist area. It crosses industrial valleys where accommodation is relatively scarce. Risca is about half way but most walkers would be advised to break themselves in by doing the Cardiff to Abergavenny stretch in 3 days.

Cardiff to Tongwynlais 5.4 miles 125 feet of ascent Maps 1 & IA

As explained under "Maps" (page 80) it is assumed that the walker has Ordnance Survey maps in addition to this guide. The description here is not a stile by stile account and only serves to supplement the maps with useful information.

The first problem may be that the gates of Bute Park at the side of Cardiff Castle are not open until after early starters will have departed. However the west bank route through Sophia Gardens is almost equally attractive. Note the grotesque animal statues on the wall of the park between the Castle and Cardiff Bridge. Return to the east bank by suspension footbridge.

Easy wide paths lead along the riverbank, under Gabalfa Bridge (detour via Llandaff Cathedral possible here returning to Llandaff Bridge. Turn away from the river after some sports grounds and make for a road going under a railway bridge. The next half mile is partly industrial but has some interest. Watch for a renovated old water wheel on left. A picturesque industrial relic follows - the Glamorgan Canal, now a nature reserve. the towpath of the old canal, a botanist' s paradise s now in the care of the Cardiff City. The canal ends abruptly at an approach road to the Coryton interchange of the M4 . This "Spaghetti" junction provides the first real test of navigation as you negotiate two footbridges and two underpasses with the help of map 1A. Be assured however that this is the only motorway to be encountered on the Cambrian Way.

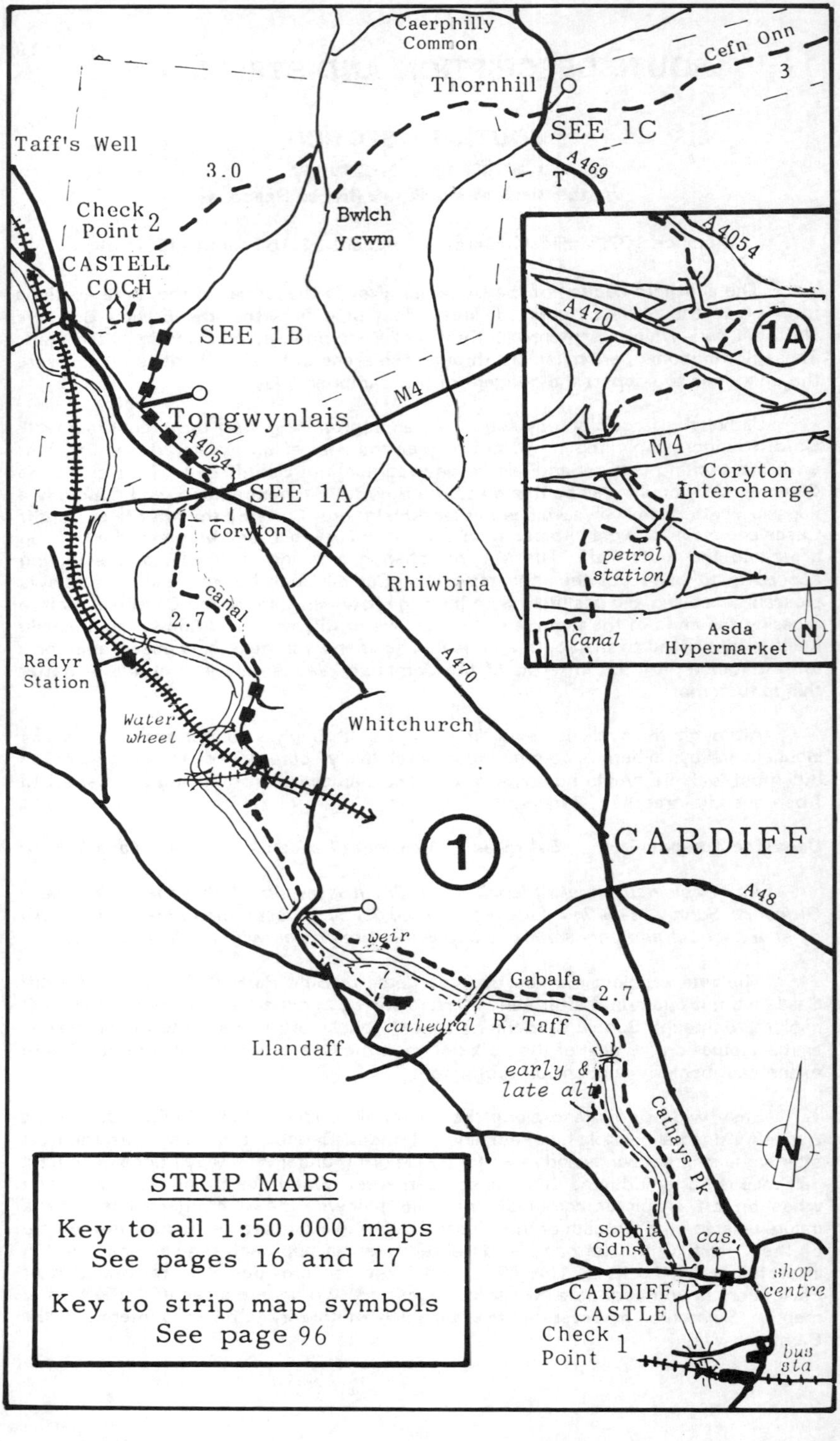
Caerphilly
Common
Thornhill
Cefn Onn
3
SEE 1C
A469
T
Taff's Well
3.0
Check
Point 2
Bwlch
y cwm
CASTELL
COCH
SEE 1B
A4054
A470
1A
M4
Coryton
Interchange
petrol
station
Canal
Asda
Hypermarket
N
M4
Tongwynlais
A4054
SEE 1A
Coryton
canal
2.7
Rhiwbina
Radyr
Station
A470
Water
wheel
Whitchurch
1
CARDIFF
A48
weir
Gabalfa
2.7
cathedral
R. Taff
Llandaff
early &
late alt
Cathays Pk
N
STRIP MAPS
Key to all 1:50,000 maps
See pages 16 and 17
Key to strip map symbols
See page 96
Sophia
Gdns
cas.
shop
centre
CARDIFF
CASTLE
Check
Point 1
bus
sta

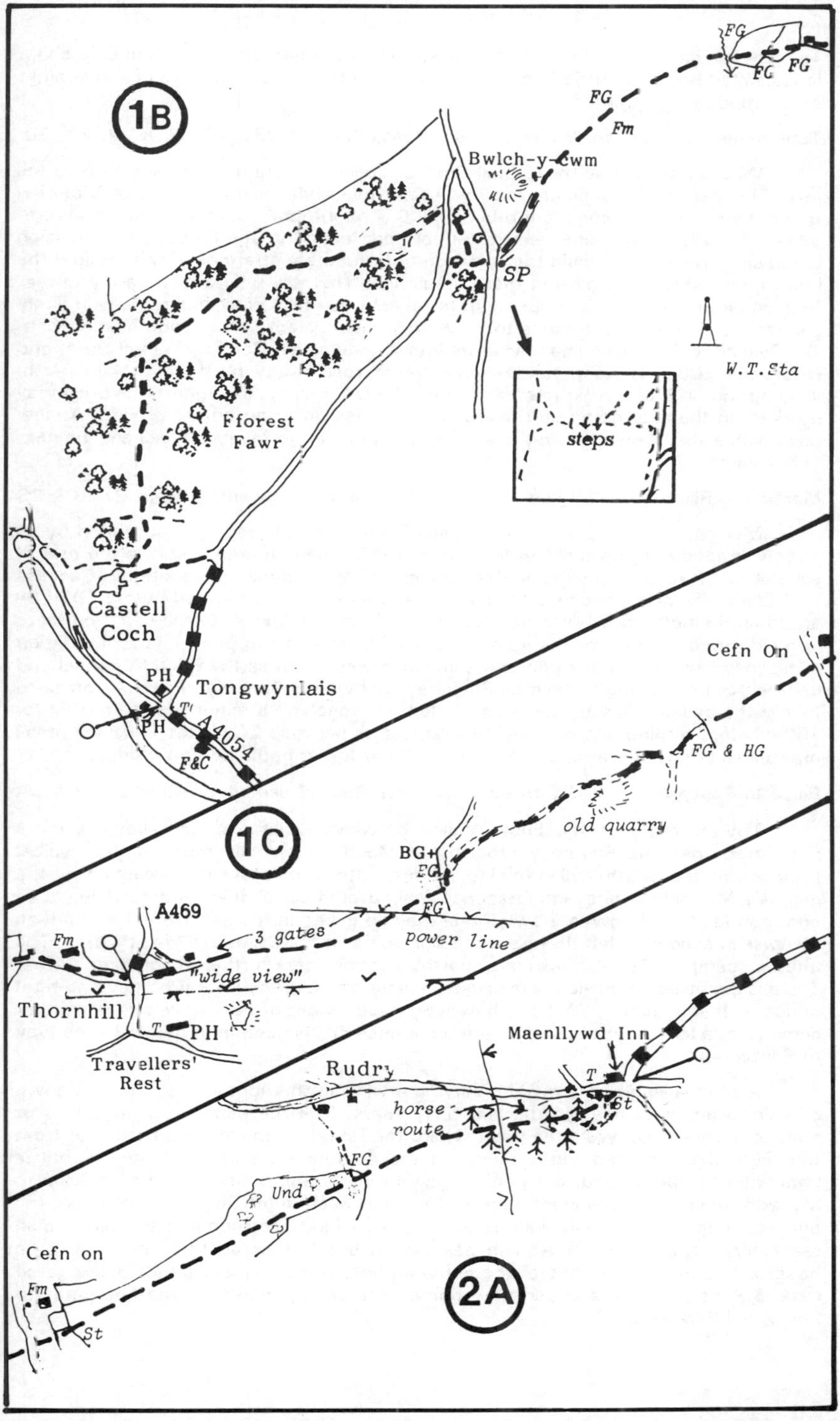
1B
FG
FG
FG
FG
Fm
Bwlch-y-cwm
SP
W.T.Sta
steps
Fforest
Fawr
Castell
Coch
PH
Tongwynlais
T
PH
A4054
F&C
1C
Cefn On
FG & HG
old quarry
BG+
FG
FG
A469
Fm
3 gates
power line
"wide view"
Thornhill
T
PH
Travellers'
Rest
Maenllywd Inn
Rudry
T
St
horse
route
FG
Und
Cefn on
Fm
St
2A

Tongwynlais has three pubs, two offering snacks at the bar, and a fish and chip shop. If a late start has been made from Cardiff, buses and trains can be taken for overnight accommodation in Cardiff.

Tongwynlais to Machen 8.3 miles 875 feet of ascent Maps 1, IB, IC, 2, 2A, 2B.

Walk up the road to the Castell Coch driveway, ignoring earlier signs off to the left. The castle *(Checkpoint No.2)* is a fairy tale style reconstruction of Victorian times, having been a complete ruin in 1870. The internal decor is lavish and worth a visit. A path up the bank behind the car park leads through Forestry Commission woodland. Keep to the main track, which unfortunately offers no views. Follow the inset map, which is shown in more detail near Thornhill where fields are crossed. Near an old quarry the view opens up to reveal Caerphilly with its large castle dimly discernible. The way continues to be well defined except in the wood beyond Cefn On. Beyond Rudry a dead end road leads into woods called Coed Cefn Pwll Du at grid reference 208871. Keep to the main forest road firstly north-east, then north, ignoring the first left forest road shown on the O.S.maps. Also ignore the bridleway marked on the map going northwards which does not exist on the ground. A view point with a seat shows the way ahead beyond Machen to Mynydd Machen, the next checkpoint.

Machen to Risca 3 miles 1022 feet of ascent Maps 2, 2B & 2C

Mynydd Machen, the first definable summit on the route, is ascended by an evenly graded path up through forestry to reach open common. This is the first of several commons encountered on this section where the public have a right of access for "air and exercise" because the land was in an area administered before 1974 by an urban district council (see note page 14). From the stile onto the common there is no defined path up to the summit, where there is a trig point and radio station *(Checkpoint No.3)*. The fine panorama includes views across the Bristol Channel and up the former mining valleys of Rhymney, Ebbw and Sirhowy. The way off is to follow the access road to the radio station. On reaching a minor road turn right for 150m before turning left into field at signpost,as per map 2C. As at 1999 OS maps omitted the right of way there. Follow field and forest paths down to Risca.

Risca to Pontypool 8.2 miles 1504 feet of ascent Maps 2C, 3 & 3A

The crossing of the Ebbw Valley between Risca and Crosskeys is more populated than the Rhymney crossing at Machen, and has many of the typical features of the South Wales mining valleys. After a pleasant short section by the disused Monmouthshire and Brecon Canal, a plod up a dead end road leads to common land. At Pegwyn-y-bwlch one may be joined in the ascent of Twmbarlwm by walkers who have left their cars at a high point on the Cwmcarn Forest Drive. The ancient camp at Twmbarlwm is a worthy summit for a further checkpoint. *(No.4)* There is a problem of erosion here caused mainly by motor cyclists who have no right to ride on this common. Walkers, however, have a right of access as this is another common in a former urban district. One continues on this common nearly all the way to Pontypool

Along the length of Mynydd Henllys the view to the right is onto the new town of Cwmbran, developed in the last forty years. It is the administrative centre of Monmouthshire County. At the point where the forest on the left starts to veer from the ridge the preferred route keeps on the contour on a public footpath that is undefined on the ground, but peak baggers may prefer to keep on the track up to Mynydd Maen. See the inset map for the short section off the common before the pleasant edge of common walk round the woodlands surrounding the Blaen Blan reservoirs. The Mountain Air Inn has closed but further on the Lamb Inn is a hospitable pub on the edge of the common before the descent by a narrow gated lane to Pontypool. Pass under new road at interchange and note the fine gates to Pontypool Park (Map3B)

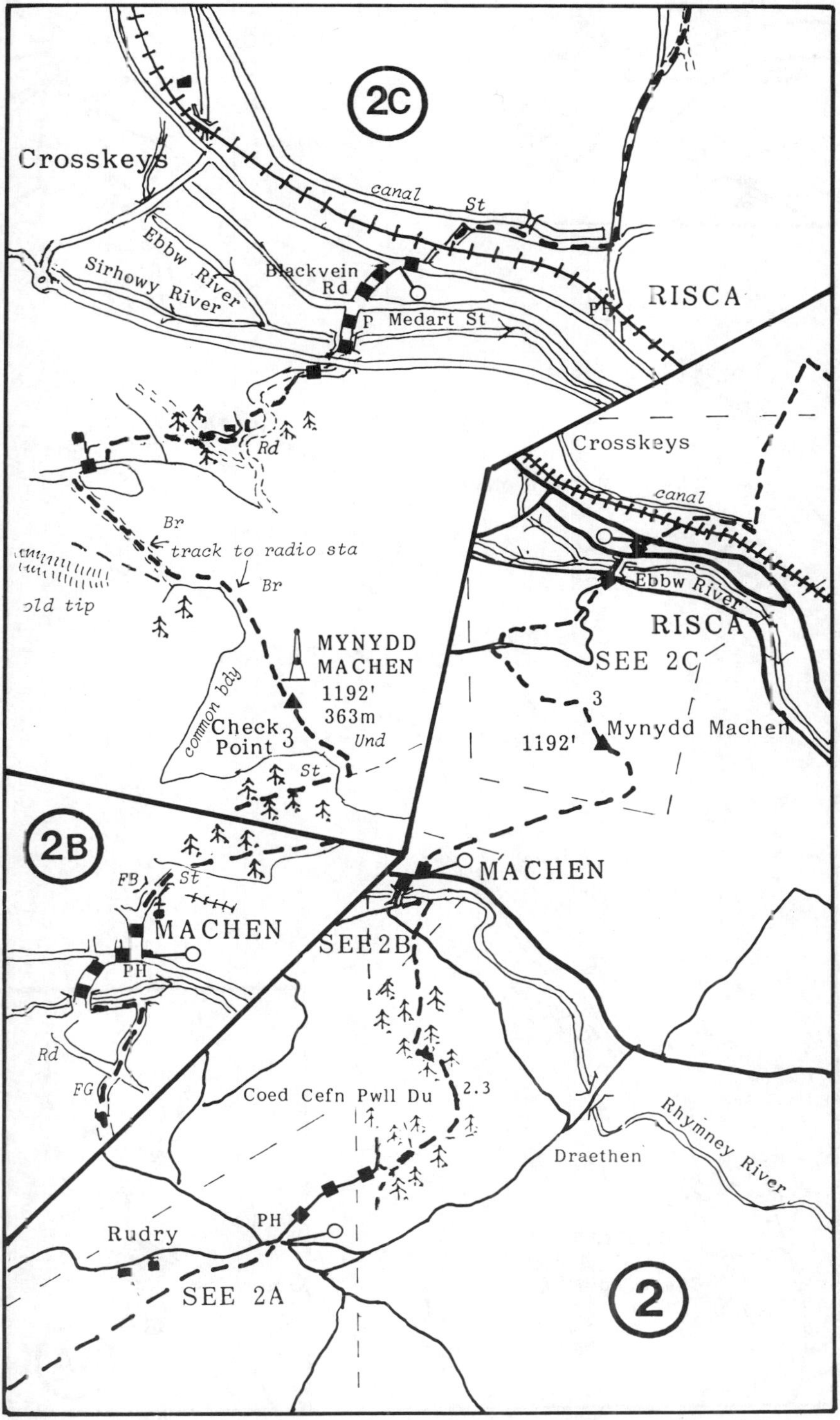
2C
Crosskeys
canal
St
Ebbw River
Sirhowy River
Blackvein Rd
P
Medart St
RISCA
PH
Rd
Br
track to radio sta
Br
old tip
MYNYDD MACHEN
1192'
363m
common bdy
Check Point
3
Und
St
Crosskeys
canal
Ebbw River
RISCA
SEE 2C
3
Mynydd Machen
1192'
2B
FB
St
MACHEN
PH
Rd
FG
MACHEN
SEE 2B
Coed Cefn Pwll Du
2.3
Draethen
Rhymney River
Rudry
PH
SEE 2A
2

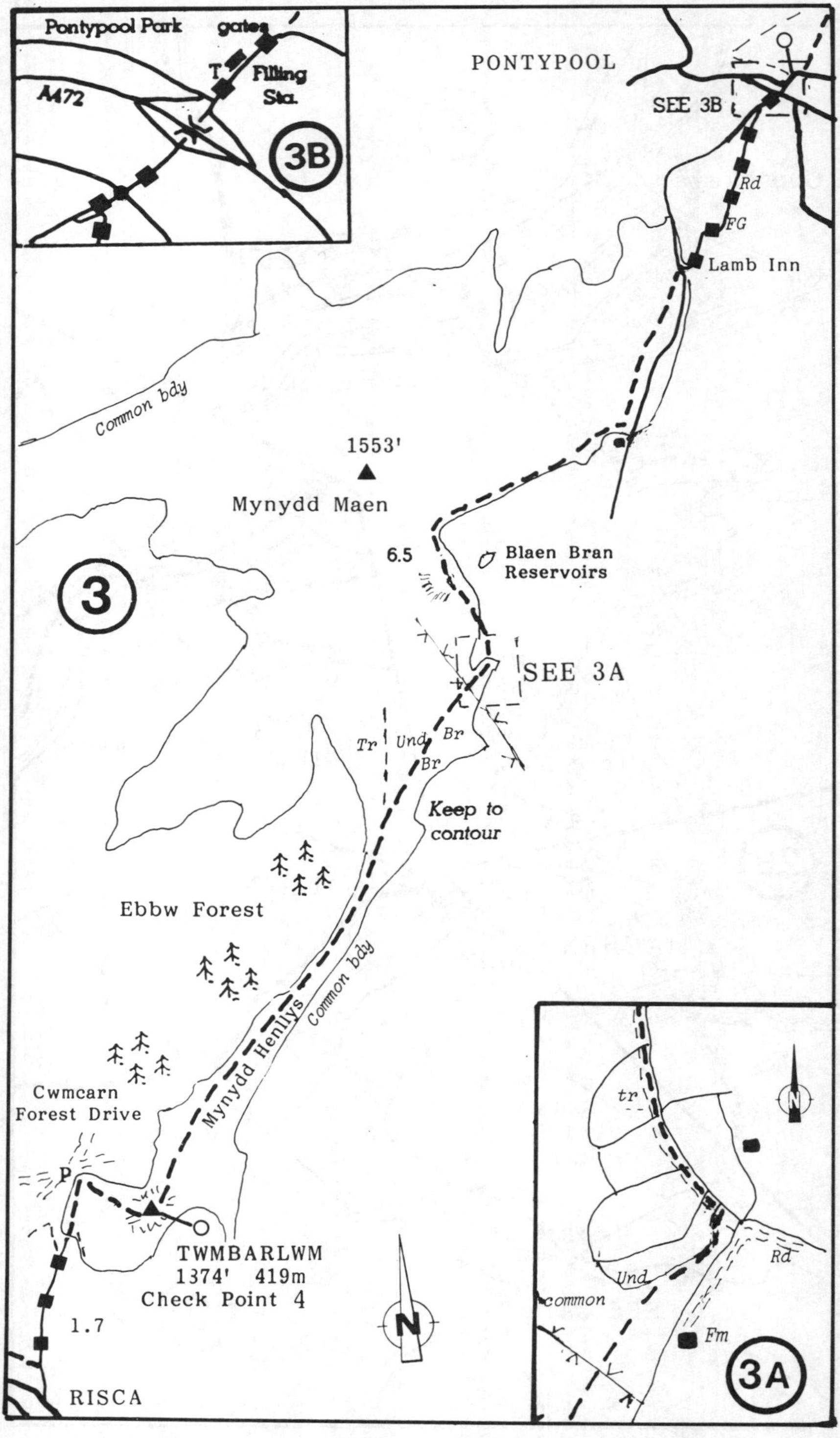
Pontypool Park
gates
T
Filling Sta.
A472
3B
PONTYPOOL
SEE 3B
Rd
FG
Lamb Inn
Common bdy
1553'
Mynydd Maen
6.5
Blaen Bran Reservoirs
3
SEE 3A
Tr
Und
Br
Br
Keep to contour
Ebbw Forest
Common bdy
Mynydd Henllys
Cwmcarn Forest Drive
P
TWMBARLWM
1374' 419m
Check Point 4
1.7
RISCA
N
tr
N
Rd
Und
common
Fm
3A

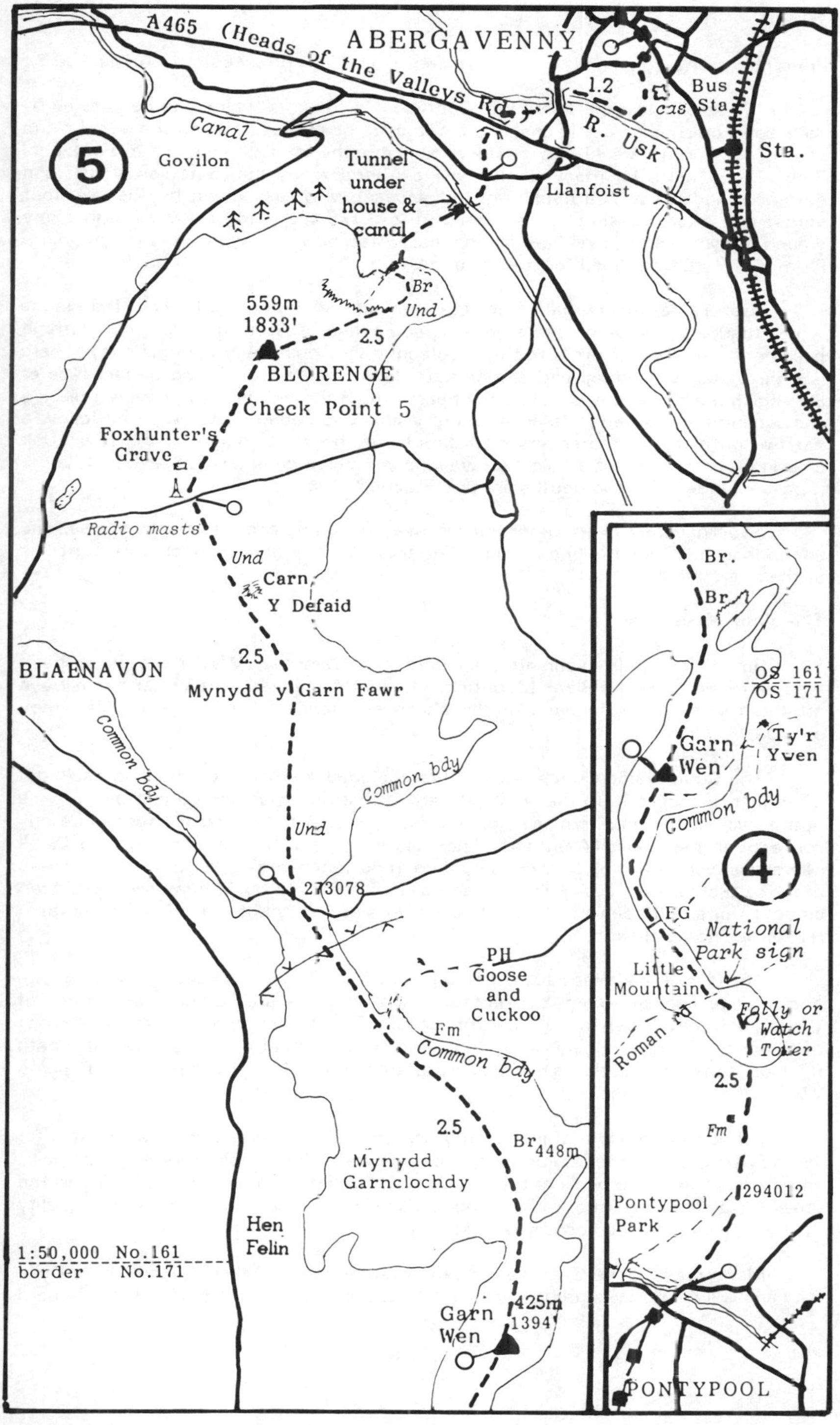
A465 (Heads of the Valleys Rd
ABERGAVENNY
1.2
cas
Bus Sta
R. Usk
Sta.
Canal
5
Govilon
Tunnel under house & canal
Llanfoist
Br
Und
559m 1833'
2.5
BLORENGE
Check Point 5
Foxhunter's Grave
Radio masts
Und
Carn Y Defaid
2.5
BLAENAVON
Mynydd y Garn Fawr
Common bdy
Common bdy
Und
273078
PH Goose and Cuckoo
Fm
Common bdy
2.5
Br 448m
Mynydd Garnclochdy
Hen Felin
1:50,000 No.161
border No.171
Garn Wen
425m 1394'
Br.
Br.
OS 161
OS 171
Garn Wen
Ty'r Ywen
Common bdy
4
FG
National Park sign
Little Mountain
Roman rd
Folly or Watch Tower
2.5
Fm
294012
Pontypool Park
PONTYPOOL

Pontypool to Abergavenny 11.3 miles 1691 ft. of ascent Maps 4 & 5 .

The most pleasant amenity of Pontypool is the Park which can be entered by the palatial ornamental gates, enabling a detour to be made, rejoining the direct route at 294012. For the direct route mostly enclosed paths are followed to the Pontypool Folly. From there, for most of the way to Abergavenny the route lies along open common land (all with a public right of access) with easy going for the first four miles, but after crossing a minor road at 273078 the going is over rough stony ground. Waymarks on posts have made it easier to find the way but it is rough going. From Carn y Defaid head for the radio masts.

Before taking the path from the east side of the car park, view the plaque which marks the grave of the famous horse Foxhunter. From the trig. point summit head north-east for half a mile to the spectacular viewpoint over Abergavenny. There is a direct but very steep and eroded path down the centre of a north-east face of Blorenge but a better way is just north of east, down through bracken covered hillside and curving round to an isolated tree (not visible until lower down) whence follow a narrow path to the aforementioned direct way down. Descent to the River Usk crossing is on the line of an old tramway incline which goes through a tunnel where it passes under the Monmouthshire and Brecon Canal..

Abergavenny is an important gateway from England into South Wales, and abounds in B.&B. and eating places. The tourist office and national park centre is at the bus station.

The Black Mountains

Since the early planning stages of the Cambrian Way there have been arguments whether the Black Mountains should be included. The writer has always argued for inclusion because of the sheer excellence of the ridge walking they provide.

The Countryside Commission at first included them in the draft proposals but bowed to pressure from the National Park authority. When the project officer was appointed for the southern third of the Way, he was not asked to investigate any route over the Black Mountains. The Park's reasons for exclusion of the Black Mountains were based on their conservation importance and sensitivity, and because of the de facto access availability to walkers. This seems to be a "can't win" situation since if there had been no access this would also, no doubt, have been given as a reason for non-inclusion.

The Black Mountains have suffered greatly from erosion caused by horse riding, and only to a lesser extent by the feet of walkers. The area around the summit of Waun Fach may never recover its grass cover. The eroded approach to the summit of Sugar Loaf is badly scarred by foot erosion. One must accept a bare earth path for a lot of the way but this is not the sort of erosion problem that besets the Pennine Way with its peat bogs.

A frequent criticism of inclusion of the Black Mountains is that two days after leaving Abergavenny one is only four miles away at Crickhowell. This is a valid point and aggravating to the beeliners who only want to get from one end of Wales to the other, to say they have "done it". For our connoisseur of mountain walking the quality of the walking and the scenery is what counts.

Many prospective Cambrian Way walkers will have followed the Offa's Dyke Path and will recall having trudged along the 12 miles of the Hatterall Ridge. It's hard

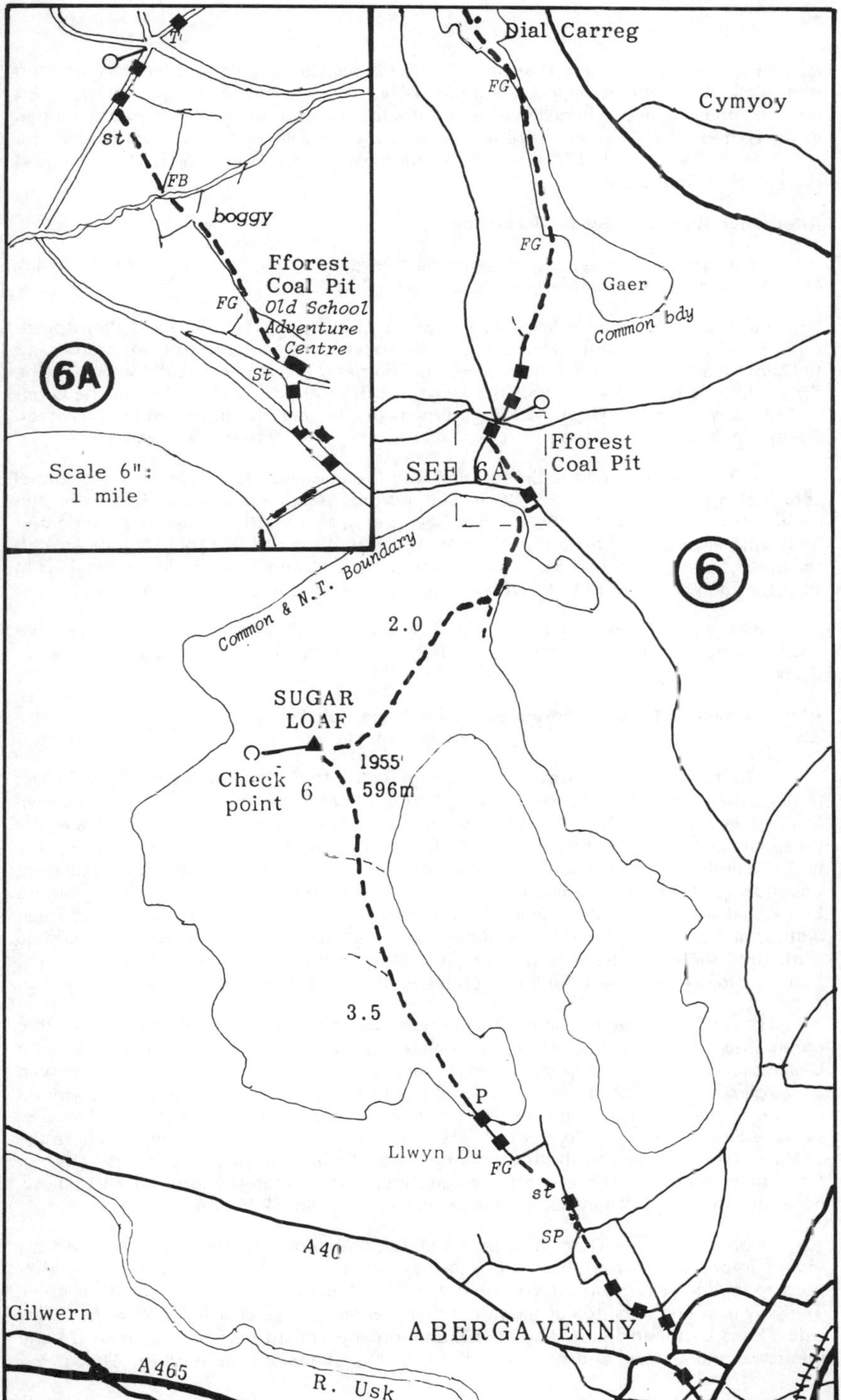
Dial Carreg
Cymyoy
FG
FG
Gaer
Common bdy
Fforest
Coal Pit
SEE 6A
6
Common & N.T. Boundary
2.0
SUGAR
LOAF
Check
point
6
1955'
596m
3.5
P
Llwyn Du
FG
st
SP
A40
Gilwern
ABERGAVENNY
A465
R. Usk
6A
st
FB
boggy
Fforest
Coal Pit
FG
Old School
Adventure
Centre
St
Scale 6":
1 mile

luck on Offa's Dyke walkers that their route follows the longest and least interesting of the Black Mountain ridges. Cambrian Way follows most of the good ridges, but never for too long in one direction or without some up and down. Whereas the slopes of the Hatterall Ridge curve to prevent views into the valleys immediately below, the opposite is true of the Bal Mawr and Pen Alltmawr ridges from which both near and distant views are superb.

Alternative Routes to Black Mountains

If despite the foregoing paragraphs the reader decides to by-pass the Black Mountains, there are several possibilities, as follows:

1. From Blorenge to Mynydd Llangattock, crossing the B4246 at Pen-ffordd-goch Pond (255108) and proceeding across open common land to Llam-march and to Cwm Clydach national nature reserve. The dramatic gorge is crossed by the Devil's Bridge thence by subway under the Heads of the Valleys road (A465) to the Drum and Monkey Inn at Blackrock. The escarpment of the east and north sides of Mynydd Llangattock can be followed to rejoin the main route at Daren Cilau (200159).

2. The towpath of the Brecon and Usk Canal can be followed from the tunnel referred to in the text at 285130 to Llangattock, near Crickhowell. Said to be the most attractive canal in Britain, it has been much restored for pleasure boating and its towpath is well maintained by the national park authority. On this six mile stretch the canal twists and turns as it follows the contours round the hillside some 150 to 200 feet above the river Usk, with consequent good views across the valley.

3. From the summit of Sugar Loaf to Crickhowell either via Mynydd Pen-y-fal and Llangenny or via Cwm Gwenffrwd, Cwrt-ygollen and riverside walk to Crickhowell Bridge.

Abergavenny to Capel-y-ffin via Sugar Loaf and Bal Mawr
13 miles 3443 feet of ascent Maps 6 to 8

The recommended way out of Abergavenny from the Town Hall Clock Tower is along the main street, thence via Pen-y-Pound (297145) and Avenue Road to Llwyn Du. One is spoilt for choice as to ways up Sugar Loaf from Abergavenny. There are pleasant routes up the east side of the Rhclben ridge and up the ridge itself but the author's preferred route is up St. Mary's Vale on the west side of that ridge. The path ascends gradually from a small car park onto the open bracken covered common. Sugar Loaf has public right of access both because it is a common in a former urban district and because it is National Trust land open to the public. Keep on ascending path until the broad ridge is gained then follow paths to the summit, avoiding the badly eroded south-west flank (which leads in from the highest car park).

Leave Sugar Loaf by the north-east ridge again taking care not to cause further erosion near the top. A short lane connects the common to a minor road at Fforest Coal Pit (charcoal, not the black variety) whence paths and minor roads are followed to Dialgarreg where the splendour of the Black Mountain ridges begins to be apparent as one looks down on the right to the Vale of Ewyas and to the left the forested Grwyne Fawr. Across the former valley is the crooked church at Cwmyoy, where the chancel tilts one way and the tower another. In the latter valley, and worth a detour from the cross roads at Fforest if time permits, is the isolated church of Partrishow, noted for its rood loft with beautiful carved oak screen, (279224).

Continuing over Garn Wen to Bal Mawr, the ridge becomes narrower and the views improve into the contrasting valleys on either side. About half a mile after passing the forest turn right for Capel-y-ffin at a stone called the Blacksmith's Anvil. The way is at first none too apparent but then becomes a steep track down the valley side . Pass between The Grange (B&B and inquiries about camping further on) and the former monastery, and so to Capel-y-ffin (The chapel on the border). *Check Pt.7*

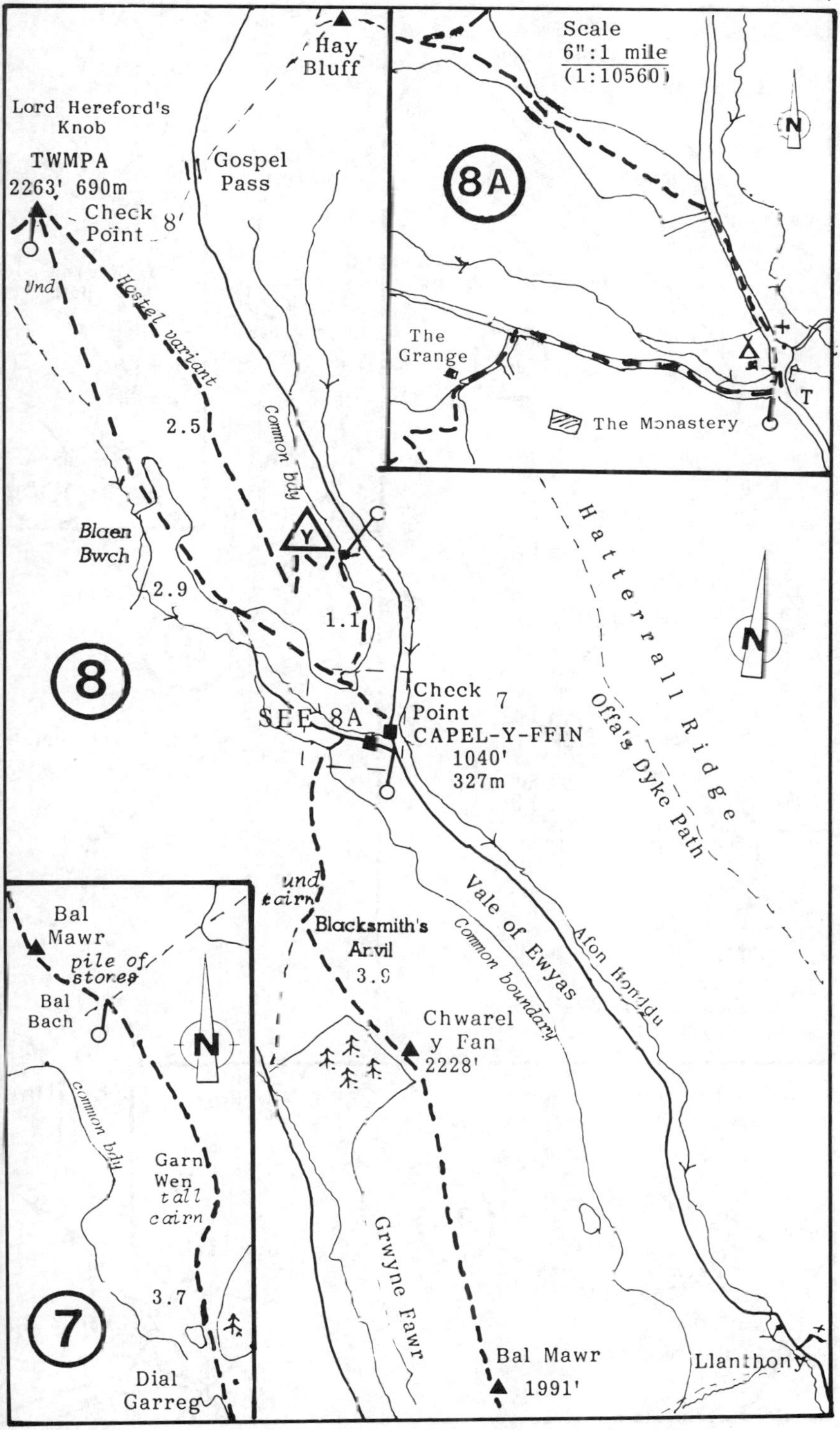
Hay Bluff
Scale
6":1 mile
(1:10560)
N
8A
Lord Hereford's Knob
TWMPA
2263' 690m
Check Point 8
Gospel Pass
Und
Hostel variant
The Grange
T
The Monastery
2.5
Common bdy
Blaen Bwch
Y
2.9
1.1
Hatterrall Ridge
N
8
Check Point 7
SEE 8A
CAPEL-Y-FFIN
1040'
327m
Offa's Dyke Path
und cairn
Bal Mawr
Blacksmith's Anvil
3.9
Vale of Ewyas
Common boundary
Afon Honddu
pile of stones
Bal Bach
N
Chwarel y Fan
2228'
common bdy
Garn Wen
tall cairn
Grwyne Fawr
3.7
7
Bal Mawr
1991'
Llanthony
Dial Garreg

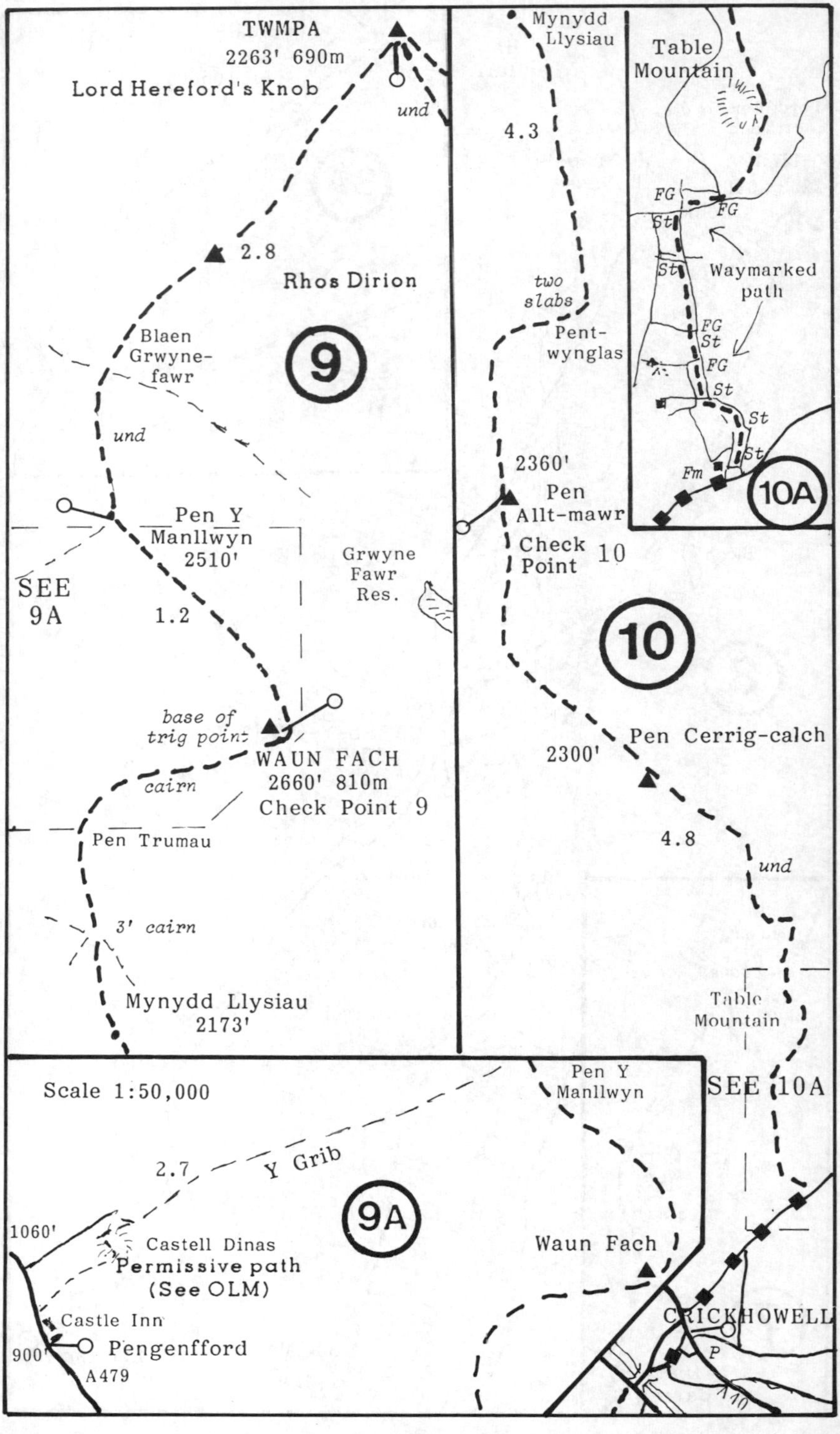
TWMPA
2263' 690m
Lord Hereford's Knob
und
2.8
Rhos Dirion
Blaen
Grwyne-
fawr
9
und
Pen Y
Manllwyn
2510'
SEE
9A
1.2
Grwyne
Fawr
Res.
base of
trig point
WAUN FACH
2660' 810m
Check Point 9
cairn
Pen Trumau
3' cairn
Mynydd Llysiau
2173'
Mynydd
Llysiau
4.3
two
slabs
Pent-
wynglas
2360'
Pen
Allt-mawr
Check
Point 10
10
Pen Cerrig-calch
2300'
4.8
und
Table
Mountain
FG
St
Waymarked
path
Fm
10A
Table
Mountain
SEE 10A
Scale 1:50,000
Pen Y
Manllwyn
2.7
Y Grib
9A
1060'
Castell Dinas
Permissive path
(See OLM)
Castle Inn
Pengenfford
900'
A479
Waun Fach
CRICKHOWELL
P

This idyllic spot at the junction of steep sided valleys was initially an idea for the starting place for the Cambrian Way. It was soon apparent that this was no equivalent of Edale on the Pennine Way and needed easier lines of communication.

For those anxious to see the impressive ruins of Llanthony Abbey and prepared to forgo the pleasures of the Bal Mawr ridge a descent can be made from Bal-bach (273267) . After visiting the abbey , follow the very minor roads and tracks on the NE side of the river Honddu via Broadley and the Vision Farm to Capel-y-ffin. The main road up the valley is narrow with high hedges and not recommended for walking.

Capel-y-ffin to Crickhowell via Twmpa, Waun Fach and Pen Allt Mawr Ridge
16 miles 2652 feet of ascent Maps 8 to 10

A section of very narrow road and a field path leads back to the open common whence the main route to Twmpa and the hostel variant divide. If going to the hostel, this way is preferable to the suicidal road route to the gate below the hostel. The Youth Hostel is a friendly old farmhouse with resident warden and is rather special in that it was provided by the King George VI Memorial Fund, which provided one hostel each in England, Scotland, Wales and Northern Ireland. The route from the hostel to Twmpa is via a steep climb at the back of the hostel and a superb viewpoint looking down the Vale of Ewyas.

Twmpa, also known as Lord Hereford's Knob, is *check point number 8* . This splendid viewpoint on the N W. escarpment of the Black Mountains looks out across the wide valley of the Wye to the hil]ls of central Wales . Two miles away to the NE is Hay Bluff, as near as Cambrian Way gets to the Offa's Dyke Path. In between is the Gospel Pass over which the icecap of the Great Ice Age overflowed to make the Vale of Ewyas the only glaciated valley of the Black Mountains.

From Twmpa to Waun Fach a path is well worn along the open common except after crossing the old track coming up from Grwyne Fawr where there are several rival paths. A compass will certainly by needed in mist. From just short of Pen y Minllwyn (small cairn) a diversion can be made down Y Grib to Pengenffordd and the Castle Inn. The summit of Waun Fach is on a flat plateau and not exactly impressive as the highest point in the Black Mountains. It is *check point number 9* but our Mountain Connoisseur is excused having to walk to the actual base of the former trig. point provided a wide circuit is taken round it, well beyond the summit area, which is devoid of vegetation due to too many feet ,both human and equine.

The eroded parts of the slope going westwards from Waun Fach can be by-passed without causing more erosion. Superb ridge walking follows over Mynydd Llysiau, Pen Allt-mawr and Pen Cerrig-calch before descent to the curious Table Mountain, an iron age hill fort, which is aptly named. The open common is left just below Table Mountain at 225203 and waymarked field paths followed (see map 10A) to a road leading into Crickhowell.

Crickhowell is a small town with many scheduled buildings. One of these was the Youth Hostel but regrettably serious structural defects were discovered which were beyond the resources of the YHA to remedy, causing its closure in 1982. There is, however, B &B, a good camp site, and many pubs providing meals.

Crickhowell to Storey Arms via Mynydd Llanynidr and Pen y Fan
20 miles & 4896 feet of ascent via Torpantau Pass (+ 1.7 miles to Llwyn y celyn YH) or 13.9 miles(1808ft) and 10.7miles (3865ft), using the **Talybont variant.**

Crickhowell Bridge, over the Usk, is a gem of an old stone bridge. From it a path leads over fields to Llangattock church and thence up to the Brecon and Usk Canal, the towpath of which is followed for half a mile, as far as the second bridge. An old tramway route, at first on the flat, then up a very steep incline, leads to the area of the former Llangattock quarries. The next two miles provide some of the most spectacular scenery on the whole Cambrian Way. The area is a nature reserve. An old

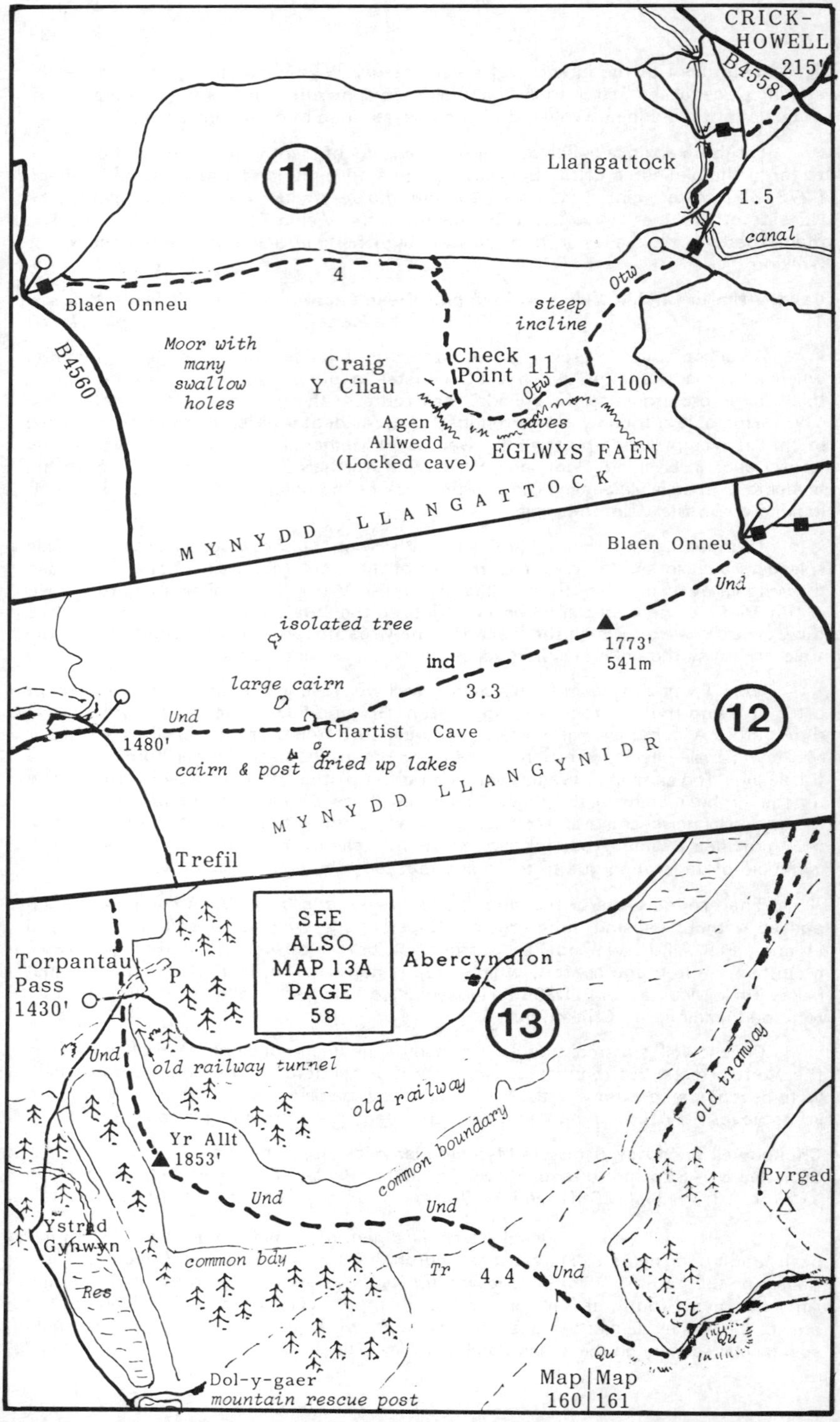
CRICK-
HOWELL
215'
B4558
Llangattock
11
1.5
canal
Blaen Onneu
4
Otw
steep
incline
B4560
Moor with
many
swallow
holes
Craig
Y Cilau
Check
Point 11
1100'
Otw
Agen
Allwedd
(Locked cave)
caves
EGLWYS FAEN
MYNYDD LLANGATTOCK
Blaen Onneu
Und
isolated tree
1773'
541m
ind
large cairn
3.3
12
Und
1480'
Chartist Cave
cairn & post
dried up lakes
MYNYDD LLANGYNIDR
Trefil
SEE
ALSO
MAP 13A
PAGE
58
Torpantau
Pass
1430'
P
Abercynafon
13
Und
old railway tunnel
old railway
old tramway
common boundary
Yr Allt
1853'
Und
Und
Pyrgad
Ystrad
Gynwyn
common bdy
Res
Tr
4.4
Und
St
Qu
Qu
Dol-y-gaer
mountain rescue post
Map 160
Map 161

tramway route on a ledge below Darren Cilau leads to a spot where a short scramble gives access into a large open cave, Eglwys Faen, which can be explored with a torch and considerable care. *(Check point no. 11.)* A different proposition is Agen Allwedd cave which is many miles long and only accessible to those with a key. Watch for a path which gradually descends off the main ledge to the base of the cliff and to an area of springs and swamp before reaching the Llangattock - Blaen Onneu road. One can walk along the grassy common land rather than the road itself.

From the road junction at Blaen Onneu across Mynydd Llangynidr is a very wild and open moor, over which careful navigation is essential, even with good visibility. This is cave country with many swallow holes and sheep tracks, but few defined paths. The rights of way do not help but de facto access is traditional here.The first objective is the trig. point at 148159 but more difficult to find is the Chartist Cave, where clandestine presses printed forbidden political papers a century and a half ago. Cairns and an isolated tree provide clues but in mist only good compass and contour navigation will enable the socialist pilgrim to find the wide open cave, facing south, and appreciate this inhospitable shelter. If the cave can be easily missed at least one should strike the road to Hendre and Ystrad quarries. Keep away from the quarries and follow the line of an old tramroad between the quarries and the top of the crop into the very steep sided valley of Dyffryn Crawnon. At a stile the main route and the Talybont Variant divide, the variant continuing on the tramroad while the main route turns left before the stile and hugs the fence round the edge of the quarry area until the open common is gained, whence strike across open moor to the ridge of Yr Allt and so down to Torpantau Pass.

From Torpantau to Pen y Fan, the highest point in the Brecon Beacons, the obvious and popular route is via Craig y Fan-ddu, Craig Cwareli and Cribin. The first of several eroded sections on this route is the ascent of Craig y Fan-ddu. This seems to have been aggravated by putting a car park in the forest near Torpantau Pass, but our Cambrian Way walker will add little to the erosion if discretion is exercised in using either the worn track or avoiding it. At a stream (050192) a line is struck across the wild moorland top for half a mile to meet the crag-top path at Craig Cwareli.

The Talybont Variant was added to the last edition to facilitate a break up of the Crickhowell to Storey Arms section. The track of the old tramroad can be followed all the way to Talybont-on-Usk, a village on the Brecon & Usk canal, or ways followed down through forest to Abercynafon (excellent B & B) or the small campsite below Talybont Reservoir. To save a major reshuffle of pages, map 13A, for the variant, is on page 58.

From Craig Cwareli,where the routes rejoin, to Pen y Fan and on to Storey Arms, the paths are all very worn, including short cuts of Fan Big and Cribin. The purists will visit all the summits but only Pen y Fan has been made a check point so as not to discourage the less eroded alternative described below. It is the south-east ridge of Pen y Fan which provides the National Park with its most intractable erosion problem, and which seems only likely to be solved by a concession to artificiality in some form of steps if the mountain is not to be gradually worn away. However Pen y Fan will not disappear for a few million years yet, so if you want to follow the most spectacular cragtop route in the Brecon Beacons you must accept the erosion eyesores and your contribution to gradual lowering of the mountains.

There is an alternative between Torpantau and Pen y Fan along the long and less interesting cragtop ridge accessible from the base of the lower Neuadd reservoir and passing along Craig Fan Ddu (no connection with crag three paragraphs ago), and Bwlch Duwynt . This route, often used as a return on a horseshoe ascent of Pen y Fan from Torpantau, was put forward in Mr. Tetlow's report as a suggested route for Cambrian Way. The owners, National Trust and Forestry Commission, were said to be agreeable. There was a naive assumption that the summit of Pen y Fan would be by-passed, but at least if it is visited the south-east ridge up it is avoided.

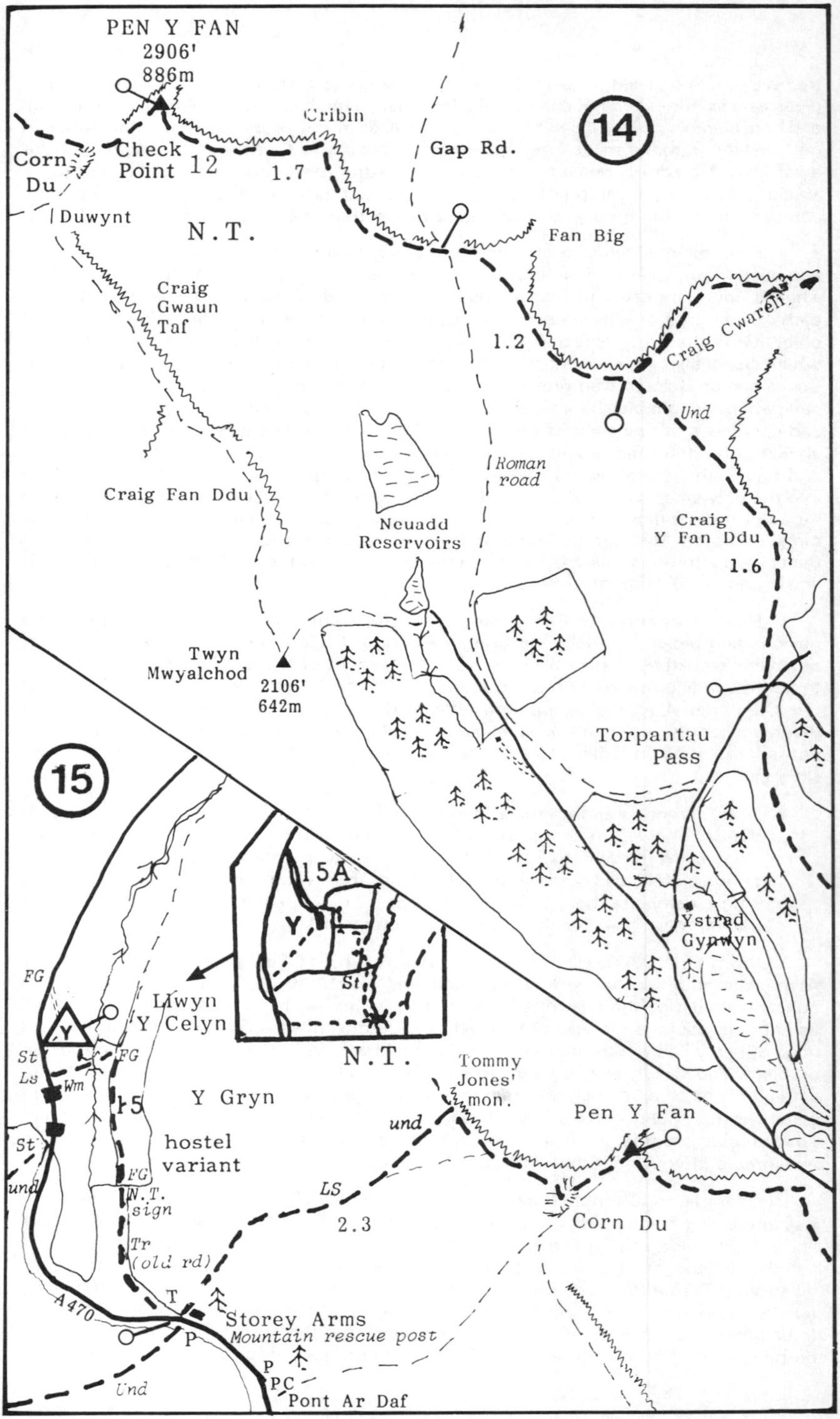
PEN Y FAN
2906'
886m
Cribin
14
Gap Rd.
Corn Du
Check Point 12
1.7
Duwynt
N.T.
Fan Big
Craig Gwaun Taf
1.2
Craig Cwareli
Und
Roman road
Craig Fan Ddu
Neuadd Reservoirs
Craig Y Fan Ddu
1.6
Twyn Mwyalchod
2106'
642m
Torpantau Pass
15
15A
Y
St
Ystrad Gynwyn
FG
Llwyn Y Celyn
Y
St
FG
Ls
Wm
N.T.
Tommy Jones' mon.
15
Y Gryn
und
Pen Y Fan
hostel variant
St
und
FG
N.T. sign
LS
2.3
Corn Du
Tr (old rd)
T
A470
Storey Arms
Mountain rescue post
P
P
PC
Und
Pont Ar Daf

There is no need to follow the grossly overused and eroded path from Bwlch Duwynt to the A470 at Pont ar Daf. More rewarding is to come off the west side of the summit plateau of Corn Du and follow the north-west ridge down to an obelisk. This is a memorial to Tommy Jones who, aged five, got lost while staying at a farm in the valley, and whose body was found at that spot nearly a month later. The more popular route leaves the ridge before the memorial, but both routes cross the valley to a ladder stile, and so by path down to Storey Arms. The former pub which gives its name to this important road pass has long since gone, so that any sustenance here is more likely to be from an ice cream van. Part of the Outdoor Education Centre at the pass used to be a Youth Hostel but now the hostel in this area is a converted farmhouse 1¾ miles towards Brecon in less bleak surroundings. A quieter route to it than the busy trunk road is along the old road on the east side of the valley and then by a new permissive route across National Trust land from 977222 (See15A.)

Storey Arms to Llandovery via Fforest Fawr and the Black Mountain

22.6 miles | 4955 ft of Ascent | Maps 16 to 20

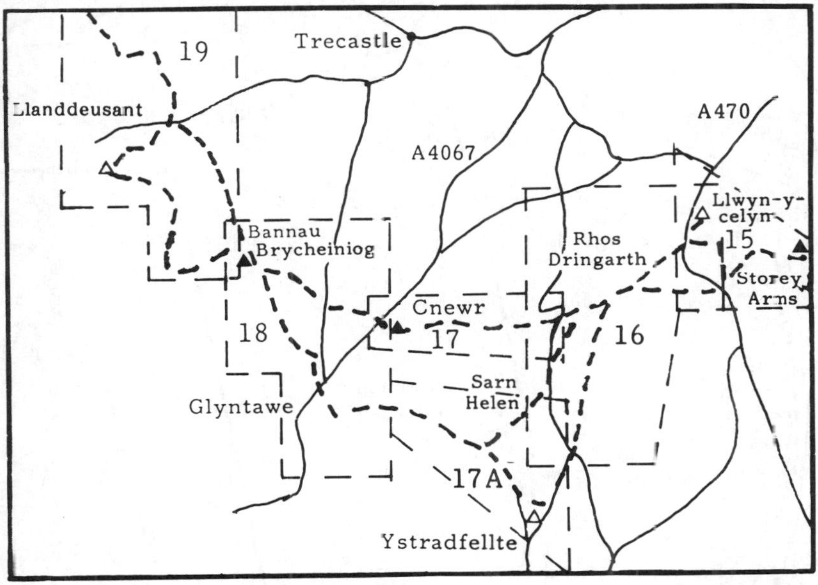

Map showing the relationship of the alternative routes between the Brecon Beacons and the Black Mountain (Carmarthen Vans), and the strip maps involved

Fforest Fawr (Great Forest) is not forest in the modern sense but is large open moorland. It is in two main sections. The eastern part is between the Brecon to Merthyr road (A470) and the minor road from Heol Senni to Ystradfellte. Another large section is on the east side of the main ridge of the Black Mountain with Bannau Brycheiniog part way along its open boundary with the Black Mountain common. These enormous commons are used for grazing by many farmers from the surrounding area. In February 1984, the National Park authority purchased the eastern part and several other sections from the Eagle Star Insurance Company for £30,000, with the help of grants from the National Heritage Memorial Fund and the Countryside Commission. The purpose of this very welcome purchase was to protect the commons, to conserve the open hill landscape and also the access on foot which the public has enjoyed in practice, if not as of right, for many years.

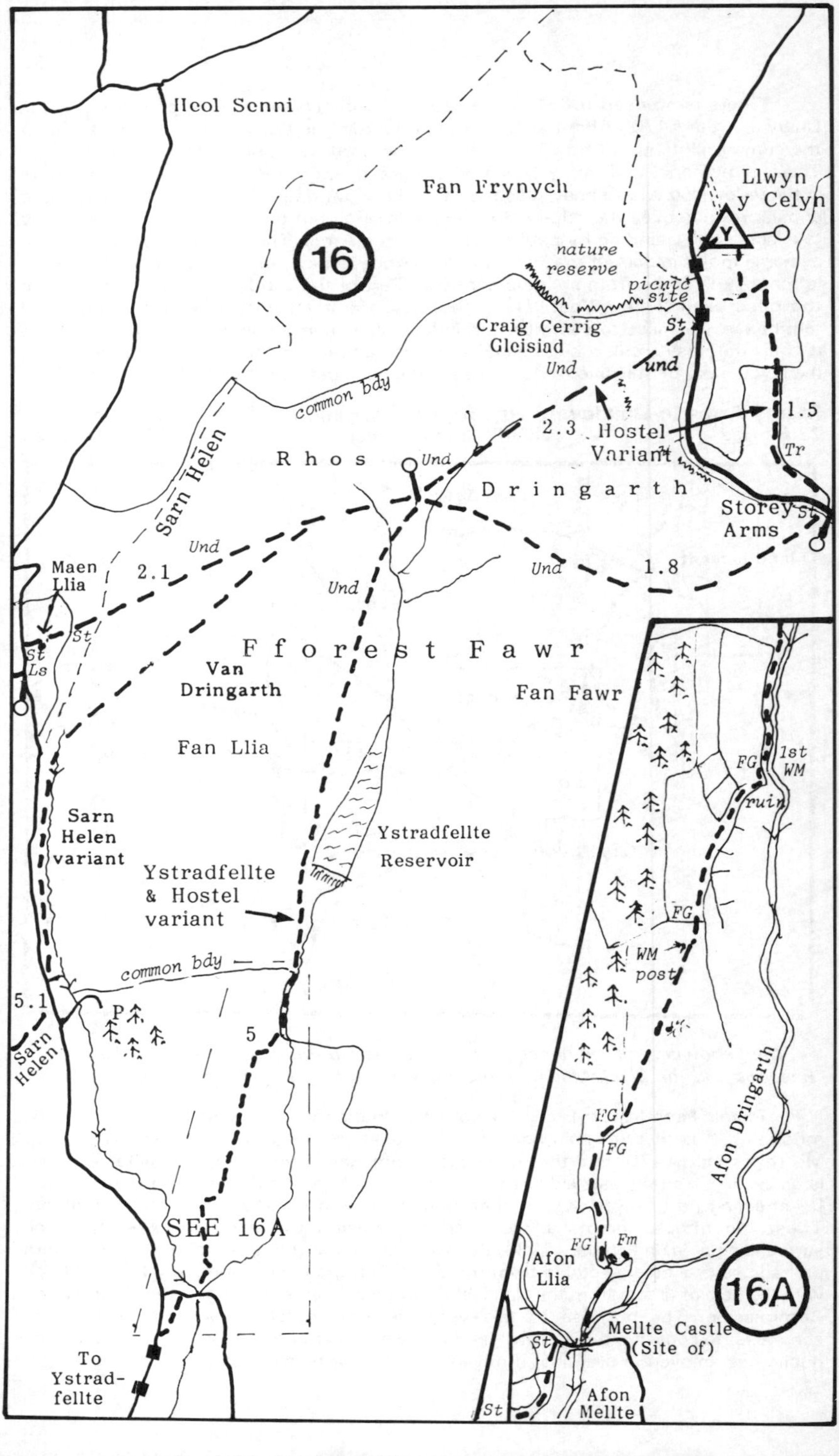
Heol Senni
Fan Frynych
16
nature reserve
picnic site
Llwyn y Celyn
Y
Craig Cerrig Gleisiad
St
Und
und
common bdy
Sarn Helen
2.3
Hostel Variant
1.5
Tr
Rhos
Und
Dringarth
Storey Arms
St
Und
2.1
Maen Llia
St
Ls
Und
1.8
Und
Fforest Fawr
Van Dringarth
Fan Fawr
Fan Llia
Sarn Helen variant
Ystradfellte Reservoir
Ystradfellte & Hostel variant
common bdy
5.1
Sarn Helen
P
5
SEE 16A
To Ystrad-fellte
FG
1st WM
ruin
FG
WM post
FG
FG
Afon Dringarth
FG
Fm
Afon Llia
16A
Mellte Castle (Site of)
St
Afon Mellte
St

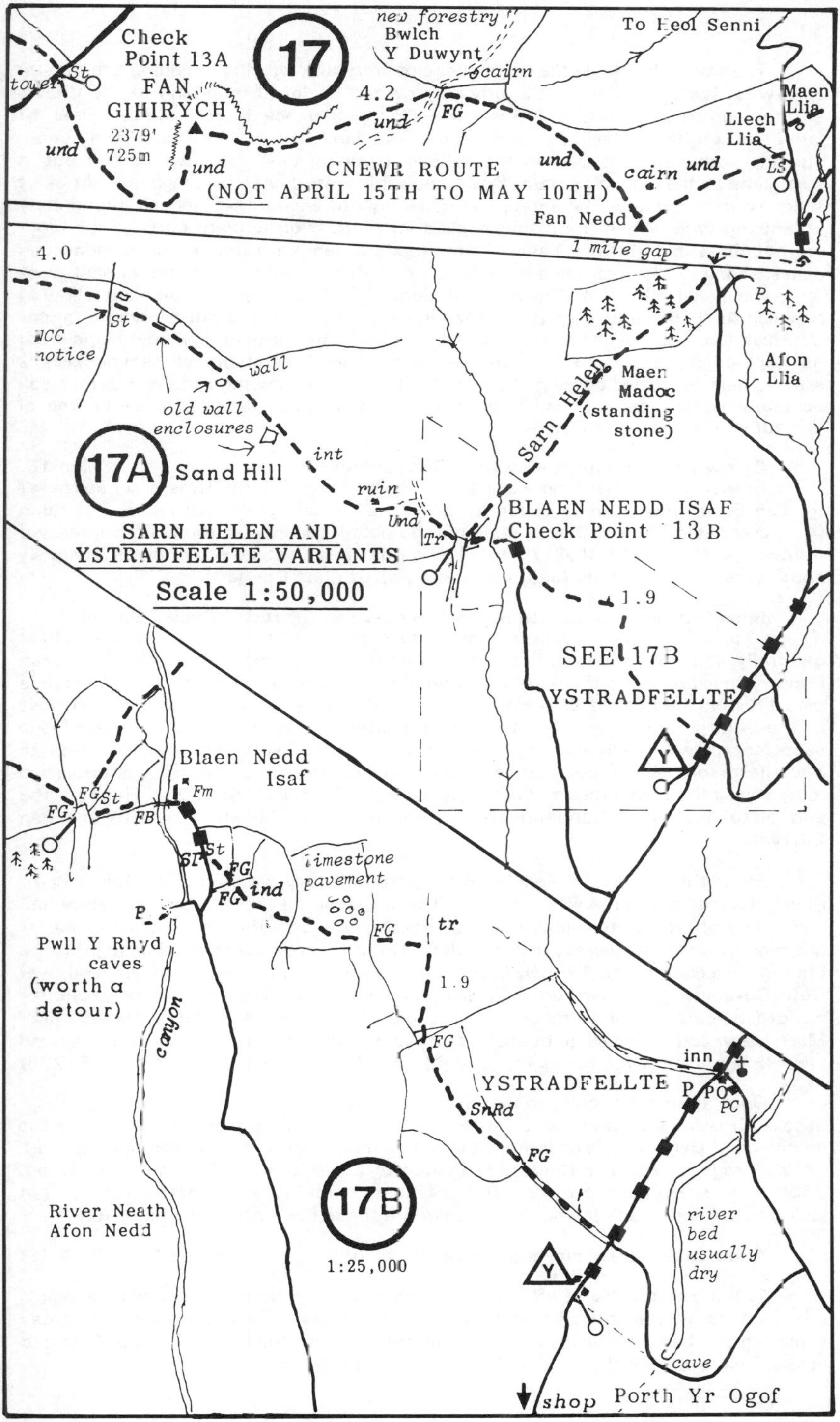
17
Check Point 13A
FAN GIHIRYCH
2379'
725m
tower
St
und
new forestry
Bwlch Y Duwynt
cairn
4.2
FG
To Heol Senni
Maen Llia
Llech Llia
LS
CNEWR ROUTE
(NOT APRIL 15TH TO MAY 10TH)
cairn
Fan Nedd
1 mile gap
4.0
St
WCC notice
wall
old wall enclosures
17A
Sand Hill
int
ruin
Und
Tr
Sarn Helen
Maen Madoc (standing stone)
Afon Llia
P
BLAEN NEDD ISAF
Check Point 13B
SARN HELEN AND YSTRADFELLTE VARIANTS
Scale 1:50,000
1.9
SEE 17B
YSTRADFELLTE
Y
Blaen Nedd Isaf
Fm
FG
St
FB
ST
ind
limestone pavement
P
tr
Pwll Y Rhyd caves
(worth a detour)
canyon
1.9
FG
YSTRADFELLTE
inn
P
PO
PC
SnRd
17B
1:25,000
River Neath
Afon Nedd
river bed usually dry
cave
shop
Porth Yr Ogof

The Cnewr Estate. In the north centre of Fforest Fawr, and including the natural east/west walking route, is the privately owned enclosed moorland of the Cnewr Estate. Lambing on sheep farms generally takes place in late winter, near to farmhouses in the valleys, but when the Cnewr land was first enclosed many years ago the estate had no land in the valleys. Lambing was therefore carried out in springtime on the open mountain. Due to possible disturbance by walkers and risk of sheep worrying by dogs the estate has generally not encouraged access, particularly at lambing time. When the estate applied for permission to plant parts of the moor with conifers in 1980 the National Park made a deal with the estate to reduce its demands and to allow access across the estate by two routes, including an east/west route via Fan Nedd, Fan Gihirych and Cefn Cul. Access is however not allowed between April 15th and May 10th , the lambing season, and is not allowed at night. Organised parties have to notify the National Park Authority in advance. Dogs must be kept on leads and no fires are permitted. Rough camping for backpackers is allowed near the ruined building of Llech Llia. During the lambing season a detour can be made via the Roman road Sarn Helen and Glyntawe, or the journey broken at Ystradfellte, as described below.

Storey Arms or Llwyn-y-celyn to Rhos Dringarth. Map 16.

Cnewr ,Sarn Helen and Ystradfellte routes leave Storey Arms and head west for Fan Fawr which can be ascended or by-passed on the northern side. If coming from Llwyn-y-celyn Youth Hostel, leave the hostel grounds at the S.W. corner and follow roadside verge of A470 for 400 yards then over stile and climb obliquely south-west onto the wide featureless expanse of Rhos Dringarth.

Rhos Dringarth to Bannau Brycheiniog via Fan Gihirych (Cnewr Estate)

Maps 16, 17 and 18. Once on the broad expanse of the rhos (moorland) strike generally south westwards. From the broad ridge between Cefn Perfedd and Fan Dringarth head towards the large standing stone, Maen Llia. A rough track, which is an old Roman road called Sarn Helen, is crossed shortly before reaching a wall. This is the edge of the Cnewr Estate. A stile invites one to cross the small enclosed section of moor to the standing stone and thence over a stile onto the Heol Senni to Ystradfellte road. A few yards south a ladder stile indicates the start of the permissive route across the Cnewr moors. *(Not between April 15th and May 10th).* Head for the summit of Fan Nedd, (undefined) then north west to Bwlch y Duwynt and Fan Gihirych.

From the summit of Fan Gihirych there is a very steep drop to Bwlch Brynrhudd, the road pass on A4067, so that it is necessary in the interests of safety and prevention of erosion to follow the edge southwards until the slope becomes easier and then to strike northwest to the bwlch. (Do not follow the suicidal descent route shown on Leisure map 12 1996 edition) The route continues on Cnewr land over Cefn Cul passing near a curious tower. Old walls and fence posts are useful for navigation across the bleak moor, and it is important to arrive at the ladder stile near Maen Mawr and stone circle because there is no other crossing of the high wall and barbed wire fence which marks the western boundary of the Cnewr Estate. (853203)

Once again one is on open land section of Fforest Fawr where there is de facto access. Crossing the Tawe can be tricky - if necessary cross higher up. Head for the south end of Llyn y Fan Fawr (not visible until almost there) then on the obvious path up the crags to Bwlch y Giedd and thence to the summit of Bannau Brycheiniog, 2630 feet, 802m,*(Check point 14)*, the highest point in the Carmarthen Vans. If in luck you will look back to the other peaks that have been ascended en route.

Alternative routes avoiding the Cnewr Estate. Maps 16, 17A & 18.

1. Via Ystradfellte. If an extra day can be spared then this variation is worth while on its own account because of the opportunity to spend at least a half day exploring the beautiful valleys around Ystradfellte with their famous waterfalls and caves. This assumes that a night is spent at Ystradfellte.

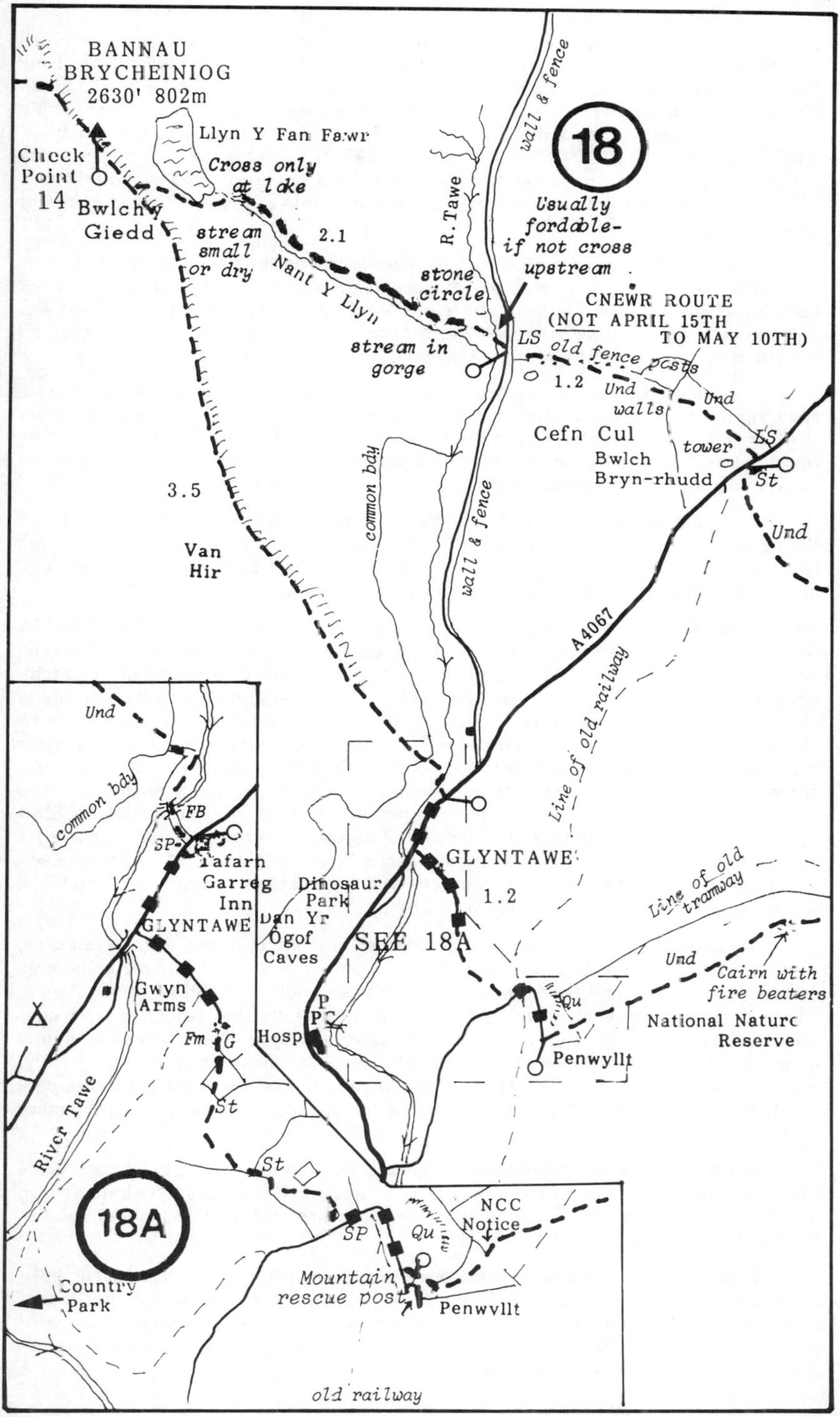
BANNAU BRYCHEINIOG
2630' 802m
Llyn Y Fan Fawr
Check Point 14
Cross only at lake
Bwlch y Giedd
stream small or dry
2.1
Nant Y Llyn
stone circle
R. Tawe
wall & fence
18
Usually fordable- if not cross upstream
CNEWR ROUTE (NOT APRIL 15TH TO MAY 10TH)
LS
stream in gorge
old fence posts
1.2
Und
walls
Cefn Cul
Bwlch Bryn-rhudd
tower
St
3.5
Van Hir
common bdy
A4067
Line of old railway
GLYNTAWE
SEE 18A
Dinosaur Park
Dan Yr Ogof Caves
Line of old tramway
Cairn with fire beaters
Qu
National Nature Reserve
Penwyllt
P
PC
Hosp
FB
SP
Tafarn Garreg Inn
Gwyn Arms
Fm
G
River Tawe
18A
Country Park
Mountain rescue post
NCC Notice
old railway

From Rhos Dringarth take a wide sweep round the moor, crossing several small tributaries of the Dringarth and then head south to pass along the west side of the Ystradfellte reservoir. Once past the dam drop down to the river and where a fence comes down from the west, turn alongside the river at 943168 and scramble between the river and the fence for about 400 yards to a gate where a waymarked public bridleway starts, near Blaen-tringarth at 942164. This is the only right of way off this part of the common and must be followed precisely. The waymarking is yellow Countryside Commission shape arrows and ends at the road near the site of Castell Mellte.

Ystradfellte. The solubility of the carboniferous limestone hereabouts has caused the rivers Mellte, Hepste and Nedd (Neath) to go underground, sometimes completely and in other parts for all except flood time. Alternate layers of hard and soft rocks have also caused waterfalls. Add to that the steep sided valleys clothed in natural woodlands and you have a wonderland of great interest and beauty.

If arriving from the Storey Arms area in the middle of the day one can, before spending the night, have a rewarding half day proceeding down the Mellte valley via Porth yr Ogof (large open cave) and the three Clun Gwyn falls to Sgwd yr Eira on the Hepste river. This latter is a waterfall with a public footpath that passes between the waterfall and the cliff it shoots over.

If two nights can be spent at Ystradfellte, a day is recommended exploring also the valleys of the Nedd, Sychryd and Pyrddin, especially if the rivers are low enough for walking along riverbeds. The cave systems should be treated with great respect, and only entered by experienced cavers with the appropriate equipment.

Ystradfellte to Glyntawe. Maps 17A,17B,18 & 18A

Routes from the youth hostel and from the area of the pub car park and church converge in a field at 920139 and then go west, past an interesting limestone pavement on the way to Blaen Nedd Isaf Farm. Go through a gate at the south end of the row of buildings. Sarn Helen, an old Roman road is crossed at 908144. Here starts a public footpath that traverses a wild open moor without touching any other highway for four miles . The 1: 50, 000 map shows little to guide one but the walls and small enclosures on the sketch map should more than suffice for navigation. The western half of the path is through a national nature reserve noted for its cave systems. The moorland path ends at a line of cottages forming a caving centre for the South Wales Caving Club.(Mountain Rescue Post) A disused railway is crossed at the Penwyllt quarries and a signpost followed on what appears to be an unofficial diversion at the start of a path down to Glyntawe.

Glyntawe, apart from being a scattered community in a very attractive valley, is noteworthy for the Dan yr Ogof Caves, claimed to be the largest showcave complex in Europe, and for Craig y nos Castle, an enormous Gothic style chateau where, at the turn of the last century Madame Adelina Patti, the famous opera singer provided lavish entertainment and was a frequent host to royalty. The castle is now a geriatric hospital but most of the fine grounds form a country park open to the public. An alternative path from Penwyllt via Rhongyr-uchaf gives access to the park at 843157. If time permits the caves should be visited and also the life size dinosaur park.

Glyntawe to Bannau Brycheiniog. Opposite the Tafarn-y-Garreg Inn a path leads to a footbridge and thence to the open common at 848173. The rough stone strewn hillside is climbed and the escarpment followed for three miles to its highest point at Bannau Brycheiniog.

2. Alternative to the Cnewr Estate via Sarn Helen. Maps 16,17A,17B,18, 18A. If seeking to avoid the Cnewr Estate but not wishing to go to Ystradfellte, take a more south-westerly line from Rhos Dringarth so as to hit the road where it is joined bv Sarn Helen at 925184 and thence via Maen Madoc to join the Ystradfellte to Glyntawe route near Blaen Nedd Isaf Farm at 908144.

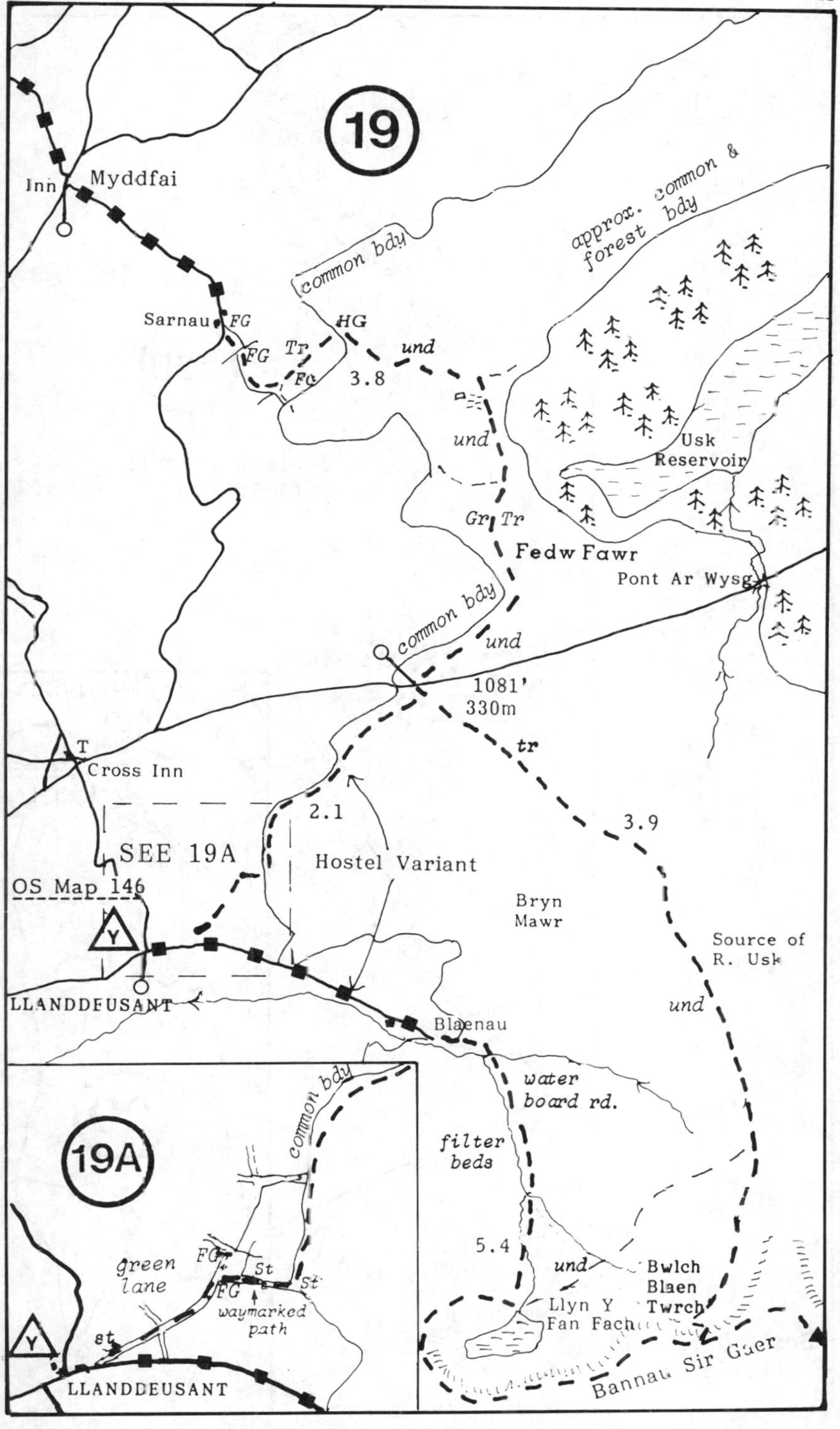
19
Inn
Myddfai
approx. common & forest bdy
common bdy
Sarnau
FG
HG
FG
Tr
Fc
und
3.8
und
Usk Reservoir
Gr Tr
Fedw Fawr
Pont Ar Wysg
common bdy
und
1081'
330m
tr
T
Cross Inn
2.1
3.9
SEE 19A
Hostel Variant
OS Map 146
Bryn Mawr
Y
Source of R. Usk
und
LLANDDEUSANT
Blaenau
water board rd.
filter beds
5.4
und
Bwlch Blaen Twrch
Llyn Y Fan Fach
Bannau Sir Gaer
19A
common bdy
green lane
FG
FG
St
St
waymarked path
st
Y
LLANDDEUSANT

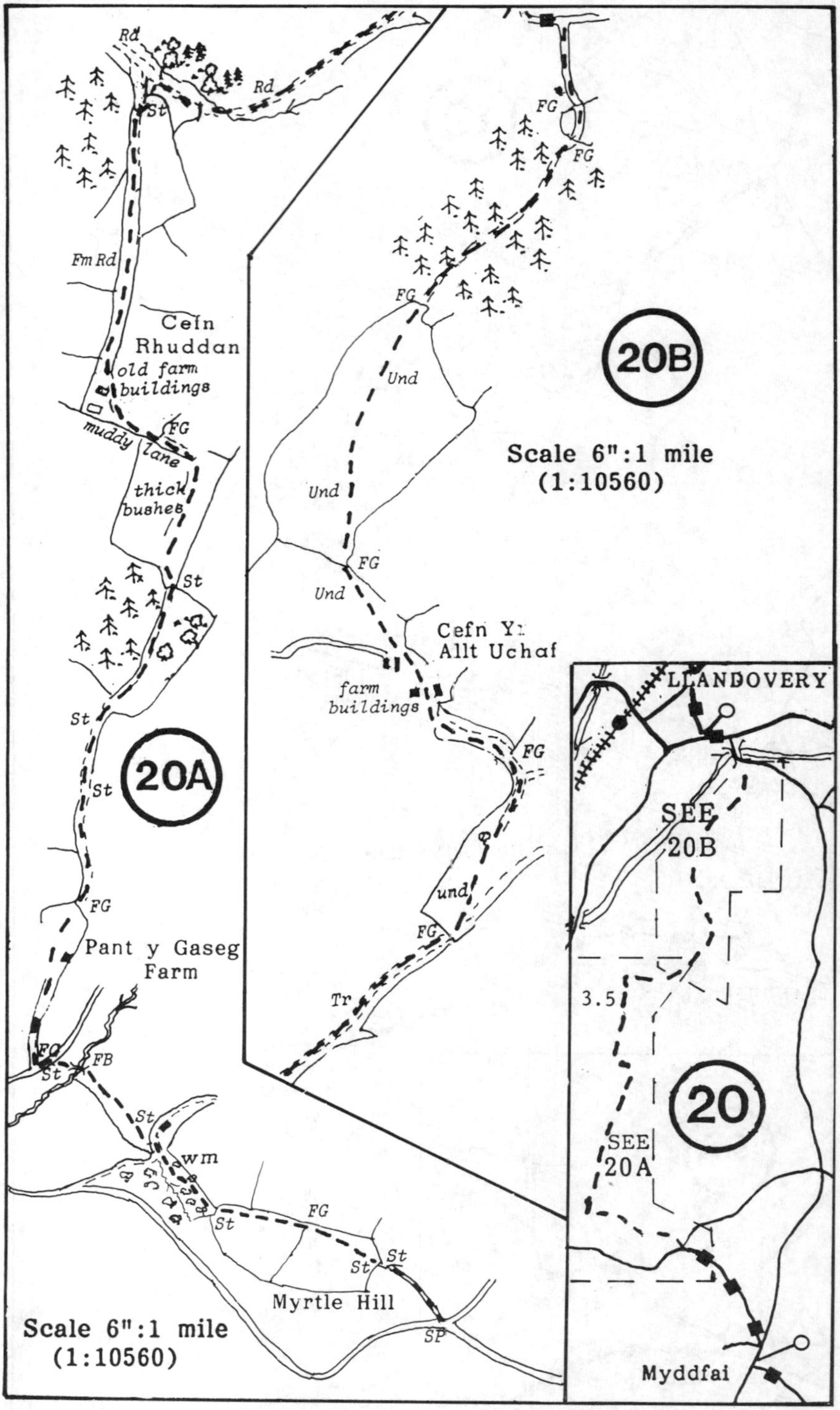
Rd
Rd
St
Fm Rd
Cefn
Rhuddan
old farm
buildings
muddy lane
FG
thick
bushes
St
St
St
20A
FG
Pant y Gaseg
Farm
FG
St
FB
St
wm
St
FG
St
St
Myrtle Hill
SP
Scale 6":1 mile
(1:10560)
FG
FG
FG
Und
Und
FG
Und
Cefn Yr
Allt Uchaf
farm
buildings
FG
und
FG
Tr
20B
Scale 6":1 mile
(1:10560)
LLANDOVERY
SEE
20B
3.5
20
SEE
20A
Myddfai

The Carmarthen Vans (Van = peak). I have always understood the term Carmarthen Vans to refer to the mountain range marked on the maps as the Black Mountain and the western end of Fforest Fawr. The Black Mountain (not to be confused with the Black Mountains at the other end of the national park) is in the former and future county of Carmarthen (Sir Gaer), though meanwhile part of Dyfed county. The Fforest Fawr section was in the county of Brecknock, also known as Breconshire, and now part of Powys county. Both constitute one enormous open moor to which there has been de facto public access from time immemorial. Farms from some distance around have grazing rights on these two commons. The Black Mountain was acquired by the national park authority in 1988 after abortive purchase by an Egyptian who was unable to complete the purchase and then by an unknown buyer.

The highest part of, the mountain range has two principal summits, thouoh neither can really be called peaks in the true sense. Bannau Brycheiniog (Brecknock Peaks) is the highest at 2630 feet / 802 metres, while the next highest is Bannau Sir Gaer at 2460 feet / 750 metres.

The walker may wonder how shepherds find their flocks if the sheep can wander anywhere on such a vast fenceless common. Under the hefting system the sheep get to know their patch and stick to it. They pass on their knowledge to their lambs. Sheep are very lost if driven off their patch and this is one reason why walkers should not have a dog with them. Sheep instinctively run away from a dog, even if it is on a lead. Unless surprised by walkers sheep are generally fairly oblivious to walkers as such and there need be no conflict of interest .

Carmarthen Vans to Llandovery. Maps 19,19A,20,20A & 20B

From the summits of the Carmarthen Vans the recommended route depends on whether the walker needs a roof for the night. The Youth Hostel in the tiny hamlet of Llanddeusant provides the excuse to walk the top of the superb escarpment of Bannau Sir Gaer, overlooking Llyn y Fan Fach and then to drop down to the lake and follow the water board road down to Blaenau and along a narrow minor road into Llanddeusant. Return route to the common is by grassy lanes.

The main route from Bannau Brycheiniog strikes northwards and continues over open land for another six miles before descending to lower levels with enclosed fields and roads. Avoid the obvious steep and erosion prone nose of Fan Foel and strike westwards to the pass of Bwlch Blaen Twrch at 816218, and down a zig-zag path before heading northwards. Our Mountain Connoisseur is however advised to do the whole circuit of Bannau Sir Gaer and down to Llyn y Fan Fach before contouring round to the direct route. Llyn y Fan Fach is the site of one of the most fascinating of Welsh legends, that of the Lady of the Lake. See Richard Sale's "A Cambrian - Way" and many other books.

The way via the source of the Usk and Bryn Mawr is fairly featureless and expert map and compass work may be necessary. About a mile after crossing the Llanddeusant to Trecastle road, north of Fedw Fawr, the track markings on the OS maps do a sharp left turn at 802278. Here strike north on an undefined route requiring expert navigation. The common is left by a grass track down to Sarnau and a narrow road followed to the village of Myddfai. Minor road walking is necessary to Myrtle Hill, whence follow little used tracks and paths to Llandovery. The maps 20A and 20B are six inch to the mile and should ensure lack of navigational problems on this very pleasant section which is in such sharp contrast to the stark open landscapes of the Brecon Beacons.

Llandovery is a natural staging and revictualling point. It has ample accommodation, eating houses, a camp site and tourist information office. Hostellers will tend to make it a midday call between Llanddeusant and Bryn Poeth. If the Cambrian Way is being walked in three sections then the rail service to Llandovery will prove useful.

CENTRAL SECTION
Llandovery to Dinas Mawddwy

Via the Elenydd and Plynlimon

Distance 79.1 miles (126.6km) Ascent 12666 feet (3863m)

After a generally east to west traverse of the Brecon Beacons National Park, our Connoisseur must now set face to the north in earnest. Let it not be thought, however, that the next few days of walking are just a beeline for Snowdonia. For those with a limited knowledge of Wales the central section is likely to be a revelation as to the wildness and beauty that is seen by few visitors to Wales.

The route crosses the Elenydd and Plynlimon ranges, both large and remote areas of mountain and moorland, which though having many crags and outcrops have few spectacular summits. In 1972 the Countryside Commission tried to designate these areas as a national park but there was much opposition locally. Much to the disgust of the Commission, and amenity and tourist interests, the Secretary of State for Wales, without even holding a public inquiry, refused to confirm the designation order. If this area had become a national park 80% of the Cambrian Way would have been in a national park. With hindsight the Commission might have been wiser to have gone for the lower status of an " Area of Outstanding Natural Beauty".

Forestry is the greatest threat to wildlife and amenity interests in this area. The many grants and tax concessions given to commercial tree growing has led to vast areas in the Elenydd being planted with conifers, though rather more on the eastern side than the western. This led Cambrian Way surveyors to suggest a line near the west side of the range, even though this meant omitting the scenic qualities of the Elan Valley reservoirs. In fact only five miles of the route in the central section goes through conifer woodlands.

There are not so many ridges and escarpments to follow in the central section but this is made up for by the attractiveness of the valleys walked, notably the Twyi (Towy), Doethie and Rheiddol.

Llandovery to Rhandirmwyn 6. 6 miles 1033 feet of ascent Map 21

From Llandovery the next objective is likely to be Rhandirmwyn. The most obvious ridge north of Llandovery has no public access at all so the choice lies between following the Towy valley by footpaths and roads through Cilycwm village or the recommended more direct route following a very minor road on the east side of Fforest ridge, then an untarred old road for 0.8 miles to 783407 (spot ht 219m). *Between there and 784418 follow map 21A. The byway followed was completely omitted from the 1991 OS 160 map (Brecon Beacons) due to Dyfed C.C.mistakenly deleting the byway because it is classified as a road, though mostly grass. It has reappeared on the latest edition and on the Explorer map.* At the road corner reached at 784418 go straight on and down to the Towy itself and follow the river path to Rhandirmwyn.

Rhandirmwyn belies its name, which means "district of mines", for the old lead mines are barely visible in the delectable valley in which this scattered village is situated. There is a large campsite, post office stores (last for 19 miles) and a pub.

This area is very much RSPB country, with many species of birds in the woods of the nature reserves. This is the most likely area on the Cambrian Way to see a kite, a species that nearly became extinct, but which is now much protected and increasing in numbers. The kite is liable to desert its young if disturbed and a year's brood may be lost . Kites do sometimes nest in the Doethie valley which lies ahead and this led to opposition to Cambrian Way going that way, but all the alternatives suggested could have similar objections. The Doethie has a public path along it and is a regular route to Tyncornel Youth Hostel, so seems a reasonable routeto adopt.It at least avoids the nature reserves.

Side excursions can be made to Dinas nature reserve and the Llyn Brianne but they involve tourist road walking, and return same way if the whole of the Doethie

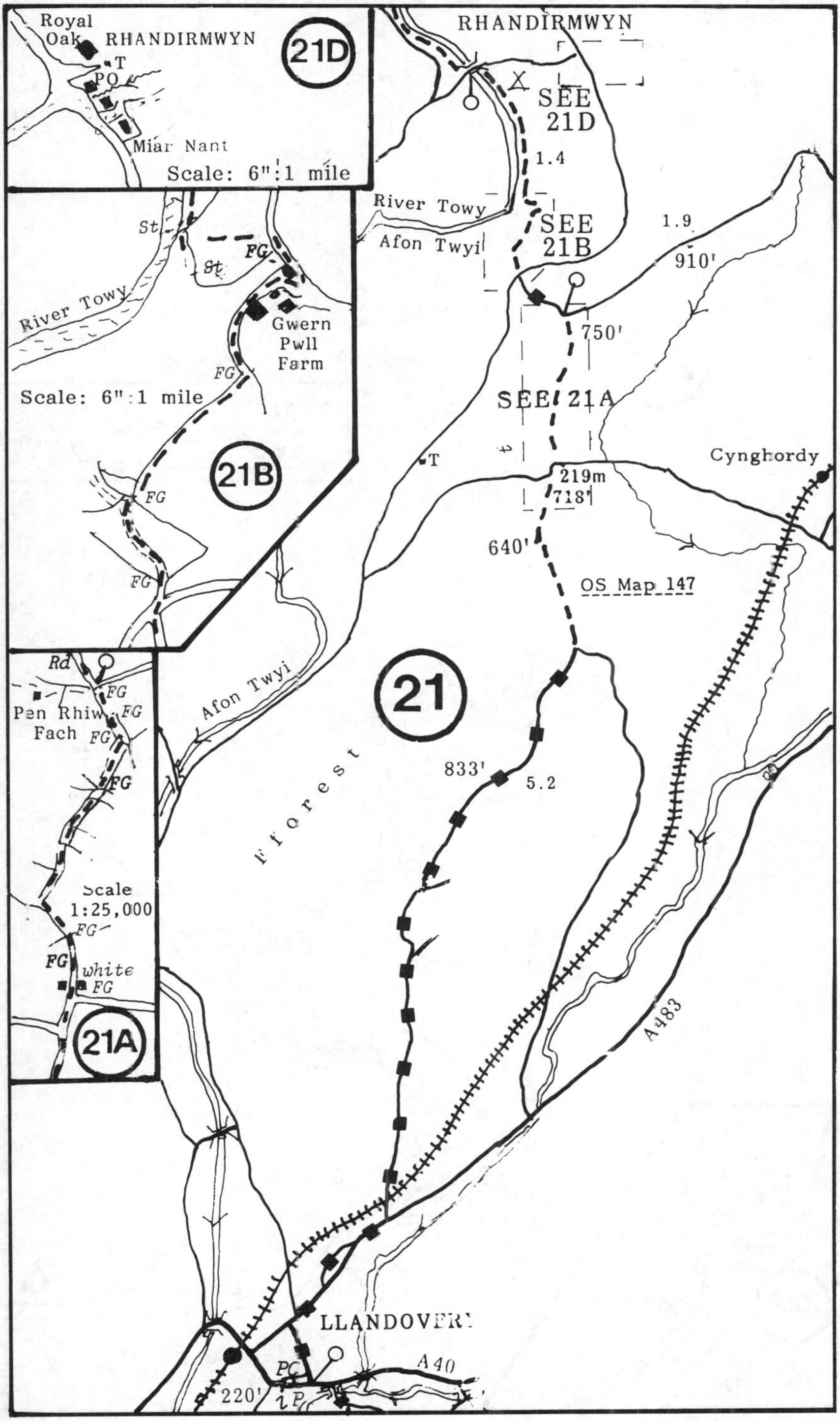

RHANDIRMWYN
SEE 21D
1.4
River Towy
Afon Twyi
SEE 21B
1.9
910'
750'
SEE 21A
Cynghordy
T
219m
718'
640'
OS Map 147
21
Afon Twyi
Fforest
833'
5.2
A483
LLANDOVERY
PC
A40
220'
iP
Royal Oak
RHANDIRMWYN
T
PO
Miar Nant
Scale: 6":1 mile
21D
St
St
FG
River Towy
Gwern Pwll Farm
FG
Scale: 6":1 mile
21B
FG
FG
Rd
FG
Pen Rhiw Fach
FG
FG
FG
Scale 1:25,000
FG
FG
white
FG
21A

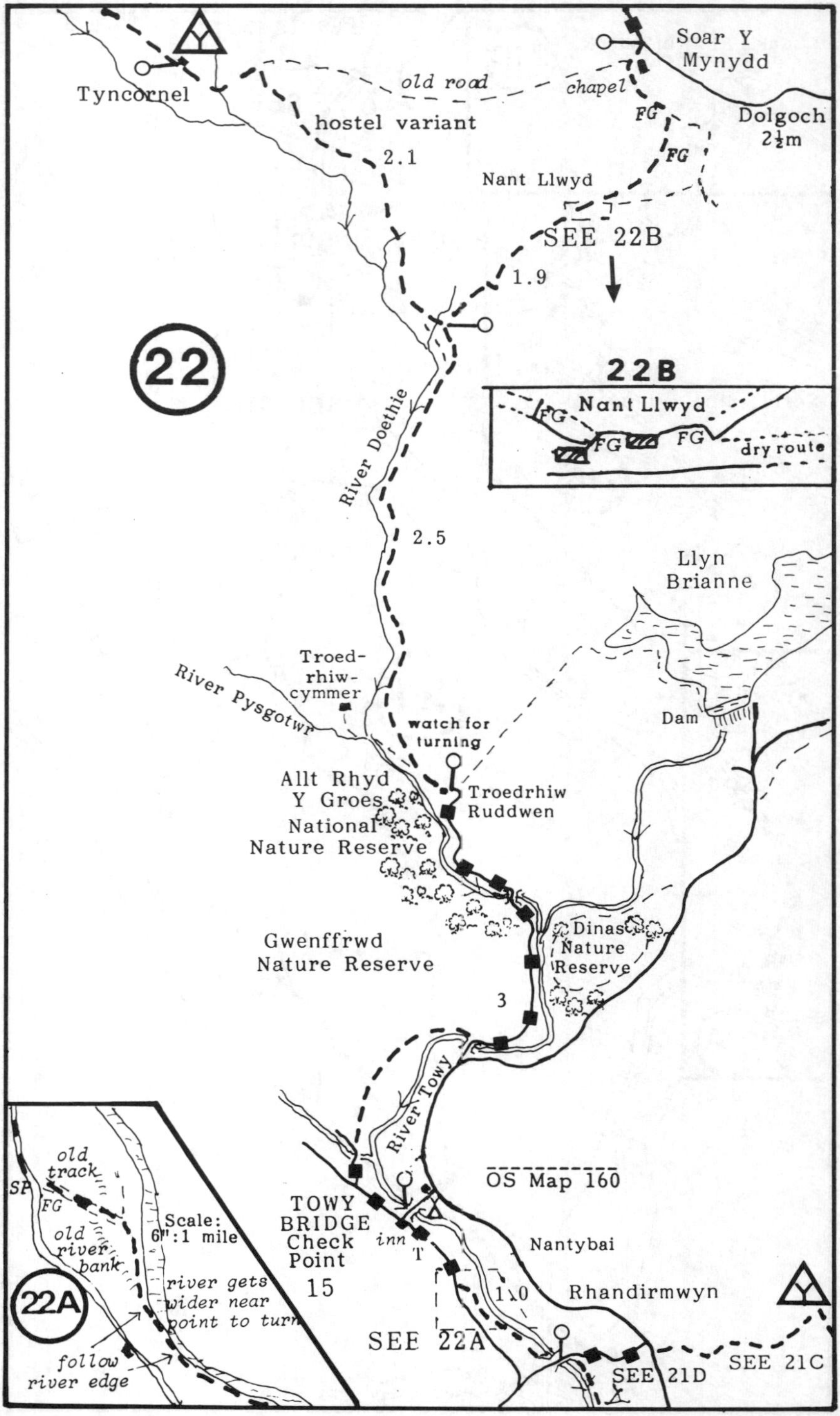
Soar Y
Mynydd
Tyncornel
old road
chapel
hostel variant
FG
Dolgoch
2½m
FG
2.1
Nant Llwyd
SEE 22B
1.9
22
22B
Nant Llwyd
FG
FG
FG
dry route
River Doethie
2.5
Llyn
Brianne
Troed-
rhiw-
cymmer
River Pysgotwr
watch for
turning
Dam
Allt Rhyd
Y Groes
Troedrhiw
Ruddwen
National
Nature Reserve
Dinas
Nature
Reserve
Gwenffrwd
Nature Reserve
3
River Towy
old
track
SP
FG
old
river
bank
Scale:
6":1 mile
OS Map 160
TOWY
BRIDGE
Check
Point
15
inn
T
Nantybai
river gets
wider near
point to turn
1.0
Rhandirmwyn
22A
SEE 22A
follow
river edge
SEE 21D
SEE 21C

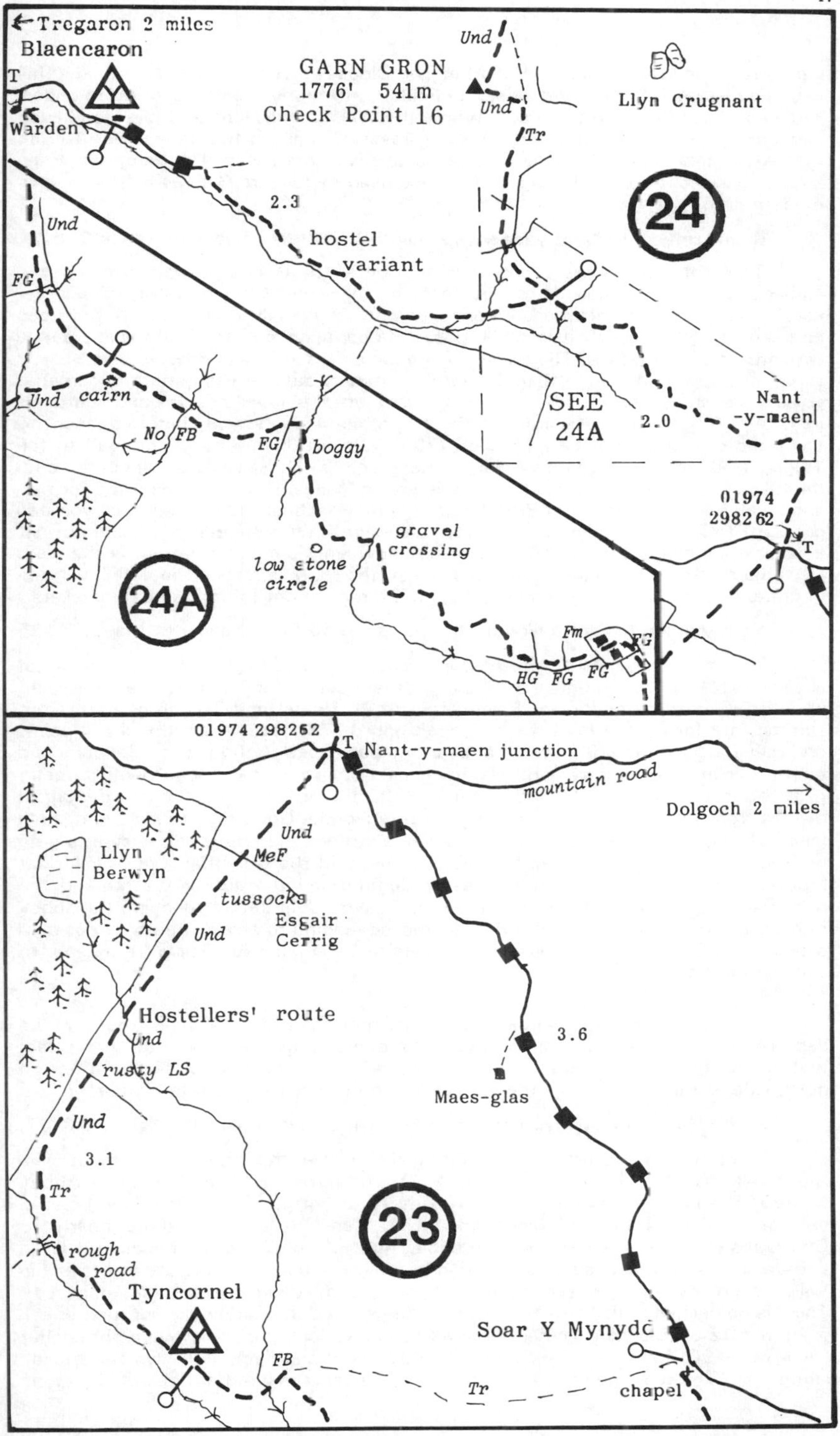

←Tregaron 2 miles
Blaencaron
T
Warden
GARN GRON
1776' 541m
Check Point 16
Und
Und
Tr
Llyn Crugnant
24
2.3
hostel
variant
Und
FG
cairn
Und
No FB
FG
boggy
SEE
24A
2.0
Nant
-y-maen
01974
298262
T
gravel
crossing
low stone
circle
24A
Fm
FG
HG
FG
FG
01974 298262
T
Nant-y-maen junction
mountain road
Dolgoch 2 miles
Und
MeF
Llyn
Berwyn
tussocks
Esgair
Cerrig
Und
Hostellers' route
Und
rusty LS
3.6
Maes-glas
Und
3.1
Tr
23
rough
road
Tyncornel
Soar Y Mynydd
FB
Tr
chapel

valley is to be walked, as it should be. The Dinas reserve is a densely wooded hill with the rushing Towy on two sides, a circular path round it and a spur up to a cleft known as Twm Shon Catti' s cave, where the Welsh equivalent of Robin Hood lived in hiding. Llyn Brianne is a large holding reservoir built in the early '70s. It is an impressive sight but it did drown a very attractive wooded valley. The dam, which the author considers the ugliest imaginable, is excused by Richard Sale as a " thoroughly modern dam "

Rhandirmwyn to Nant-y-maen 12 miles 1579 feet of ascent Maps 22&23.

To return to the main route, we now enter the Doethie valley, which in the author's opinion is the most attractive valley on the whole Cambrian Way. The lower part has extensive natural woods on one side and craggy hillside with scattered trees on the other. A particularly delectable spot is the confluence of the Towy and Doethie with attractive waterfalls. The tarred road ends at Troedrhiw Ruddwen farm.Shortly after, a rough road leads off to Troedrhiwcymmer, but the valley path becomes a grass route, sometimes muddy, but always with attractive valley sides and scattered trees. At 771514 non-hostellers must bear right and climb steeply before descent to the remote chapel at Soar y Mynydd (784533) and thence by minor road to the Tregaron- Abergwesyn road near Nant-y-maen (762577). Hostellers will continue up the valley to Tyncornel, the most remote hostel in Wales. Compared with the former, and much lamented, hostel at Bryn Poeth it is more accessible inasmuch as you can get a car to it by a long lonely road from Llandewi Brefi, whereas you could not get a car anywhere near Bryn Poeth. Tyncornel, however, is much more out in the wild. From the hostel road onwards to Nant y Maen, the route is not on the definitive map of rights of way, but there is a long standing arrangement for its use by hostellers .

Nant-y-maen to Strata Florida 6½ miles 946 feet of ascent Maps 24&25

From the farm at Nant-y-maen careful navigation is necessary as the path is not always visible and both rough ground and streams have to be crossed. The large cairn at 745595 is the junction for Blaencaron Youth Hostel and Tregaron. Garn Gron summit, not far off the faint track, though only 1776 feet is a worthy check point, and gives a good distant view on a clear day both back to the Brecon Beacons and on to Plynlimon. The way continues over wild open country, though with forestry growing up to the east. Around about 738623 the diversion for Pontrhydfendigaid divides from the main route heading for Strata Florida. Good map reading is needed here. The latter route, still undefined, crosses a stream and enters forestry at a gate with white post marking, blue bridleway arrow and the Cambrian Way Welsh hat logo. By arrangement with the Forestry Commission the author waymarked the bridleway route with blue arrows as far as Talwrn. Just before reaching the abbey remains at Strata Florida a footbridge is crossed leading to a raised path alongside a side stream. This stream was over boot tops until Ceredigion Council were persuaded to build up the path.

A visit to Pontrhydfendigaid (Bridge at the ford of the Blessed One) may be desirable for accommodation and for the bird watcher could be a place for a rest day, with a visit to Tregaron Bog, a national nature reserve nearby. A footpath on the north side of the Teifi returns the walker to the main route at Strata Florida.

Strata Florida to Cwmystwyth 9 miles 1408 feet of ascent Maps 26 & 27.

The remains of Strata Florida Abbey are open to the public on payment. The route follows part of the ancient monks' route across wild moorlands to Abbey Cwmhir. This is a road as far as Ty'n-y-cwm. A turn off is made below Llyn Egnant, one of the series of wild lakes known as Teifi Pools. From there nearly to Cwmystwyth one is on land with a public right of access either because it is on Crown common or because it is on land within the gathering grounds of the Elan Valley reservoirs which are subject to the famous Birmingham Clauses (see page 14). There is no defined route acros the moorland to get to Domen Milwyn, our next check point, but the old Claerddu farmhouse (likely to be available for basic overnight shelter see page 90), and three lakes, Llyn Fyrddin Fawr and Fach and Llyn Du provide landmarks. The watershed of the gathering grounds is marked at intervals by stone

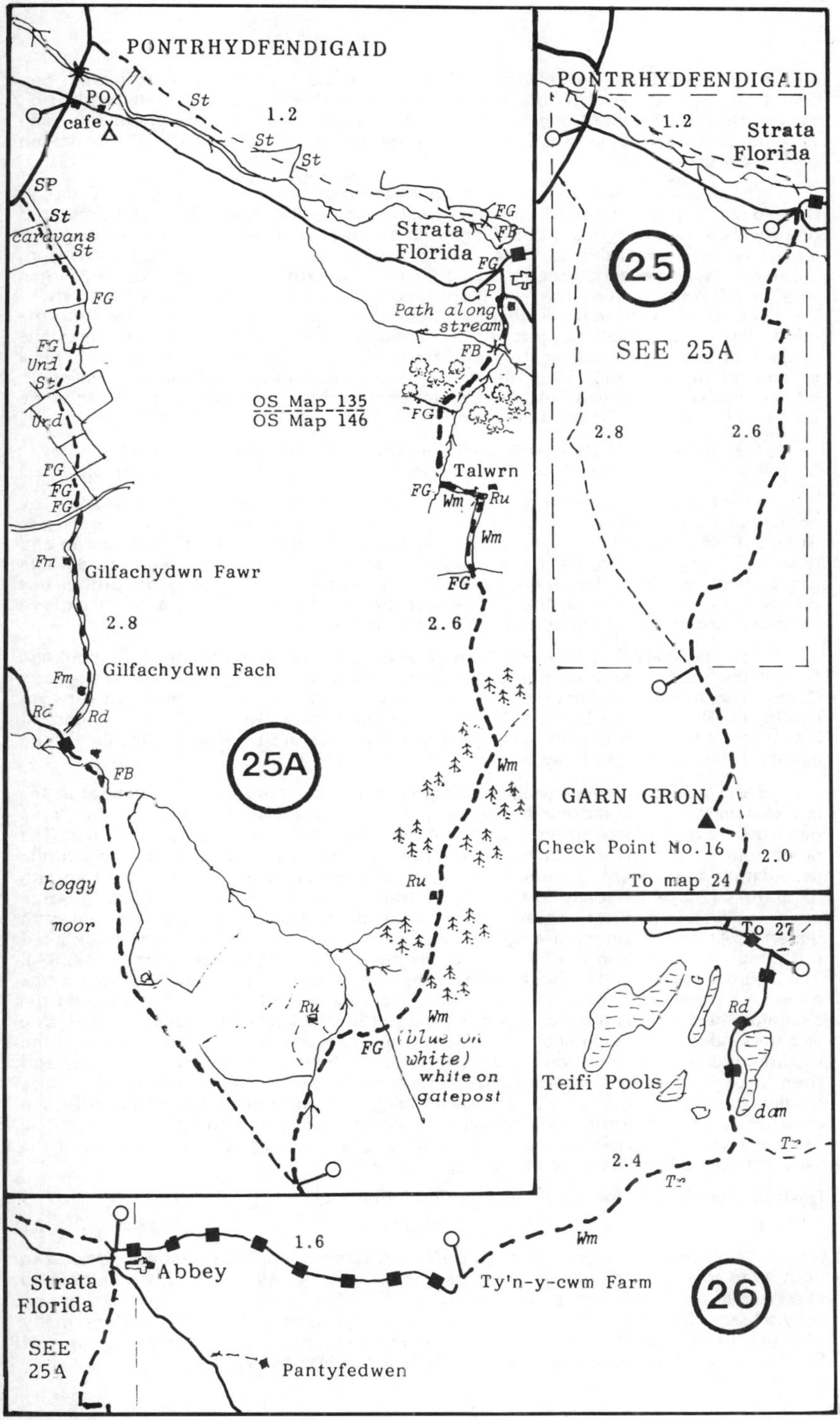
PONTRHYDFENDIGAID
PO
cafe
St
1.2
St
St
SP
St
caravans
St
FG
FG
Und
St
Und
FG
FG
FG
Fm
Gilfachydwn Fawr
2.8
Gilfachydwn Fach
Fm
Rd
Rd
FB
boggy
moor
OS Map 135
OS Map 146
FG
FB
Strata
Florida
FG
P
Path along
stream
FB
FG
Talwrn
FG
Wm
Ru
Wm
FG
2.6
Wm
Ru
Ru
Wm
(blue on
white)
white on
gatepost
FG
25A
PONTRHYDFENDIGAID
1.2
Strata
Florida
25
SEE 25A
2.8
2.6
GARN GRON
Check Point No.16
2.0
To map 24
To 27
Rd
Teifi Pools
dam
2.4
Wm
1.6
Strata
Florida
Abbey
Ty'n-y-cwm Farm
26
SEE
25A
Pantyfedwen

pillars. The panorama from Domen Milwyn on a clear day is even more wild than Garn Gron. From the summit descend NW to a stile,then follow footpath marked on map on NE side of Nant Milwyn towards Cwmystwyth . Follow route marked on map 27A into Cwmystwyth (amended route since last edition). A stile at 791733 is hidden from view until close by.

Cwmystwyth was the scene of much lead mining, which was in its heyday at the end of the 19th century. Enormous mine buildings, closed in 1921, were situated one mile up the valley from the village and stood as a monstrous eyesore or gaunt industrial relic according to taste. Those with time to spare can keep north from Domen Milwyn,descend steeply, and ford the Ystwyth to visit the site. See Simon Hughes "The Cwmystwyth Mine" (published by Northern Mine Research Society) . The river below the mine has incidentally been irrevocably polluted by water from the mine. The village itself has attractive surroundings. Donald Hoare, who was the project officer appointed by the Countryside Commission to report on the central section of the Cambrian Way (see page 7) lives in Cwmystwyth and is willing to advise walkers and hear of any problems they have encountered . He can be contacted at the Old School (see map) .

Cwmystwyth to Dyffryn Castell via Devil's Bridge and Ponterwyd

11 miles 1930 feet of ascent Maps 28 & 29

From the Cwmystwyth area it is possible to make a beeline for Plynlimon by going via Llethr Nant-Hylles or Myherin Forest and crossing the A44 at Eisteddfa Gurig or Dyffryn Castell, but this route would omit the spectacular Rheidol gorge and the fascinating areas of Devil's Bridge and Ystumtuen. As it requires considerable extra effort to follow the recommended route via the Rheidol valley the author has nominated Pontbren Plwca, the bridge over the Rheidol at 727782, as a checkpoint for achievement of his version of the Cambrian Way.

For the Rheidol route leave Cwmystwyth by gate opposite the old school and follow the map closely on some ill-defined paths, and boggy ground to Forestry Commission forest and thence to The Arch, a stone structure over the Cwmystwyth to Devil's Bridge road built in 1810 to commemorate George III's accession. A pleasant track commencing shortly to west of the arch leads to Devil's Bridge avoiding the sometimes busy tourist road .

Devil's Bridge (Pontarfrynach) is a somewhat congested tourist honeypot at the end of a narrow gauge railway. It is nevertheless worth a visit if only to see the three generations of bridges, one above the other, the oldest being 900 years old. The splendour of the Mynach Falls, which you have to pay to see, varies, of course, according to the amount of water flowing. The Cambrian Way route takes a footpath off the A4120 which leads to the railway track but do not cross it yet. 300 metres on cross line into nature reserve then cross back again 110 metres on, near a waterfall. At time of writing the right of way is then alongside the railway track itself but a legal diversion on the upper side has been imminent for some time (see29A). The diverted route doubles back to the original path which descends to a footbridge called Pontbren Plwca (check point 18). This superb spot, with waterfalls and the beautiful Rheidol valley around, has been marred by the Cwm Rheidol lead mine. Due to a man induced landslide and the danger from toxic water from mine workings the recommended route has been altered to follow a low class road up the valley and thence to Ystumtuen, where sadly there is no longer a Youth Hostel. The route continues to Dyffryn Castell via Ponterwyd using two short stretches of the A44. An alternative from Ystumtuen is to follow a waymarked route to Parson's Bridge, a recently replaced footbridge over a really dramatic and deep gorge, but the rest of the way involves 2½ miles of road walking.

Dyffryn Castell to Dylife via Plynlimon (Punlumon)

11½- miles 2560 feet of ascent Maps 30 31

The approach to Plynlimon from Dyffryn Castell is long and relatively little used compared to the shorter route from Eisteddfa Gurig. Much of the way is undefined and in cloud a compass will be necessary until the fence is reached, after which one is by a fence almost to the summit. There one will find a ring of stones in which many walkers have sought shelter from wind and rain. Here on the main summit of Plynlimon one can really feel one is at the heart of Wildest Wales.

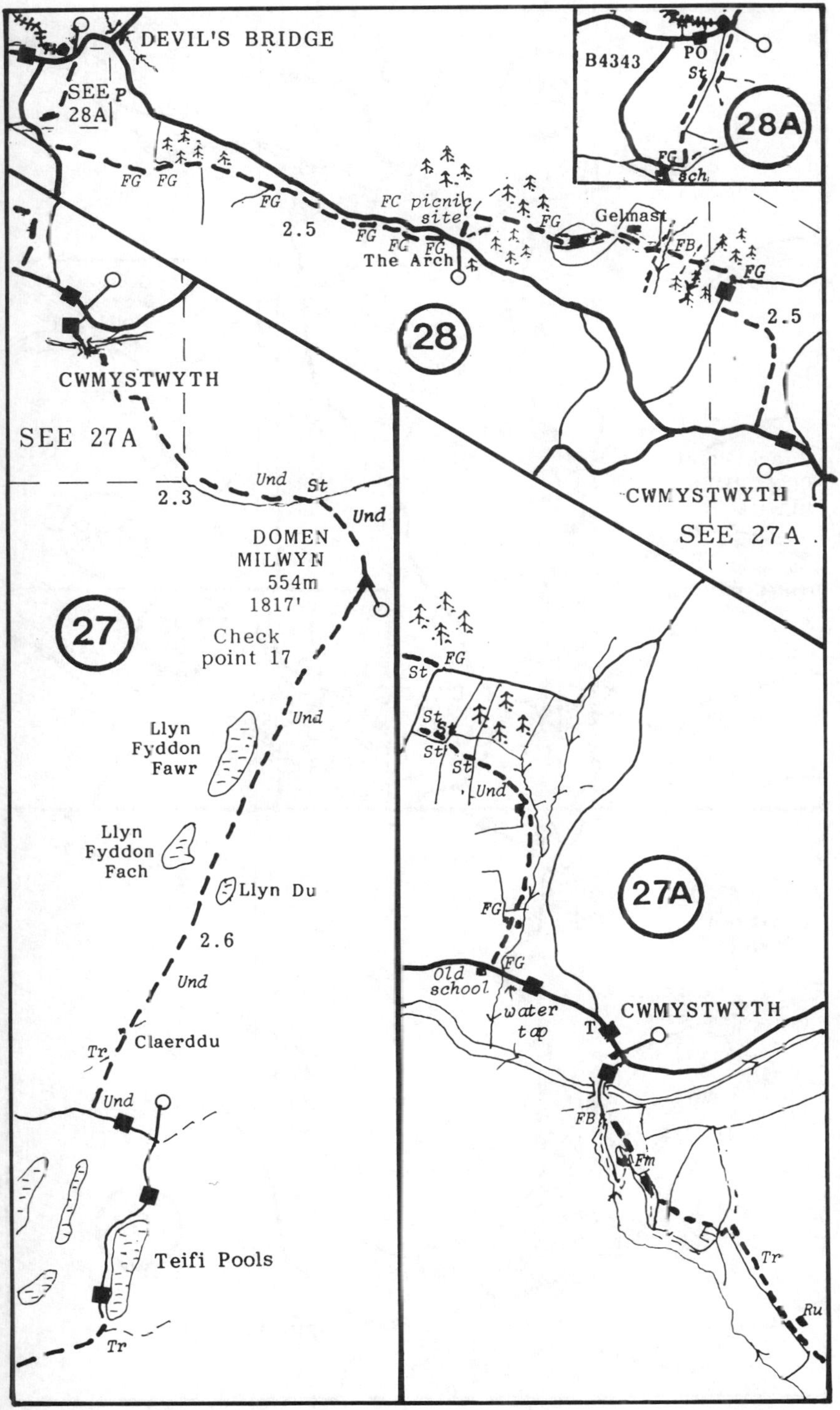
DEVIL'S BRIDGE
SEE 28A
P
FG FG
FG
2.5
FC picnic site
FG
FG FG
The Arch
Gelmast
FB
FG
2.5
28
B4343
PO
St
28A
FG
sch
CWMYSTWYTH
SEE 27A
2.3
Und
St
Und
DOMEN MILWYN
554m
1817'
27
Check point 17
Und
Llyn Fyddon Fawr
Llyn Fyddon Fach
Llyn Du
2.6
Und
Tr
Claerddu
Und
Teifi Pools
Tr
CWMYSTWYTH
SEE 27A
FG
St
St
St
St
St
Und
27A
FG
FG
Old school
water tap
T
CWMYSTWYTH
FB
Fm
Tr
Ru

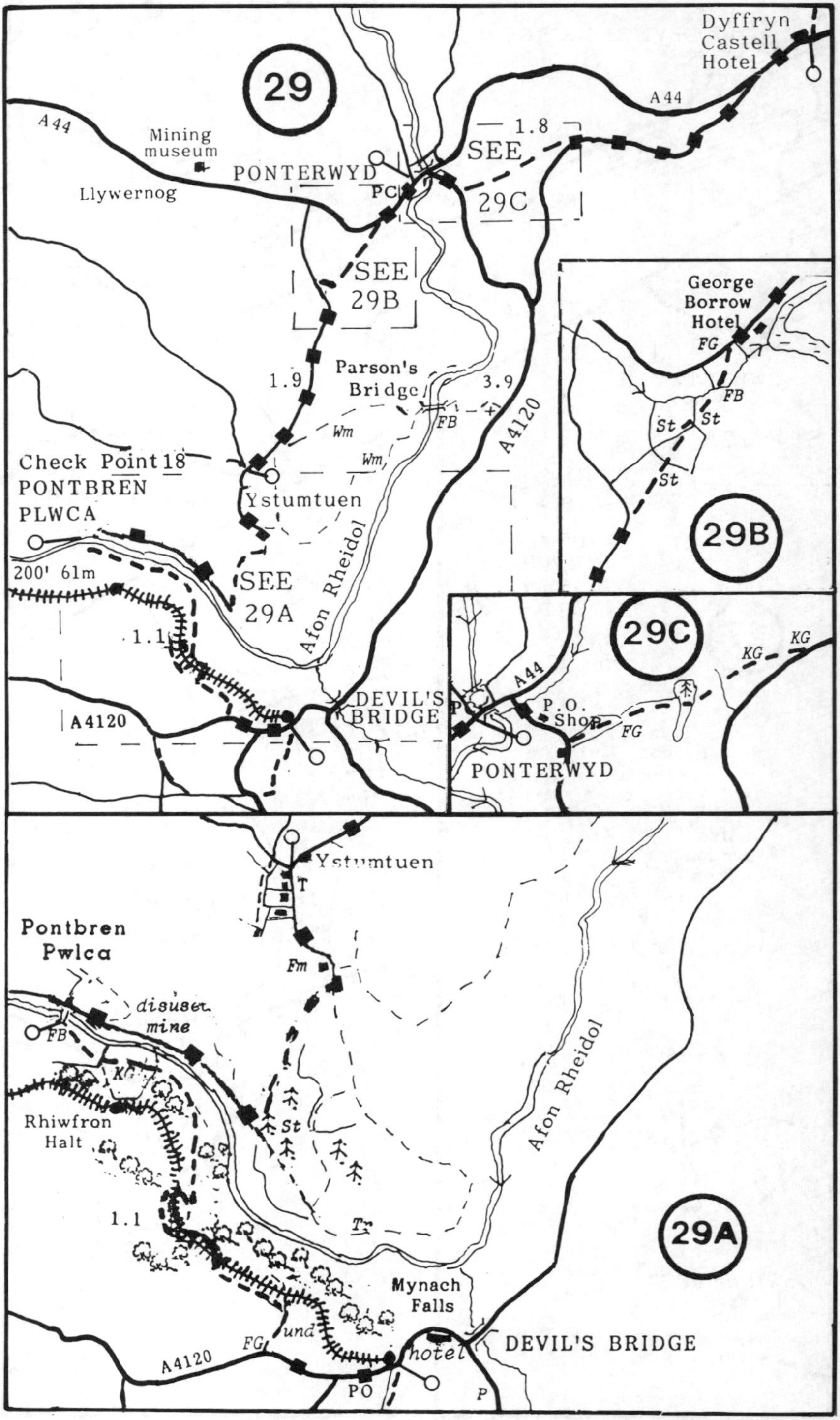
29
A44
Mining museum
Llywernog
PONTERWYD
PC
SEE
29B
1.8
SEE
29C
Dyffryn Castell Hotel
A44
1.9
Parson's Bridge
3.9
FB
Wm
Wm
A4120
Check Point 18
PONTBREN
PLWCA
Ystumtuen
200' 61m
SEE
29A
Afon Rheidol
1.1
DEVIL'S BRIDGE
A4120
George Borrow Hotel
FG
FB
St
St
St
29B
29C
A44
P
P.O. Shop
FG
KG
KG
PONTERWYD
Ystumtuen
T
Pontbren Pwlca
Fm
disused mine
FB
KG
Rhiwfron Halt
St
Afon Rheidol
1.1
Tr
29A
Mynach Falls
FG
und
DEVIL'S BRIDGE
hotel
A4120
PO
P

Plynlimon is Crown common with a legal right of public access (see page 14) but this right was under threat in 1983 due to a misguided scheme of the Crown Estate Commissioners, following buying up of the last remaining commoner, to fence off certain areas to provide shelter belts for tree planting and to improve other areas. The scheme was to be in commemoration of the marriage of the Prince and Princess of Wales but this gesture was not at all appreciated by the Countryside Commission or any of the amenity bodies such as the Ramblers' Association, Council for the Protection of Rural Wales and the Youth Hostels Association. They were particularly incensed that the Crown Estate erected a long barbed wire fence before the Secretary of State for the Environment had had a chance to decide if it was for the "benefit of the neighbourhood ". In the event the Secretary of State settled for a compromise so that no new fences appear near the summit but the prematurely erected fence (not seen from Cambrian Way) has periodic stiles in it.

The Machynlleth Variant. The summit of Plynlimon is a possible junction for beeliners determined to get to Cader Idris via Machynlleth. This saves 16 miles compared with the recommended route. There is a fine route on rights of way via Hyddgen, the escarpment of Creigiau Bwlch Hyddgen and passing east of Glanmerin Lake to Machynlleth. This busy little market town may prove an attraction with its better supplies than those available from the village post offices recently encountered. Looking ahead on the main route in this guide one can expect good grocery shops at Mallwyd and then not until Barmouth. Beyond Machynlleth there are routes into a much forested area but except for the A487 through Corris there is no right of way into the Talyllyn valley to the SE of Cader Idris between the way to Abergynolwyn via Foel y Geifr and the footpath to Bwlch Lynn Bach from Cwm Ratgoed. The Abergynolwyn approach to Cader Idris is long and involving a repeat of the top section on the descent, and is not nearly such a good way up as the two offered in this guide. The road route from Corris is preceeded by more road walking from Machynlleth, although the Centre for Alternative Technology can be visited on the way. It is because of these problems but rather more the scenic qualities and interest of the route via Dylife, Mynydd Cemmaes, Dinas Mawddwy and the Maesglasau ridge that the Connoisseur is advised to stick to the route in this guide.

Plynlimon has several summits and several sources of famous rivers. The Wye source lies a mile away to the east but more on the route is the source of the Severn, the longest river in Britain, and which is reached by a short deviation to the east of the main fence line. Returning to the common go north and cross the valley to hit the track leading round a headland to bring Lake Bugeilyn into view. Follow the bridleway between the two parts of the lake and at the ruins of the Bugeilyn farm cross the stream and go over the bank on an undefined public footpath. Watch for the site of an old reservoir which served the disused mine beyond. Follow the map into Dylife.

Glyndwr's Way. Half a mile before Dylife there is a crossing with a long distance footpath route devised and waymarked by Powys County Council. Glyndwr's Way is in two sections, each crossing from near the Welsh coast at Machynlleth to the Offa's Dyke Path along the border with England. This is the southern section to Knighton. The northern section to Welshpool will be crossed near Commins Coch. It traverses quiet and attractive Welsh countryside but the route as devised by Powys C.C.has 36 of its 120 miles along tarred roads, i.e. 30% compared to 11% for Cambrian Way. In particular, it currently follows 3 miles of the busy A489 from Machynlleth.

Glyndwr's Way is being groomed for national trail status and a project officer is seeking to negotiate new rights of way, often with reluctant landowners. Aim is to reduce road walking to 20% but it looks like being 25%, still vastly more than Cambrian Way. The terrain generally is more akin to the Offa's Dyke Path and has nothing like the proportion of wild open country. Unless much improved, properly waymarked, and many miles of new rights of way created it is unlikely to appeal greatly to our Mountain Connoisseur.

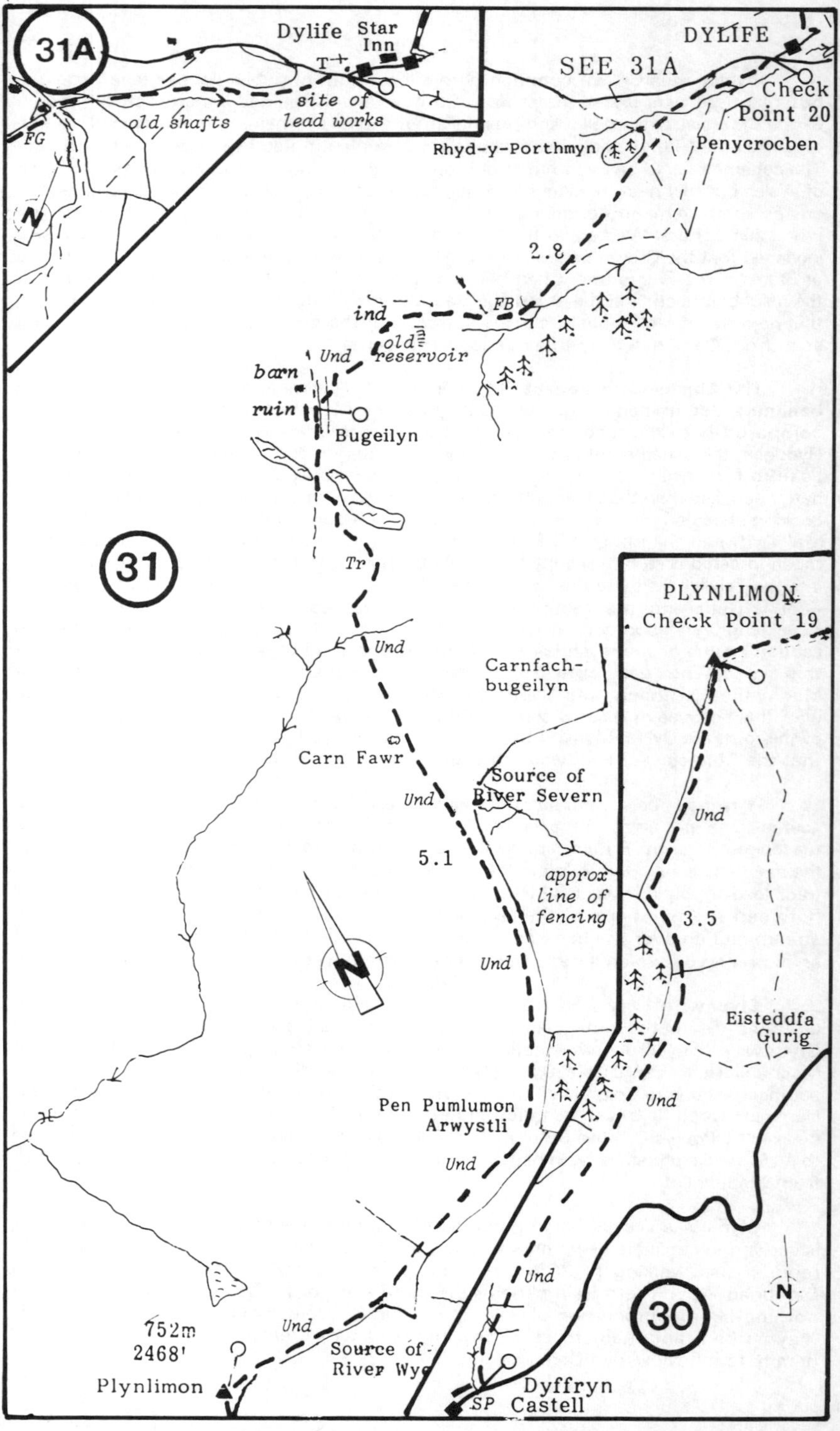
31A
Dylife
Star Inn
T
site of lead works
old shafts
FG
N
DYLIFE
SEE 31A
Check Point 20
Penycrocben
Rhyd-y-Porthmyn
2.8
FB
ind
old reservoir
Und
barn
ruin
Bugeilyn
31
Tr
Und
PLYNLIMON
Check Point 19
Carnfach-bugeilyn
Carn Fawr
Source of River Severn
Und
5.1
Und
approx line of fencing
3.5
N
Und
Eisteddfa Gurig
Pen Pumlumon Arwystli
Und
Und
Und
N
30
752m
2468'
Und
Plynlimon
Source of River Wye
SP
Dyffryn Castell

Dylife. It is hard to believe that this quiet hamlet, 1200 feet up in the hills, with only a few houses and a pub, was, just over a century ago, the scene of intense mining activity. At that time vast quantities of lead were being mined, also copper and zinc, and many hundreds of miners were employed. The Romans almost certainly mined here and there was a fortlet on Penycrocbren, the hill to the south. It is a ghostly place with bare areas where the mine buildings have been removed and a churchyard with tombstones but no church left. The derelict barrack buildings are a reminder of the overcrowding that went on here with one bed shared by two miners who each did a 12-hour shift and got into the warm bed left by the other. Pencrocbren (meaning gallows hill) has a gruesome tale to tell of a blacksmith at the mine who murdered his wife and daughter and threw their bodies down a disused shaft. At that time it was the custom to hang murderers near the scene of their crime and for the head to hang in a metal cage. His last job was to make his own cage, which is still preserved at St. Fagans Folk museum at Cardiff.

The Star Inn is partly very old, with modern additions for a restaurant and bedrooms. If time permits a stroll should be made down the road from the village until the magnificent view down into the Pennant valley is obtained with the crags on the left and the waterfall of Ffrwd Fawr. For further reading see " Dylife" written and published by David Bick, Pound House, Newent, Glos. (1985 edition £2.10 post free).

Dylife to Commins Coch 8½ miles 750 feet of ascent Map 32

The next section of the Cambrian Way is in complete contrast to the starkness of Plynlimon. It is a fascinating undulating walk over two attractive passes, with a mixture of rough and improved grassland, forest and heather moorland. The whole route is shown at 1:25,000 scale as well as 1:50,000 because many field boundaries have to be crossed and it is necessary to have maps showing relevant boundaries to help the walker to keep to public rights of way. Paths are less used in these parts and some minor diversions are necessary where paths are obstructed but hopefully these will be dealt with by Powys C.C..

In the woods west of Esgair Geulan follow the paths and forest roads as shown on the map. Part of the right of way was planted on but a legal diversion between 848975 and 849979 was stimulated by the author and became operative in July 1984, and is waymarked. At Maesteg the Forestry Commission allows the use of the forest road but watch for the public footpath which turns sharply down at a bend in the forest road. (See page 14). Watch for waymark post at right turn.

Commins Coch is a small village with a post office/shop but no pub Trains pass through but do not stop nearer than Machynlleth to the west and Caersws to the east. There is a pleasant spot for a picnic on common land alongside the rushing river Twymyn to the south-east of the village at 849029. The nearest B&B is 377feet up to a magnificent viewpoint at Cefn Coch Uchaf, or you can press on to a rambler's welcome at "Gwalia". A path route for diversion to Cemmaes is shown as map 33B

Commins Coch to Dinas Mawddwy 13 miles 2460 feet of ascent Map 33

Mynydd y Cemmaes is a broad ridge of some 2½ miles length giving fine views of the surrounding valleys and of Snowdonia's principal summits. Until 1992 It was a quiet and wild place with little sign of the bridleways to be followed on the Cambrian Way route. Now there is a line of 24 wind generators along the ridge, constituting the first windfarm in Wales. The author protested at the public inquiry in support of the Countryside Council for Wales and many amenity bodies, putting the view that the visual effect and fears of the precedent created for other parts of the Cambrian Way was not justified for the relatively small amount of "green" power to be produced. Our Mountain Connoisseur will either be horrified or fascinated, but should be warned not to go too close in a gale, as blades have been known to come off when the power supply line came down which operates the mechanism to turn the turbines off and face the wind.

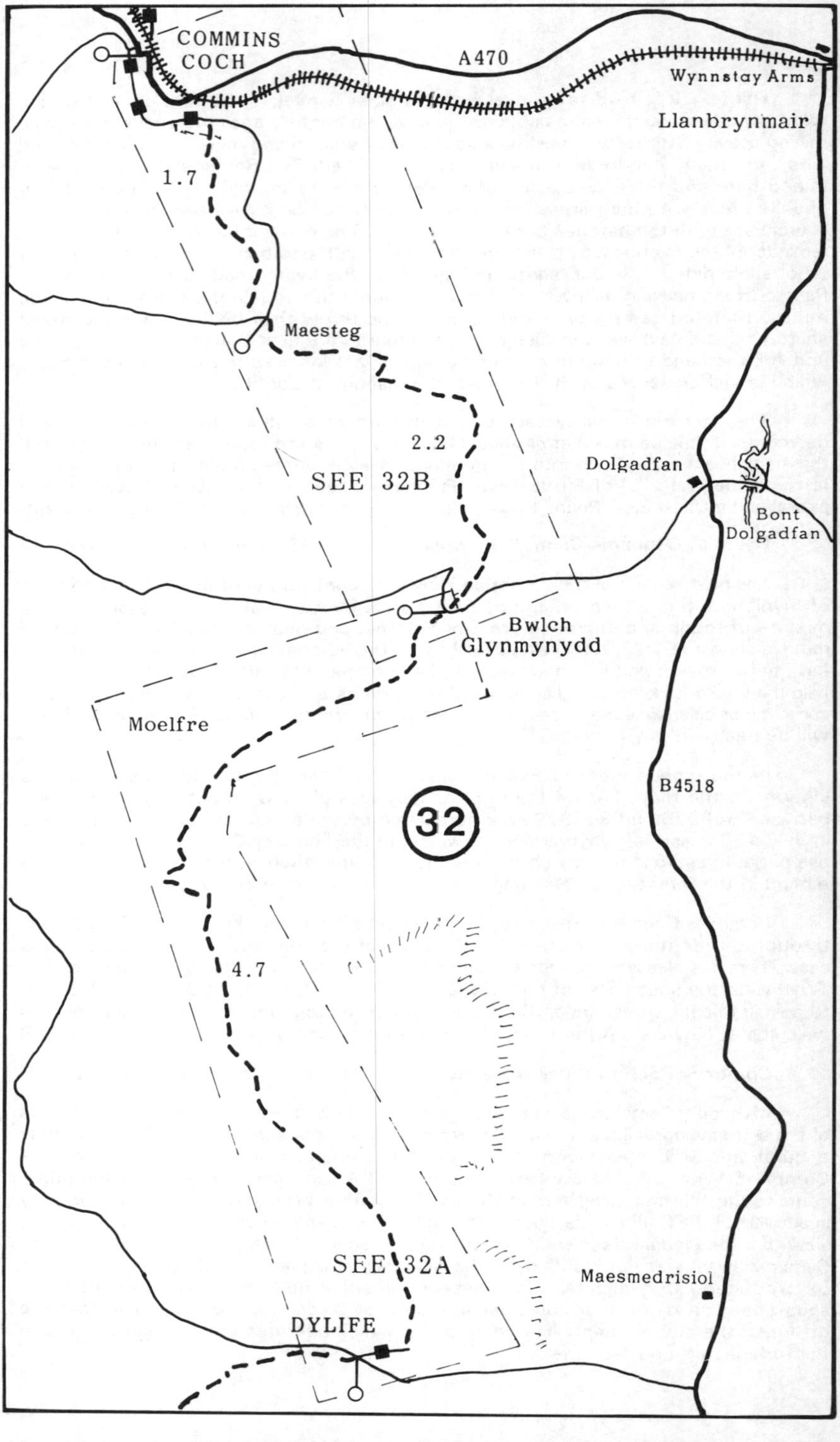
COMMINS
COCH
A470
Wynnstay Arms
Llanbrynmair
1.7
Maesteg
2.2
Dolgadfan
SEE 32B
Bont
Dolgadfan
Bwlch
Glynmynydd
Moelfre
B4518
32
4.7
SEE 32A
Maesmedrisiol
DYLIFE

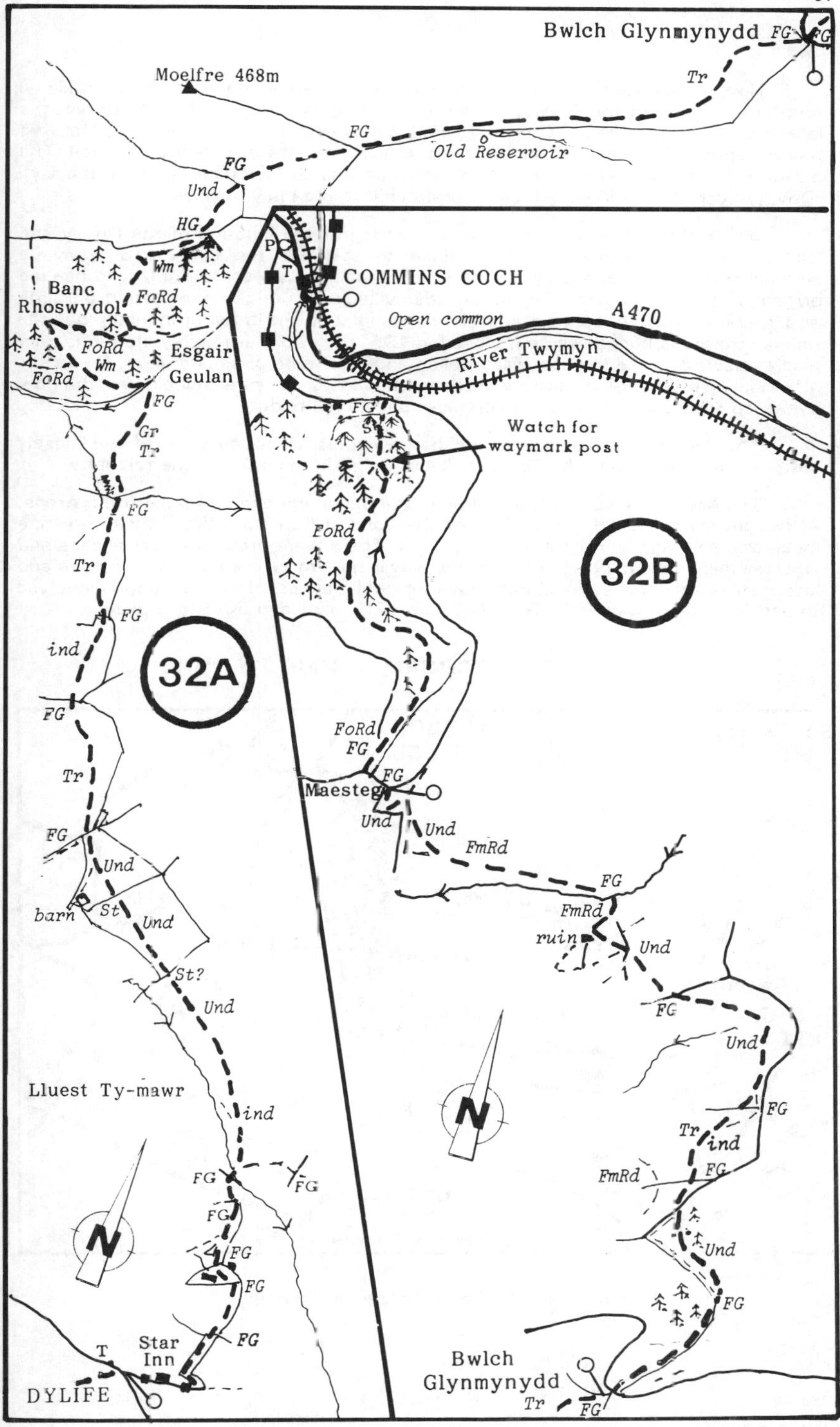
Bwlch Glynmynydd
FG
FG
Tr
Moelfre 468m
FG
Old Reservoir
FG
Und
HG
Wm
Banc
Rhoswydol
FoRd
FoRd
Wm
FoRd
Esgair
Geulan
P
T
COMMINS COCH
Open common
A470
River Twymyn
FG
St
Watch for
waymark post
FG
Gr
Tr
FG
Tr
FG
ind
32A
FoRd
32B
FG
Tr
FG
Und
barn
St
Und
St?
Und
Lluest Ty-mawr
ind
FG
FG
FG
FG
FG
FG
T
Star
Inn
DYLIFE
FoRd
FG
FG
Maesteg
Und
Und
FmRd
FG
FmRd
ruin
Und
FG
Und
FG
Tr
ind
FmRd
FG
Und
FG
Bwlch
Glynmynydd
Tr
FG
N
N

North of Mynydd Cemmaes the only route zig zags somewhat via Waun Llinau and Esgair Ddu into the Tafalog valley and thence by stony road to Mallwyd, the latter marked in spots as an "Other route with public access" (see page 13) . Mallwyd has a supermarket and the Brigands Inn, which only has a restaurant licence. The minor road suggested to Dinas Mawddwy passes a delectable spot by the Dyfi (Dovey) river at Pont Mallwyd and is preferable to the busy main road.

Dinas Mawddwy with its majestic setting at the junction of the Dovey and Cerist rivers will prove a worthy place to stay for the sheer beauty of its surroundings. Dinas Mawwdwy was once noted for the lawlessness of its red headed brigands. It is diifficult to imagine how this village was once an important borough and market town. A century ago slate mining was the thriving industry but the railway that was built to serve it closed in 1951. The former railway station is now a cafe attached to the Meirion Mill woollen and craft enterprise and shop. On sale is a fascinating booklet on the history of Dinas Mawddwy. Be sure to look over the now bypassed road bridge to see a much older packhorse bridge.

The camp site, Celyn Brithion, has a superb all round view of the closely surrounding mountains. The Red Lion (Llew Coch) is the older of the two inns.

The Arans. From Dinas Mawddwy a side excursion can be made to the Arans. Although never part of the author's route for the Cambrian Way, these are fine mountains and slightly higher than Cader Idris. There were problems over access and whereas there used to be open access the way is now more confined with fences and ladder stiles and the National Park pays for public access Road walking is involved to and from Cwm Cywarch. Total distance 12½ miles and 3000ft of ascent

END OF CENTRAL SECTION

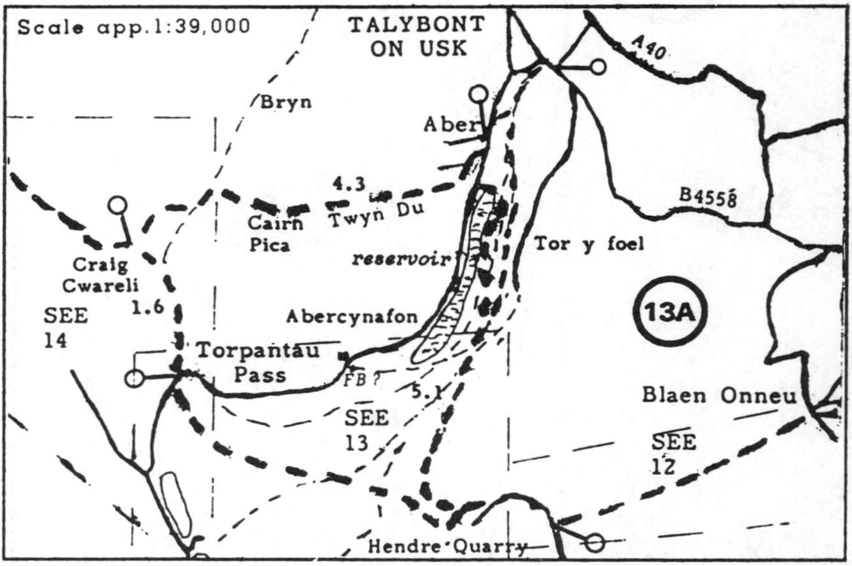

Map showing the **Talybont Variant** (see page 33)

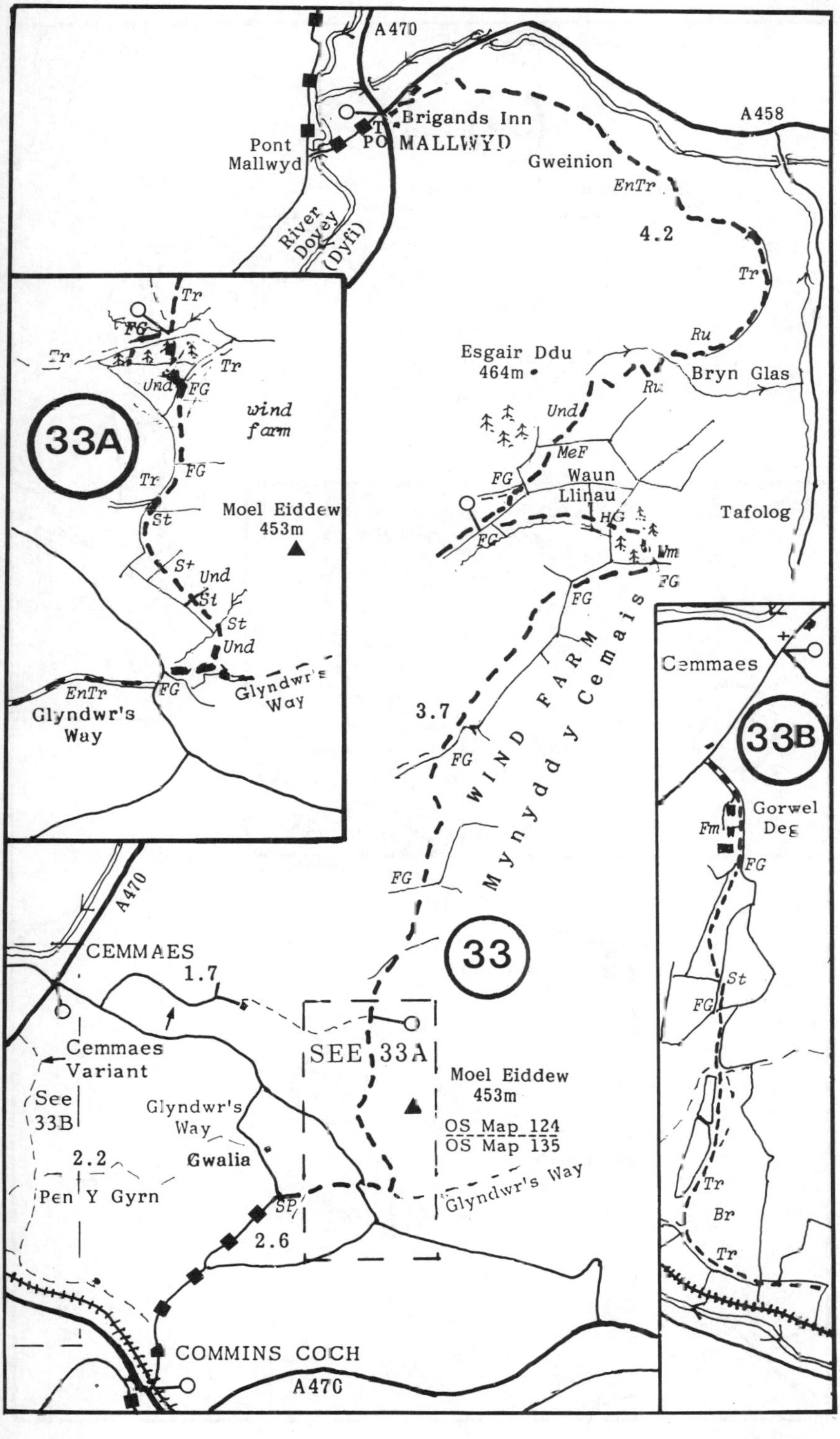
A470
Brigands Inn
PO MALLWYD
Pont Mallwyd
Gweinion
A458
River Dovey (Dyfi)
EnTr
4.2
Tr
Ru
Esgair Ddu
464m
Bryn Glas
Und
MeF
FG
Waun Llinau
HG
Tafolog
Wm
WIND FARM
Mynydd y Cemais
3.7
33A
wind farm
Moel Eiddew
453m
St
Glyndwr's Way
33B
Cemmaes
Gorwel Deg
Fm
Br
A470
CEMMAES
1.7
Cemmaes Variant
See 33B
SEE 33A
Moel Eiddew
453m
OS Map 124
OS Map 135
Glyndwr's Way
Gwalia
2.2
Pen Y Gyrn
SP
2.6
33
COMMINS COCH
A470

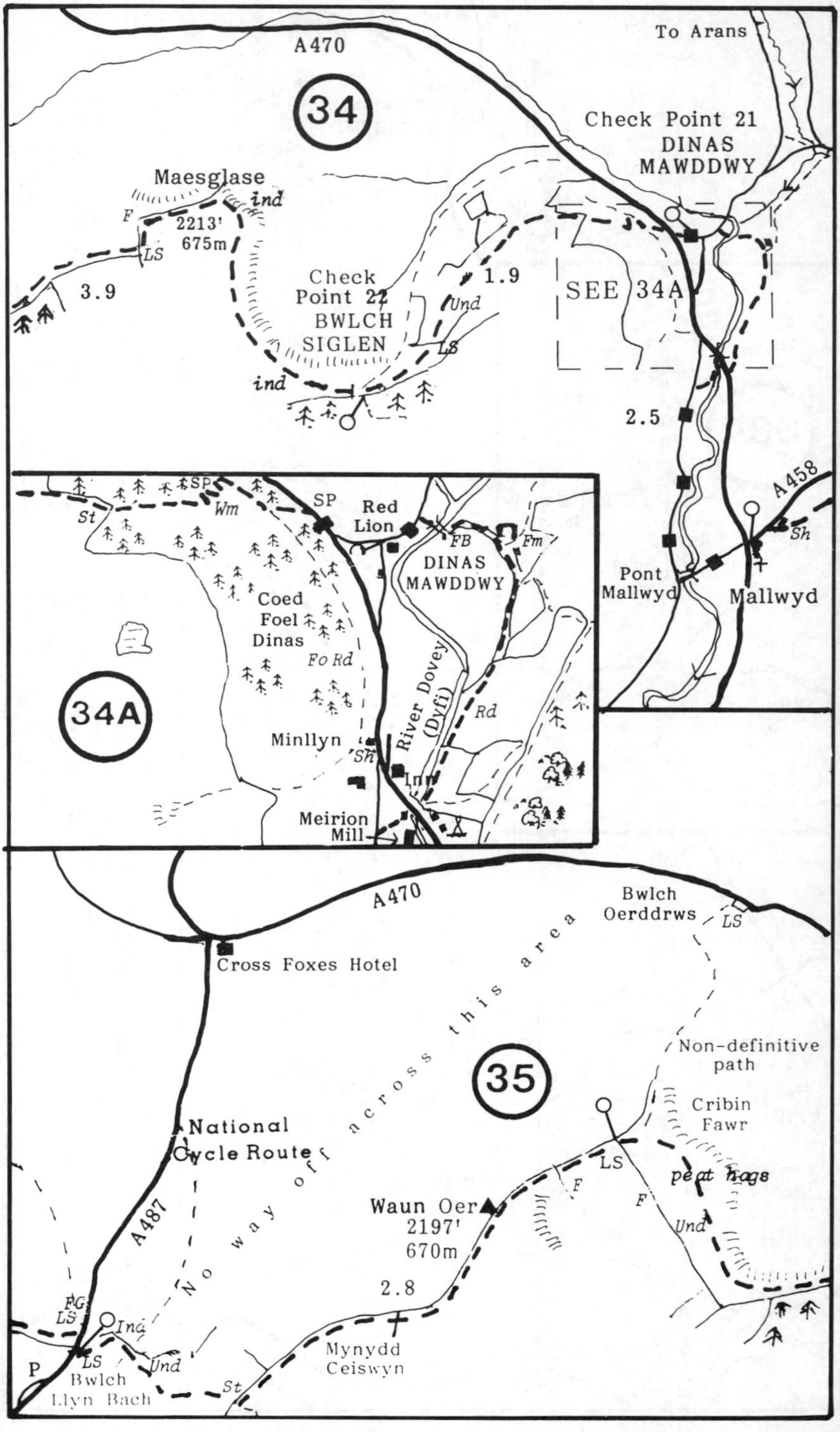
A470
34
To Arans
Check Point 21
DINAS
MAWDDWY
Maesglase
ind
F
2213'
675m
LS
3.9
Check
Point 22
BWLCH
SIGLEN
1.9
Und
SEE 34A
LS
ind
2.5
A458
Sh
Pont
Mallwyd
Mallwyd
St
SP
Wm
SP
Red
Lion
FB
Fm
DINAS
MAWDDWY
Coed
Foel
Dinas
Fo Rd
River Dovey
(Dyfi)
Rd
34A
Minllyn
Sh
Inn
Meirion
Mill
A470
Bwlch
Oerddrws
LS
Cross Foxes Hotel
No way off across this area
Non-definitive
path
35
Cribin
Fawr
National
Cycle Route
LS
peat hags
F
F
Waun Oer
2197'
670m
Und
A487
2.8
FG
LS
Ind
LS
Und
Mynydd
Ceiswyn
P
Bwlch
Llyn Bach
St

NORTHERN SECTION
Dinas Mawddwy to Conwy
Through Snowdonia National Park

88.1 miles (141.8 km) 27,711 ft ascent (8452m)

Dinas Mawddwy to Barmouth via Maesglase, Waun-oer and Cader Idris
20 miles 5526 feet of ascent Maps 34 to 38

Part of the obliquely ascending path through the forest of Coed Foel Dinas has been diverted, necessitating a detour along a forest road and then a steep zig zag climb back to the line of the original right of way. The author originally complained in 1979 about the obstruction caused by a cliff formed when the forest road was made, It took from 1984 to 1995 for Gwynedd County Council to process a proper diversion, no less than 26 letters being sent by the author over the period. Beyond the diversion the rough and gradually ascending path gets steeper before emerging onto the open hillside at a corner of the moor.

Bwlch Siglen to Mynydd Ceiswyn via Maesglase and Waun Oer is one of the finest sections of Cambrian Way with superb crag top walking ,wild moorland and superb views. Between Bwlch Siglen and Cribin Fawr the route is across public access land provided under a Tir Cymen agreement (see page 15) and is mostly clearly defined on the ground with ladder stiles at fences. A short peaty section on Cribin Fawr is best passed on the north side. The fine ridge walking continues south-westwards and is eroded on the steep approach to Waun-oer. Turn down off Mynydd Ceiswyn onto the path coming from Aberllefenni. The crossing of the national cycle route may be a more sheltered place than most for turning the Leisure map 23 over.

Bwlch Llyn Bach is presumably the name of the pass on the A487 despite being wrongly marked on the Ordnance maps. The lake that gives it its name was filled in alongside a layby on the SW side of the pass. At the pass a decision has to be made as to alternatives. The main route makes the approach to Cader Idris involving the least ascent. From a ladder stile off the road on the north side of the pass, follow up a well worn path by a fence for about a mile before a steeper scramble onto the broad main ridge of the mountain.

The alternative route, involving descent, partly by old road, to the area of Minffordd and Lake Talyllyn, enables a night to be spent there before making the most exciting approach to Cader Idris. This involves a steep wooded ascent by cascading waterfalls followed by a spectacular ridge climb, marked as the Minffordd Path, round the enormous cwm surrounding Llyn Cau..

On the writer's first visit to Cader Idris a man in a little hut on the summit dispensed cups of tea but there is no such hospitality there today to greet the many who climb this deservedly popular mountain. Perhaps more practically useful on occasions is the emergency shelter just to the north of the summit. The whole mountain is a national nature reserve.

It is tempting to descend by Fox's Path but this is very steep, terribly eroded and strongly advised against. Much the better route is westwards by gradual descent to the Pony Path at Rhiw Gwredydd, thence north-east down a maintained path. Half way down, (unless making for the national park car park), go left through gate, before a hunting gate on main path, and follow less used right of way down to the road.

Hostellers may make a beeline for Kings but they must also be planning ahead and decide whether to press on to Barmouth. Few will be capable of reaching Llanbedr and certainly not Ffestiniog along the Cambrian Way route in one day from Kings. Maybe an easy 5½ mile day to Barmouth with an indulgence in candyfloss and sea bathing is called for before tackling the Rhinogs.

The walk to Barmouth through the lower foothills of Cader, past the Cregennen Lakes and a waymarked path route, partly non-definitive, leading down past Arthog waterfalls to the Mawddach estuary is a fascinating walk. Lovers of walking old railway routes could, as an alternative, follow the beautiful wooded valley down from Kings to the Mawddach estuary and follow the scenic cycle route to Arthog.

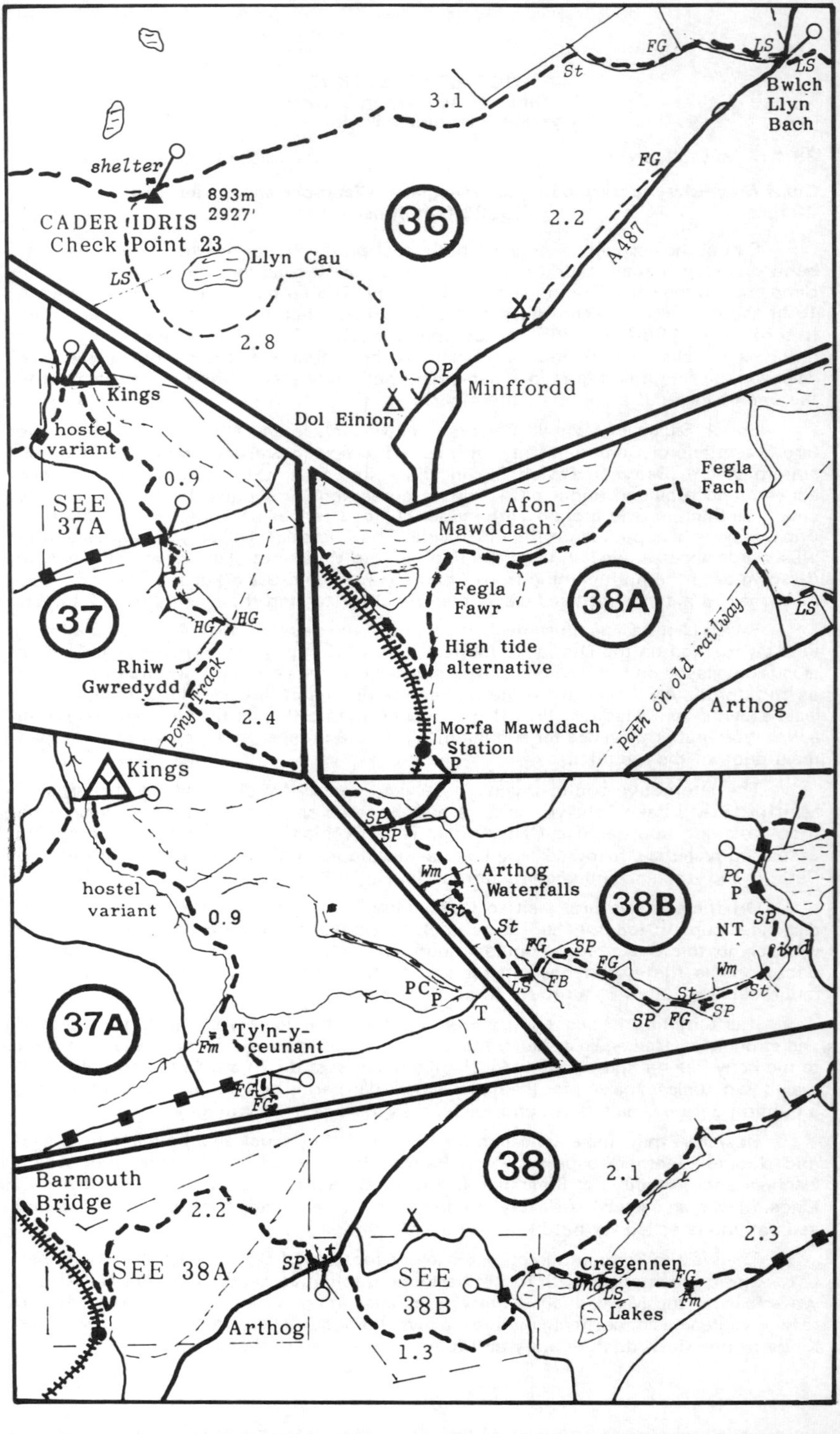
shelter
893m
2927'
CADER IDRIS
Check Point 23
3.1
FG
LS
St
Bwlch
Llyn
Bach
36
2.2
A487
Llyn Cau
LS
2.8
P
Minffordd
Dol Einion
Kings
hostel
variant
0.9
SEE
37A
37
HG
Rhiw
Gwredydd
Pony Track
2.4
Fegla
Fach
Afon
Mawddach
Fegla
Fawr
38A
High tide
alternative
Path on old railway
Arthog
Morfa Mawddach
Station
Kings
hostel
variant
0.9
SP
Wm
Arthog
Waterfalls
38B
PC
NT
37A
PC
T
Ty'n-y-
ceunant
Fm
FG
FB
38
2.1
Barmouth
Bridge
2.2
SEE 38A
SEE
38B
Arthog
1.3
Cregennen
Lakes
2.3

Barmouth Bridge carries both the Cambrian Coast railway line and a footbridge, for which there is a small toll. The future of the bridge and of the whole line was in some jeopardy in 1980 when it was thought the Teredo beetle was destroying the bridge timbers, but the damage was not as bad as was thought.

Barmouth to Maentwrog or Ffestiniog via the Rhinogs
22½ miles 7928 feet of Ascent Maps 39 to 41

Barmouth is a fascinating seaside resort sandwiched between the cliffs and either the sea or the Mawddach estuary. Depart by a path which starts as a steep flight of steps alongside an enormous gash of an old quarry. Good navigation is required up to the radio mast and Bwlch y Llan. Thence follows a superb ridge walk that would have been impossible but for negotiation by the national park with the owner for a permissive route with ladder stiles over the high walls The action of the owners is much appreciated but it should be noted that to emphasise that the route is not a public right of way, it is closed on February 5th each year. February is an unlikely and highly dangerous time of year to make an expedition along the Cambrian Way, but an alternative " February 5th Route" is shown on map 39.

The Rhinog section of the Cambrian Way is at the same time the most demanding, the most rewarding and the most controversial part of the whole route. The traverse of the range should not be undertaken unless the walker is capable of moving safely over difficult terrain and capable of easy climbing with a pack on., Good navigational ability is essential and **one must be prepared to take much longer than the distances suggest will be necessary.**

Going is reasonably easy as far as the summit of Y Llethr the highest point in the range, but the central and northern sections involve much rock scrambling, often where heather obscures the boulders below. Lone walkers particularly must appreciate the dangers of a sprained ankle or other accident in places where no one will hear or see them. The local volunteer mountain rescue organisation was very apprehensive of the creation of the Cambrian Way, not least -because of the difficulty of finding an injured person amongst the rocks.

Very few walkers will be capable of doing the whole range in one day and many will find even half the way more than enough for one day. Those who want a roof over their head will find there is limited accommodation in Cwm Nantcol but none in Cwm Bychan. A Youth Hostel was opened at Gerddi Bluog, between Cwm Bychan and Harlech, with the help of the Countryside Commission, with Cambrian Way in mind and before the project foundered, but it was neither very near the route or easily accessible from the coast road and was closed.The backpacker scores on this part of the route in being able to stay in the mountains.

Stage planning for the normal distance walker, if not camping, or being car assisted from road heads at Cwm Nantcol or Cwm Bychan, is likely to involve a detour to Llanbedr or Harlech. The stage planning chart gives distances involved for a taxi assisted detour and return. For a two day Rhinogs schedule descent is made from the route at Bwlch Drws Ardudwy and Cwm Nantcol followed to Llanbedr or a taxi phoned for from the call box at 623262. Return next day by taxi could be to Maes-y-Garnedd. (See accommodation list for taxi details). For a three day schedule, descent to Cwm Nantcol can be made from Crib y rhiw down gentle slopes on Tir Cymen access land to a gate at 636246,and thence by gated path to the Cwm Nantcol road at 630257, returning to Crib y rhiw same way following day. Cwm Bychan has no convenient phone box for taxi calling but one could do this section in reverse to use the Nantcol phonebox again.This is one part of Cambrian Way where a mobile phone would be useful (if it worked in the mountains)

Exhilarating ridge walking along Crib-y-rhiw leads to Y Llethr the highest point on the range. Beyond the summit keep to the end of the plateau and descend down a gully. Do not be tempted by a much eroded steep descent which leads more directly to Llyn Hywel. Rhinog Fach is suggested as a spur route using the scramble up the south end and same route for return to avoid steep and erosion prone descents elsewhere off the mountain.

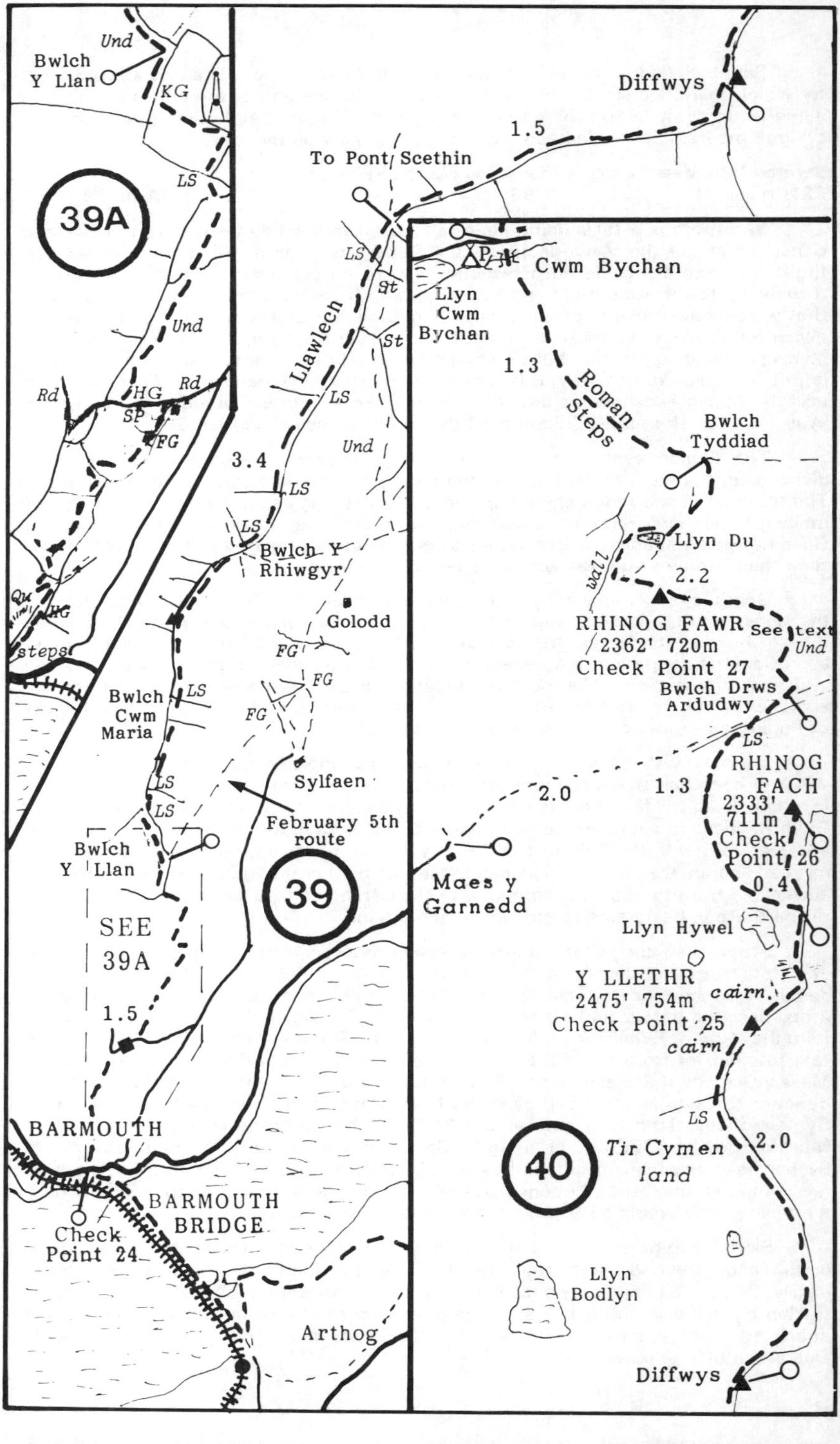
39A
Und
Bwlch
Y Llan
KG
LS
Und
Rd
HG
Rd
SP
FG
Qu
HG
steps
To Pont Scethin
LS
St
St
Llawlech
LS
Und
3.4
LS
LS
Bwlch Y
Rhiwgyr
Golodd
FG
FG
FG
Bwlch
Cwm
Maria
LS
LS
LS
Sylfaen
February 5th
route
Bwlch
Y Llan
39
SEE
39A
1.5
BARMOUTH
BARMOUTH
BRIDGE
Check
Point 24
Arthog
Diffwys
1.5
P
Cwm Bychan
Llyn
Cwm
Bychan
1.3
Roman
Steps
Bwlch
Tyddiad
Llyn Du
wall
2.2
RHINOG FAWR
2362' 720m
Check Point 27
See text
Und
Bwlch Drws
Ardudwy
LS
RHINOG
FACH
2333'
711m
Check
Point 26
1.3
2.0
Maes y
Garnedd
0.4
Llyn Hywel
Y LLETHR
2475' 754m
Check Point 25
cairn
cairn
LS
2.0
40
Tir Cymen
land
Llyn
Bodlyn
Diffwys

Rhinog Fawr is, next to Tryfan, probably the rockiest mountain in Wales. Geologically and ecologically, however, it is very different, which is no doubt partly why the Nature Conservancy acquired it. Finding the best of many possible routes can be the most difficult piece of navigation on the whole route. Do not be deceived by the wide gradually ascending ledges as seen from the south side, but start scrambling up from just beyond the wall at the actual pass of Bwlch Drws Ardudwy and climb steeply and slightly right, aiming for a small vulnerable cairn on the skyline. Beyond the cairn, if it still exists and you find it, the gradient eases off and one is on a broad rock terrace. Strike half right for a way up the cliff ahead onto one of the more definite paths that lead to the summit.

Descent north-westwards is eroded but unavoidable. Avoid direct descent to Llyn Du and make for wall, then follow wall and north side of lake. North-east from the lake a path leads round to Bwlch Tyddiad but avoid spurious path to left which would take you too high.

The so-called Roman Steps are now agreed as being of later origin. The ready supply of large boulders were used to make a packhorse route over these inhospitable mountains. They now provide thousands of tourists much pleasure and Cambrian Way walkers welcome faster progress than may have been experienced on the Rhinogs. The national park has carried out much improvement to the Steps path with the assistance of working parties of the B.T.C.V. An alternative to the Steps path is to press on along the main ridge via Craig Wion, but the going is very slow and probably not worth the saving of height against the drop to Cwm Bychan.

Cwm Bychan is a grand spot surrounded by rocky mountains and with a most attractive lake. The camp site has only recently acquired toilets. It is just out of sight from where the cover picture was taken. The picture, incidentally, portrays your author before he took to walking poles. These can be recommended, are said to take 30% of weight off the feet, give the arms something useful to do and bring a new dimension to country walking.

The northern Rhinogs are more rocky but less heathery than the central section. From just north of Clip to just west of Moel y Gyrafolen (535m) there is a public right of access because it is a Welsh Crown common. The approach to Clip, and Moel y Gyrafolen are currently permissive access under a Tir Cymen agreement. A steep scramble from just before Bwlch Gwylim is probably the easiest way up to Clip, but it is undefined. Thence follows a remarkable walk, mostly along a bare rock plateau, interspersed with chasms that have to be climbed down and up again. Easy climbing is needed up a rock face but can be circumvented round the sides if necessary. Two small lakes should be identified for help in navigation, especially if the area is in cloud. In contrast Moel Ysgyfarnogod is a grassy mound followed by another dip and cliff to the even flatter rock plateau of Diffwys (not to be confused with the Diffwys at the southern end of the Rhinogs). It is important to come off the open land by the public footpath at the hunting gate at 674358 to the north of Moel y Gyrafolen. Any other ways in that area would involve climbing over walls, something our Connoisseur never does.

At the minor road at Moelfryn main route walkers will go north by the signposted and waymarked path to the new Trawsfynydd dam and so down to Maentwrog. A variant route can be via Trawsfynydd and Ffestiniog, passing round the south and east side of Llyn Trawsfynydd. This alternative was put in before the Youth Hostel at Ffestiniog closed. It passes near a Roman amphitheatre, now only grassy mounds, with nearby Tomen-y-mur, a Roman fort which Richard Sale describes as "the very frontier of the Empire with pouring rain and pagan savages for company"

Either way one gets a view of the controversial former Trawsfynydd nuclear power station and one can assess whether Sir Basil Spence and Sylvia Crowe made a good job of designing the nuclear power station. Major development, possibly as a factory, was rejected after inquiry in 1998. Burying for 135 years is one option and at the time of writing the Welsh Office was likely to hold a public inquiry into its future.

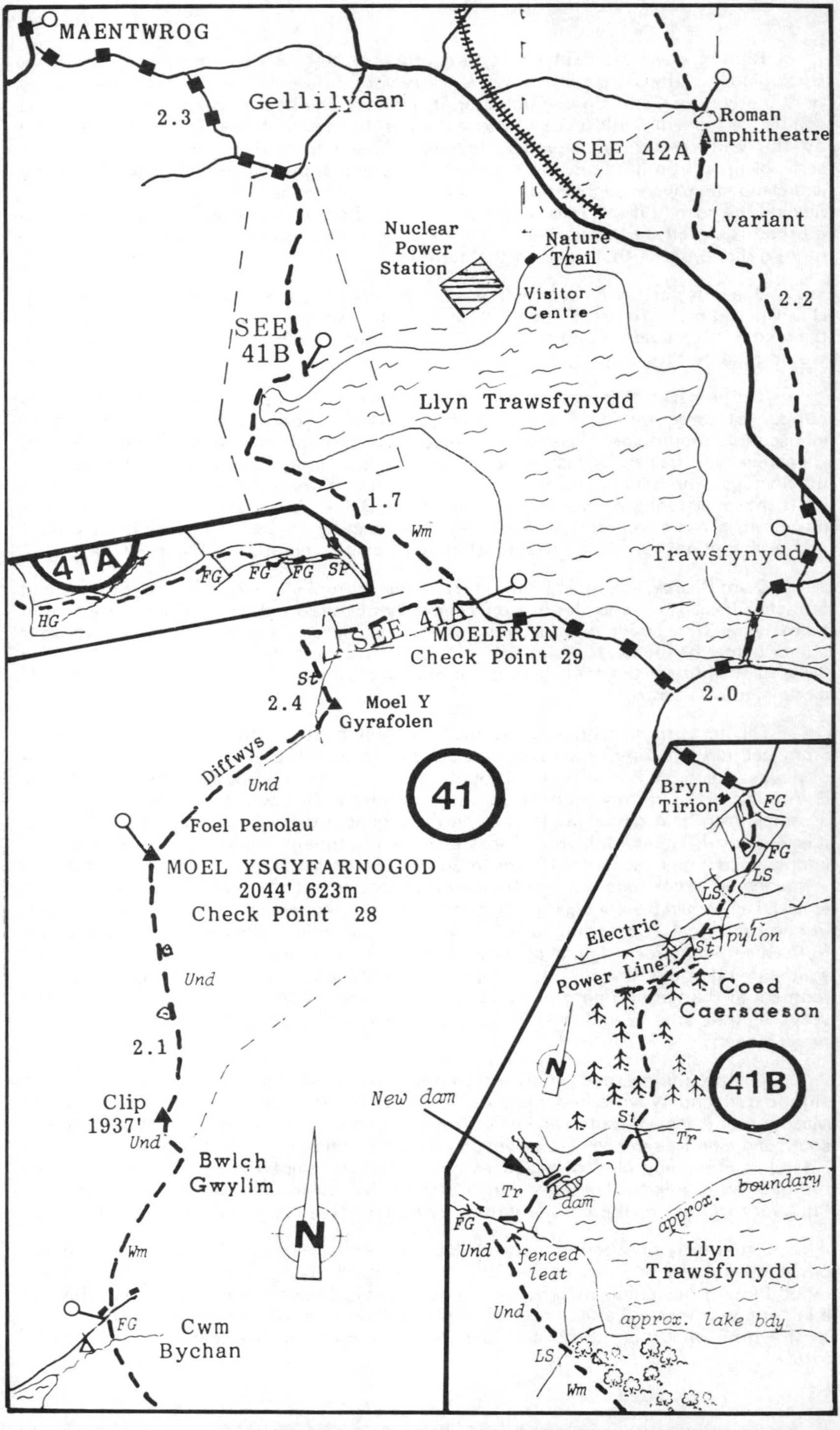
MAENTWROG
Gellilydan
2.3
SEE 42A
Roman Amphitheatre
variant
Nuclear Power Station
Nature Trail
Visitor Centre
2.2
SEE 41B
Llyn Trawsfynydd
1.7
Wm
41A
FG
FG
FG
SP
HG
Trawsfynydd
SEE 41A
MOELFRYN
Check Point 29
2.0
St
2.4
Moel Y Gyrafolen
Diffwys
Und
41
Bryn Tirion
FG
FG
LS
LS
Foel Penolau
MOEL YSGYFARNOGOD
2044' 623m
Check Point 28
Electric Power Line
St
pylon
Coed Caersaeson
Und
2.1
N
41B
Clip 1937'
Und
New dam
St
Tr
Bwlch Gwylim
Tr
dam
approx. boundary
FG
N
Und
fenced leat
Llyn Trawsfynydd
Wm
Und
approx. lake bdy
FG
Cwm Bychan
LS
Wm

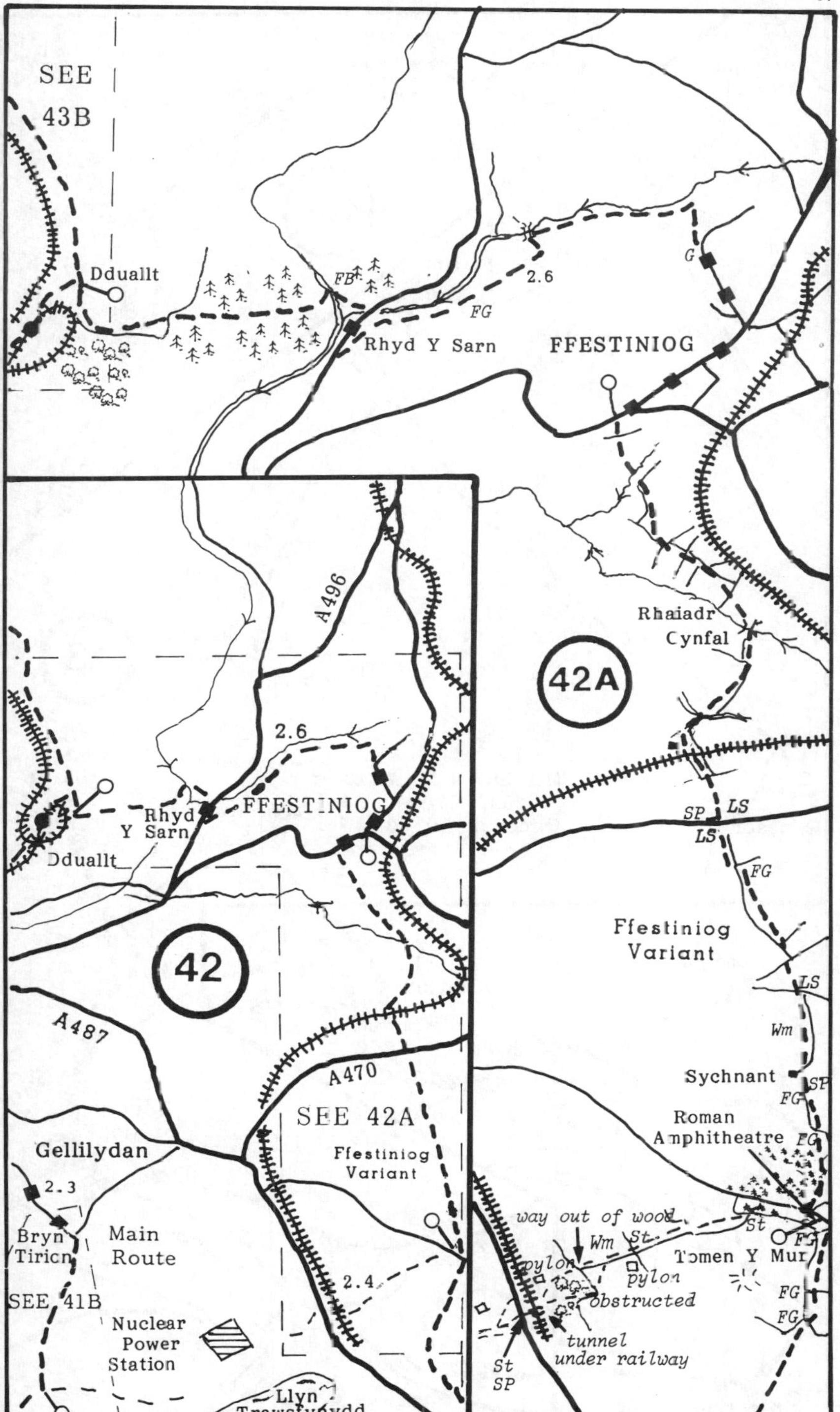
SEE 43B
Dduallt
FB
Rhyd Y Sarn
2.6
FG
G
FFESTINIOG
Rhaiadr Cynfal
42A
SP
LS
LS
FG
Ffestiniog Variant
LS
Wm
Sychnant
SP
FG
Roman Amphitheatre
FG
way out of wood
Wm
St
St
Tomen Y Mur
FG
pylon
pylon
obstructed
tunnel under railway
FG
FG
St SP
A496
2.6
Rhyd Y Sarn
FFESTINIOG
Dduallt
42
A487
A470
SEE 42A
Ffestiniog Variant
Gellilydan
2.3
Bryn Tirion
Main Route
SEE 41B
2.4
Nuclear Power Station
Llyn Trawsfynydd

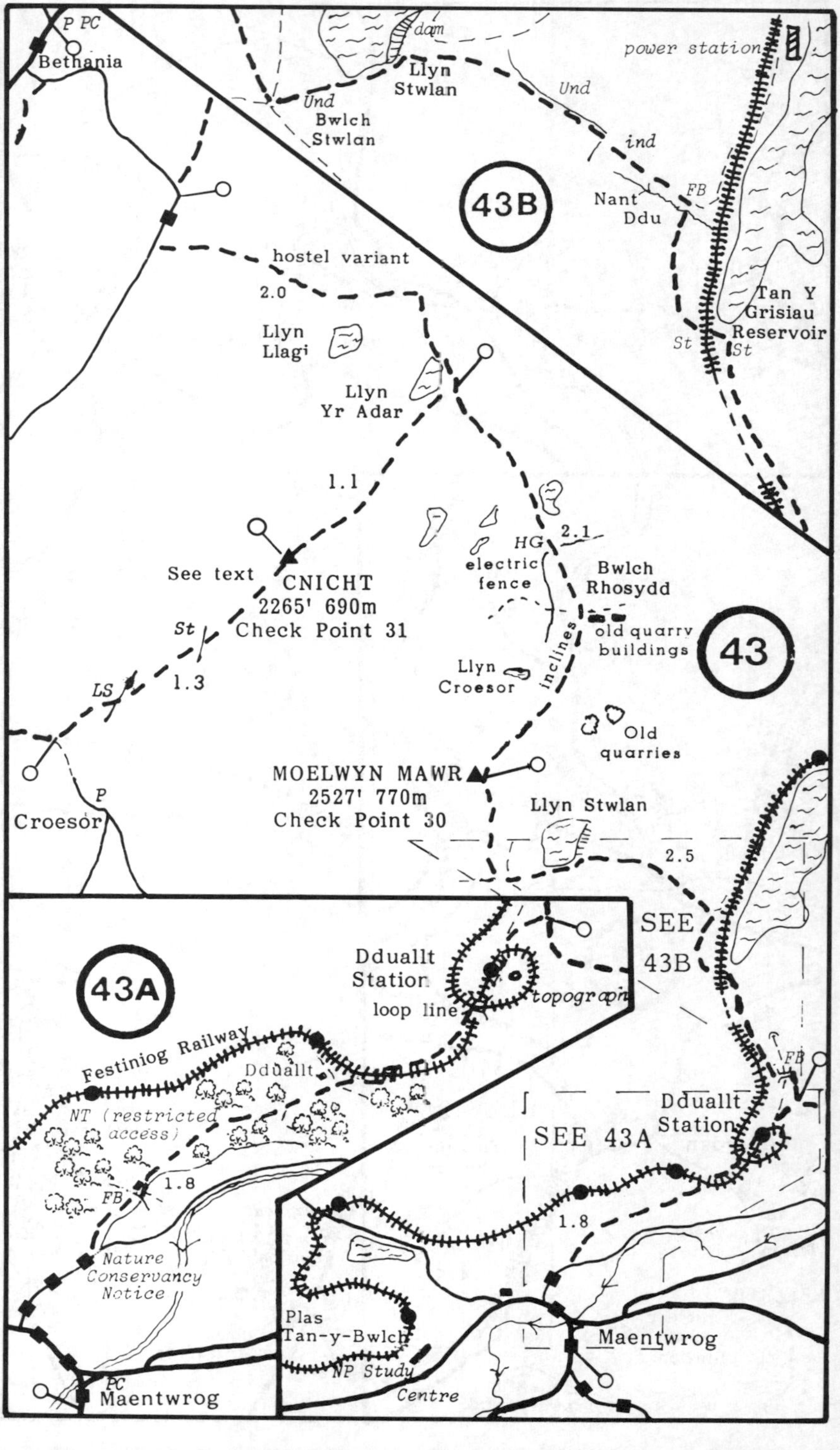
P PC
Bethania
dam
Llyn
Stwlan
power station
Und
Bwlch
Stwlan
Und
ind
43B
Nant
Ddu
FB
hostel variant
2.0
Tan Y
Grisiau
Reservoir
Llyn
Llagi
St
St
Llyn
Yr Adar
1.1
2.1
HG
See text
CNICHT
2265' 690m
Check Point 31
electric
fence
Bwlch
Rhosydd
St
old quarry
buildings
43
LS
1.3
Llyn
Croesor
inclines
Old
quarries
MOELWYN MAWR
2527' 770m
Check Point 30
P
Croesor
Llyn Stwlan
2.5
SEE
43B
43A
Dduallt
Station
loop line
topograph
Festiniog Railway
Dduallt
NT (restricted
access)
FB
Dduallt
Station
SEE 43A
1.8
FB
1.8
Nature
Conservancy
Notice
Plas
Tan-y-Bwlch
NP Study
Centre
Maentwrog
PC
Maentwrog

Maentwrog to Beddgelert via Moelwyn Mawr and Cnicht
12.8 miles, 3617' ascent Maps 42 - 45
To Bryn Gwynant Y.H. 12.0 miles, 3457' ascent.

From Maentwrog a path leads through beautiful woods forming part of the Coed Maentwrog national nature reserve. The National Trust allows restricted access and one is asked to keep to the paths. Our particular path leads round the lower side of a house called Bronturnoruchaf, and thence up to a crossing of the Festiniog railway, which is crossed again at Dduallt station. Due to submergence of part of the disused line when the Tan-y-grisiau reservoir was made, the enterprising organisation seeking to reopen this unique narrow gauge railway had to make a new route at a higher level, involving a new tunnel and the loop under which you pass before reaching the station. The train could be used by Cambrian Way walkers seeking bed and breakfast in Portmadoc or Blaenau Ffestiniog. Beyond the station the path runs a short distance away on the east side of the railway.

Those using the Ffestiniog variant descend by a cascading Afon Teigl to Rhyd-y-sarn and then over the Afon Goedol and through a conifer plantation to rejoin the main route below Dduallt station.

The right of way previously passing across the south end of Tan-y-grisiau reservoir has been diverted to the west side of the railway and should be followed to a footbridge over Nant Ddu, before striking up to Llyn Stwlan on a none too obvious footpath. At the dam go round the south end.

Llyn Stwlan is the upper reservoir of a pump storage system built to enable power from Trawsfynydd nuclear power station to be used at night to pump water from Tan-y-grisiau reservoir up to Llyn Stwlan, then let out to generate power at peak times.

Moelwyn Mawr is a worthy summit with fine views (if clear of course) of the Snowdon range, the coastline and the Rhinogs. Beneath one is a mountain riddled with mines which have been used for the storage of explosives. A few years ago a scare about danger of deterioration of the explosives led to a panic emptying of Llyn Stwlan as the dam was thought to be at risk.

This is one of the wildest and most desolate sections of the Cambrian Way and can be very inhospitable in rain and cloudy conditions. Good map reading is particularly important here. Be prepared for a new menace in the form of electric fencing on what has hitherto been unfenced open moorland. If you do not find the crossing points you may need a dry insulator to place over the fence in order to get over without shock. From Moelwyn Mawr summit descent is made down the broad NE flank to old quarry inclines leading to the gaunt ruins of the Rhosydd quarry buildings and barracks. From the pass the route is undefined through very boggy ground to a gate in the electric fence before passing small lakes and thence to a point near Llyn yr Adar, where a left turn is made onto the ridge to the summit of Cnicht. (Check Point 31). This section is on the edge of part of the National Trust acquisition in 1998 (see page 70)

At this point hostellers can retrace their steps to Llyn yr Adar and follow the path down to a minor road and thence by footpath, partly through forest, to Bryn Gwynant Youth Hostel. The latter part of this route (see map 45) leaves the public footpath shortly after leaving the forest, just beyond an old stone barn (marked on OS maps), and follows a permissive route for hostellers negotiated by the YHA with the landowner. The route is waymarked with white arrows and crosses into the extensive woods of the hostel grounds by a ladder stile and so down steep paths to the hostel.

The main route continues down the south-west ridge of Cnicht, shown on OS maps as a black dashed line. Some scrambling down is needed at a steep section not far below the summit where the best route is down an open chimney to the left (SE) side of the ridge. The gradient eases off and the route continues as a courtesy path waymarked by the national park. A look back to Cnicht (The Knight) shows it as quite an imposing mountain, but it is really an insult to the most famous mountain in the Alps to call it the "Welsh Matterhorn". A rough track/old road is followed to Bwlchgwernog then a minor road to Nantmor.

In the Aberglaslyn area there are problems arising from the controversial decision to allow the reopening of the Welsh Highland Railway (Dinas, near Caernarfon, to Portmadoc). The old trackbed in Aberglaslyn Pass has been a very popular walk, including a 280metre tunnel and two short tunnels. At a long inquiry in 1997/8 the National Park, National Trust, Snowdonia Society, the landowners, Ramblers Association etc opposed reopening whilst the County Council, and the tourism and railway interests supported. Mr Prescott, as Sec. of State for DETR overruled the inspector and allowed reopening subject to assurances about safety from rock falls at Aberglaslyn.

Previous editions have insisted that the tunnel should not be used as a short cut to Beddgelert and that the magnificent and exciting Fishermen's Path through the Aberglaslyn Pass should not be missed. There is no choice now as the tunnels have been firmly closed, prior to railway reopening, and the section of trackbed north of the long tunnel has been fenced off, forcing walkers into an adventurous scramble close to the torrent, particularly below the northernmost of the short tunnels,. If in doubt there is no alternative but to follow the A498 until one can join the west bank footpath, with its optional deviation to the grave of the faithful dog of Llewelyn the Great (see Richard Sales's book). At the time of going to press there were many ideas in the air as to improvements to the Fishermen's Path and/or a new footbridge across the Glaslyn. Watch the updates for latest situation.

Beddgelert to Pen-y-Pass via Snowdon

10 miles 3590 feet of ascent Maps 44 & 45

Beddgelert is a deservedly popular tourist village, its main disadvantage being the traffic that pours through it and which in particular goes over the attractive bridge in the village centre. There are inns, shops, cafes and accommodation here. Beddgelert has no direct path to Snowdon and the route chosen for Cambrian Way follows the atttractive Nant Gwynant and alongside Llyn Dinas before ascending Snowdon partly by the Watkin path. Hostellers from Bryn Gwynant come along the main road to join the main route at Pont Bethania, near the car park and toilets.

The Watkin Path is in many ways the most attractive approach to Snowdon, albeit the one involving the greatest ascent. The lower part is on the track going to the old mines and quarries in Cwm Llan, and this has been skilfully restored in recent years by expert boulder movers as part of the Snowdon Management Scheme.The whole of the mountain in view as one ascends was acquired by the National Trust in 1998 after a fantastically successful appeal to buy it for the nation. Altogether over £5 million was raised.

The Watkin Path was opened by Gladstone in 1892, at the age of 84, during his fourth term of office as prime minister, the occasion being commemorated by a plaque on the Gladstone Rock. Supposedly Sir Edward Watkin had the path above the quarries made to the summit by a route to take in the view of the Snowdon Horseshoe but no account was taken of the impracticability of maintaining a good path across the very unstable south flank of Snowdon summit. Although large sums of money have been apent on Snowdon's paths, the upper part of the Watkin Path remains an unsolved and most intractable erosion problem. Fortunately however for Cambrian Way, there is no need to go that way at all as there is a better way up Allt Maenderyn and Bwlch Main ridge.

Just after passing some waterfalls and before the ruin of the mine manager's house, at 621520, an unsigned public footpath goes sharply left up an old incline. After 300 metres turn right onto the line of an old tramway and follow this for about another 300 metres, then strike half left towards the pass of Bwlch Cwm Llan.The line of the right of way is only vaguely discernible and peters out altogether nearer the pass. Once on Allt Maenderyn the way is up a broad rocky ridge. Some sections are

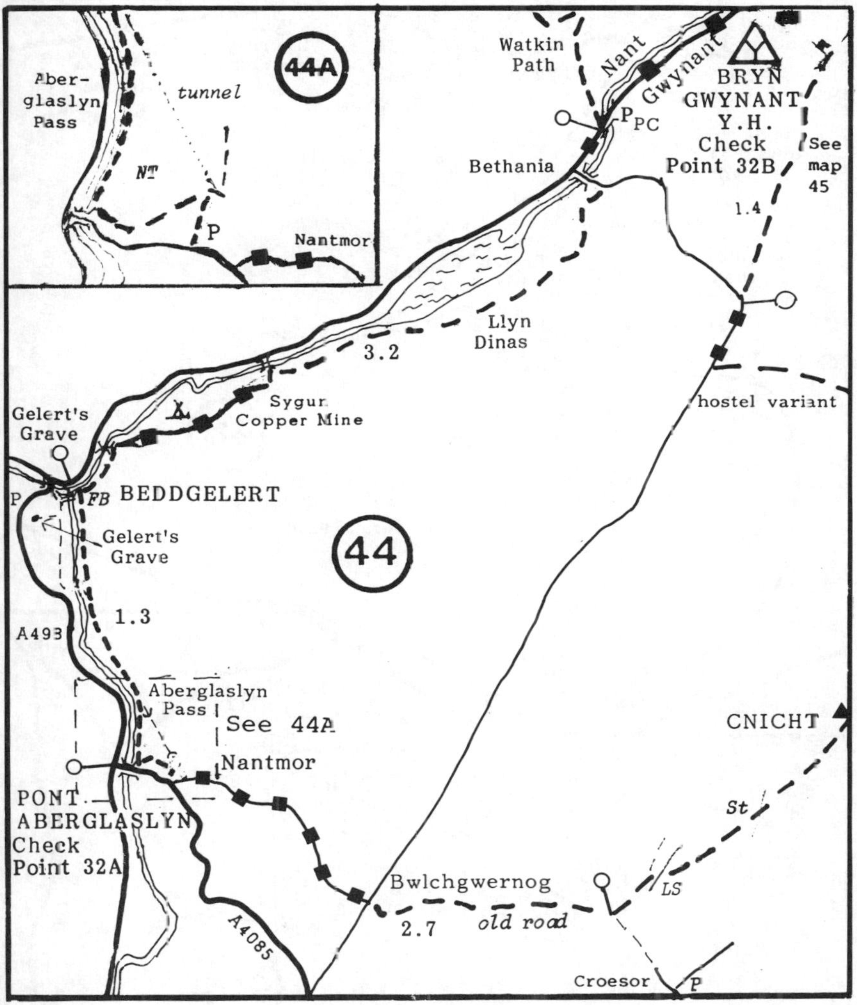

getting eroded, mostly by those dashing down this ridge, but our Connoisseur, being on the ascent will add little to the erosion. The ridge is broad enough for the eroded parts to be bypassed but do not just walk on the edge of the erosion - thats the next bit to go . Walk well away from the worn route - if all use was spread out the grass cover would not be damaged. Higher up the ridge narrows, particularly after being joined by the Llechog ridge and the route is slightly airy before the final scramble to the summit.

Snowdon summit will, more likely than not, be in cloud, even if the rest of the way up has been clear. Chris Jesty in his admirable panorama guide to Snowdon summit, reckons that the odds against seeing the nearby peak of Lliwedd as 1.1 to 1, with 400 to 1 against seeing Scafell Pike, the highest point in England.

The summit receives about 200 inches of rain and many hundreds of thousands of visitors a year. If you have ideas of celebrating reaching the climax of

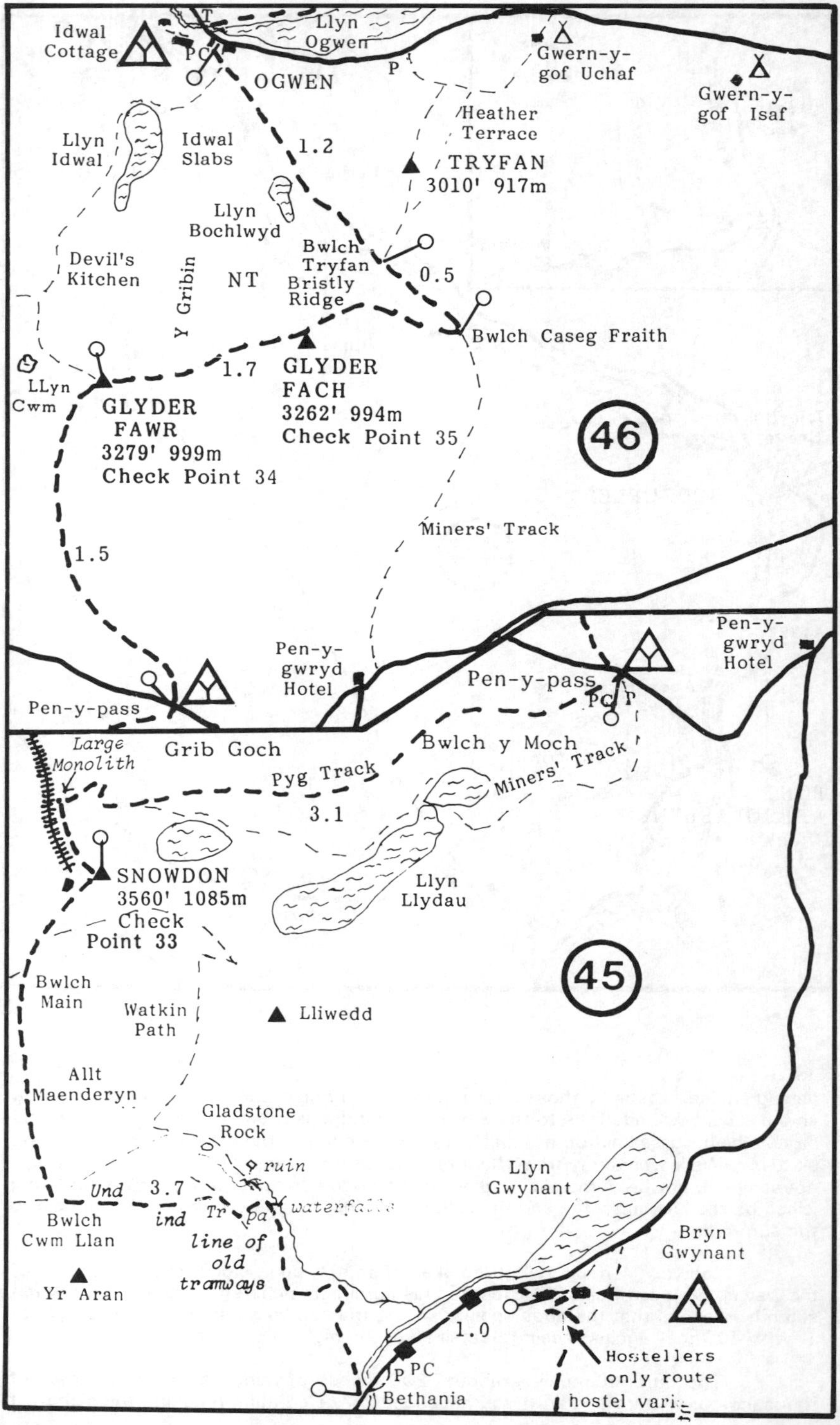
Idwal Cottage
PC
T
Llyn Ogwen
OGWEN
P
Gwern-y-gof Uchaf
Gwern-y-gof Isaf
Heather Terrace
TRYFAN
3010' 917m
Llyn Idwal
Idwal Slabs
1.2
Llyn Bochlwyd
Devil's Kitchen
Y Gribin
NT
Bwlch Tryfan
0.5
Bristly Ridge
Bwlch Caseg Fraith
LLyn Cwm
1.7
GLYDER FACH
3262' 994m
Check Point 35
GLYDER FAWR
3279' 999m
Check Point 34
46
Miners' Track
1.5
Pen-y-gwryd Hotel
Pen-y-pass
PC T
Pen-y-pass
Pen-y-gwryd Hotel
Large Monolith
Grib Goch
Bwlch y Moch
Pyg Track
Miners' Track
3.1
SNOWDON
3560' 1085m
Check Point 33
Llyn Llydau
45
Bwlch Main
Watkin Path
Lliwedd
Allt Maenderyn
Gladstone Rock
ruin
Llyn Gwynant
Und
3.7
Bwlch Cwm Llan
ind
Tr
pa
waterfalls
line of old tramways
Bryn Gwynant
Yr Aran
1.0
P PC
Bethania
Hostellers only route
hostel vari

the Cambrian Way by sitting admiring the view with a pint of beer, at a table on a terrace at the cafe, then dispel this idea quickly. There may be so many in the cafe that you refuse to wait to be served, there are no terraces with tables, and the cafe may be closed. It is only open when the railway is running, and does not open until some time after Easter because of snow in the railway cuttings.

Any soil that there once was near the summit pyramid has gone and serious suggestions have been made for people to be asked to carry small bags of earth up with them. The surroundings of the cafe and station are such that Prince Charles is said to have remarked that this is the highest slum in Britain. There have been plans for improvements but the costs of working at such a site are enormous.

Despite all the problems besetting Snowdon summit these do not alter the importance of Snowdon as the worthy climax of the Cambrian Way. It is a mountain on the grander scale than anything else en route and its magnificence is not belittled by its popularity.

From the summit area follow the path parallel to the railway to the enormous stone monolith at Bwlch Glas (spot height 993m) put up to indicate the vital point at which to hit the top of the Pyg or Pig Track. There is uncertainty as to whether the name of this famous path is derived from an abbreviation of the Pen-y-gwyrd Hotel beyond the end of the path or from the Welsh word "moch", sometimes meaning pig, in the title of the pass called Bwlch y Moch part way up the path. At the monolith a decision must be made whether to follow the Pyg Track down or whether to take the more exciting but very exposed Crib Goch ridge route to Bwlch y Moch. This classic part of the Snowdon Horseshoe route is strongly advised against if carrying a heavy pack, or if the walker is not very sure footed or if there are bad weather conditions. The ridge is really very knife-edged and quite sheer for hundreds of feet either side.

The Pyg Track has carried many millions intent on reaching the highest point in England and Wales under their own steam. It is only in recent years that it has been fully appreciated that such usage on such terrain requires maintenance to prevent the path becoming most unpleasant and dangerous to walk. This path is where most effort has been expended but the cost has been considerably reduced by the use of volunteers from several organisations notably the British Trust for Conservation Volunteers. If the idea of such public spirited work appeals to you, not necessarily on such arduous projects, contact B.T.C.V. at 35 St. Mary's Street, Wallingford, Oxon. for details of their national and local tasks.

The first section below the pass is appropriately called the Zig Zags and has been much improved. Do not be tempted to short cut as this is what caused such terrible erosion in the past. Further on there is another option, this time to descend to the Miners Track that runs up to the old mines by Llyn Glaslyn. This follows a wider path, crosses Llyn Llydaw by a causeway, and a much improved track to Peny-Pass. The Pyg track keeps higher up and crosses into the Llanberis valley at Bwlch y Moch at the end of the Crib Goch ridge.

Pen-y-Pass, popular because at 1168 feet (356m) it is the highest road pass from which to climb Snowdon, consists of a youth hostel, restaurant and car park. Much to the disgust of many of the climbing fraternity the old Gorphwysfa Hotel at the pass was converted and extended, with large government grants, to become a very well appointed Youth Hostel. On the opposite side of the road is a cafe and toilets. If your mode of walking Cambrian Way involves the use of the car park, note that it is expensive and strictly limited in size. Hostel visitors have free overnight parking. There is nowhere else to park legally near the pass. The Snowdon Sherpa bus service calls here. A timetable is available from Snowdonia National Park Office; (see page 85). It is possible to use the buses so as to spend the night at say Peny Gwryd, Llanberis, Beddgelert or Bryn Gwynant and return to resume the walk at Pen-y-Pass next day, thus allowing a light rucksack for Snowdon.

Pen-y-Pass to Ogwen via the Glyders
4.8 miles | 2353 feet of ascent | Map 46

The path leading onto the Glyders is over a ladder stile on the Llanberis side of the hostel building. The way up the broad south ridge of Glyder Fawr gets more defined as the years pass and is now marked as black dashes on the Ordnance maps. Compass and map work will be necessary in cloud in this area.. Assuming that the Ogwen valley is to be a staging point before the long trek over the Carneddau, our Connoisseur is advised either to have a short day from Pen-y-Pass to Ogwen or to get to Ogwen early enough to make separate sorties in this superb mountain area to, say, Tryfan or Cwm Idwal. By making Glyder Fach a checkpoint as well as Glyder Fawr use will be discouraged of the eroded descent from Glyder Fawr to Llyn Cwm and the frustrating boulder descent below the Devil's Kitchen. From Glyder Fach there are several possible descents, such as the Gribin or the very airy Bristly Ridge, but the recommended safe way is to proceed further east along the Glyder plateau to Bwlch Caseg Fraith, where the Miner's Track from Pen-y-Gwryd to Ogwen crosses over.

The south facing land hereabouts and nearly to Capel Curig was farmed from the 1930s until her death in 1999 by Mrs. Esme Kirby. Her first husband Thomas Firbank wrote the best selling book "I Bought a Mountain". The book is well worth reading, particularly for its insight into the problems of sheep farming in the wilder parts of Wales. Esme founded and was the driving force of the Snowdonia National Park Society, now renamed the Snowdonia Society.

Tryfan, as the rockiest mountain in Wales is ideal for learning to climb (and the author has happy memories of the easier climbs there), but the north ridge is not for the uninitiated to descend with a large rucksack and therefore Tryfan has not been made a Cambrian Way checkpoint. The traverse of Tryfan is however a splendid expedition, but best achieved from north to south. On the top (3010 ft.) there are two prominent boulders, Adam and Eve. A mountaineer's initiation is sometimes to jump from one to the other.

From Bwlch Tryfan the Miner's Track passes Llyn Bochlwyd, an attractive spot, or a rougher way down is by Heather Terrace on the east side of Tryfan.

Ogwen has probably the finest panorama of mountains around it of anywhere in Wales and maybe this was why it gave its name to a rural district of Caernarvonshire before local government reorganisation in 1974. Certainly it was not the population living at Ogwen which gave it importance, since the place consists only of a mountain school, a Youth Hostel, tea bar, toilets and small car park. There is no pub or B&B . The National Trust owns virtually all the land you can see and does not allow camping except at the organised sites which are at Gwern Gof Isaf and Uchaf. This sounds a rather inhospitable place but it could be easily spoiled. Nearby at Cwm Idwal is a national nature reserve, and a pleasant evening stroll can be made from the hostel to follow the nature trail round Llyn Idwal, amidst the spellbinding scenery of the glacially carved valley.

Ogwen to Conwy via the Carneddau
18 miles | 4697 feet of ascent | Maps 47 - 49

The final section of the Cambrian Way is longer than most other stages suggested but is not as long as the 28 mile final stretch of the Pennine Way. The journey can more easily be broken as there is a Youth Hostel about two-thirds of the way along, and a roadhead for car assisted parties near the Bwlch y Ddeufaen. On the other hand, this section has other hazards which can have serious consequences since 4½ miles run at over 3000 feet.At that level the mountains are more often in cloud than not, and just as much so in summer as winter. Conditions of rain, wind or snow can be unbelievably treacherous, as the author found with wind that just knocked one over and necessitated a retreat.There are escape routes but these can leave the walker in remote valleys miles from anywhere. There seems to be no satisfactory low level alternative route. If bad weather prevails on the last day of a

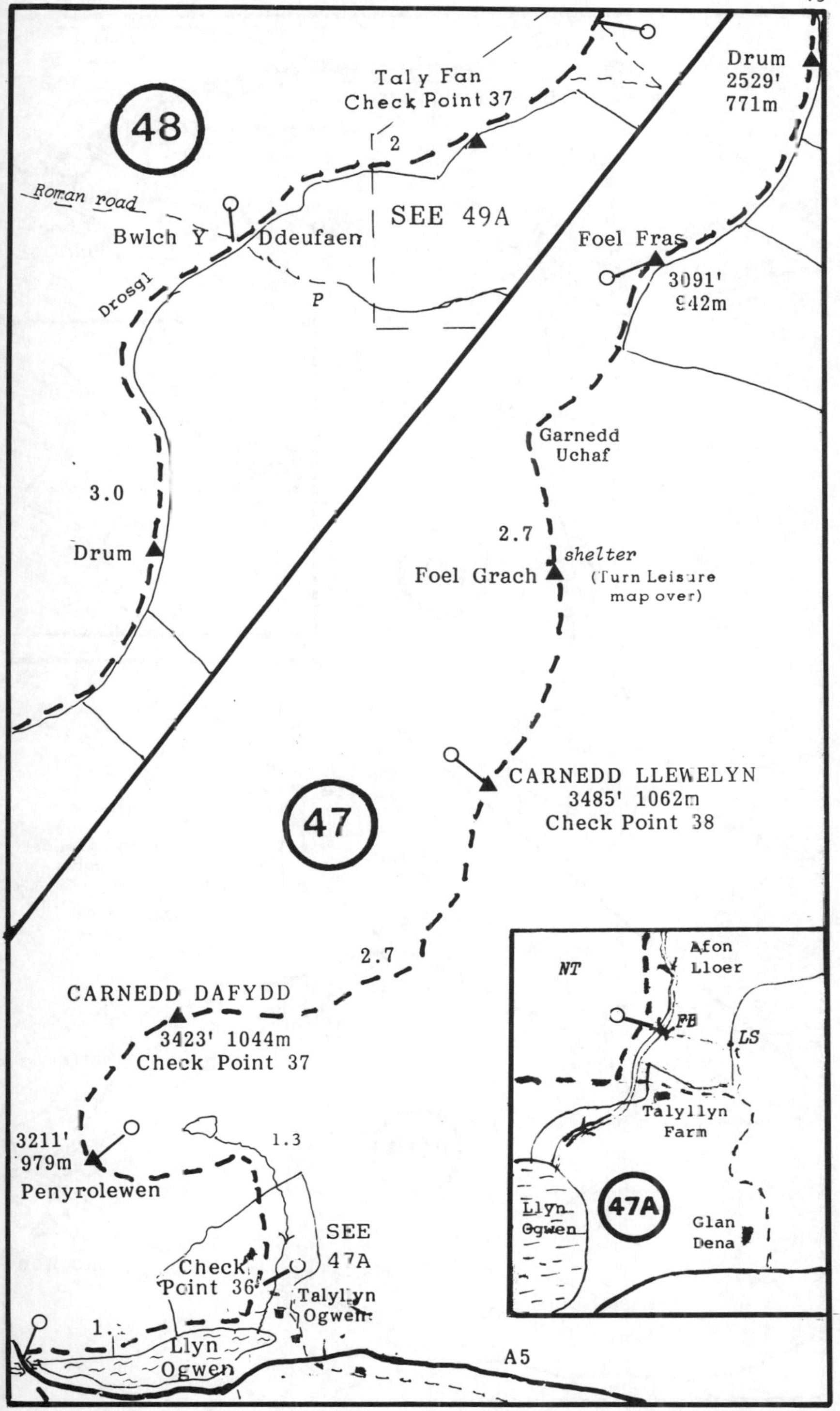

48
Taly Fan
Check Point 37
2
SEE 49A
Roman road
Bwlch Y Ddeufaen
Drosgl
P
3.0
Drum
Drum
2529'
771m
Foel Fras
3091'
942m
Garnedd
Uchaf
2.7
shelter
Foel Grach
(Turn Leisure
map over)
CARNEDD LLEWELYN
3485' 1062m
Check Point 38
47
2.7
CARNEDD DAFYDD
3423' 1044m
Check Point 37
3211'
979m
Penyrolewen
1.3
SEE
47A
Check
Point 36
Talyllyn
Ogwen
Llyn
Ogwen
A5
Afon
Lloer
NT
FB
LS
Talyllyn
Farm
Llyn
Ogwen
47A
Glan
Dena

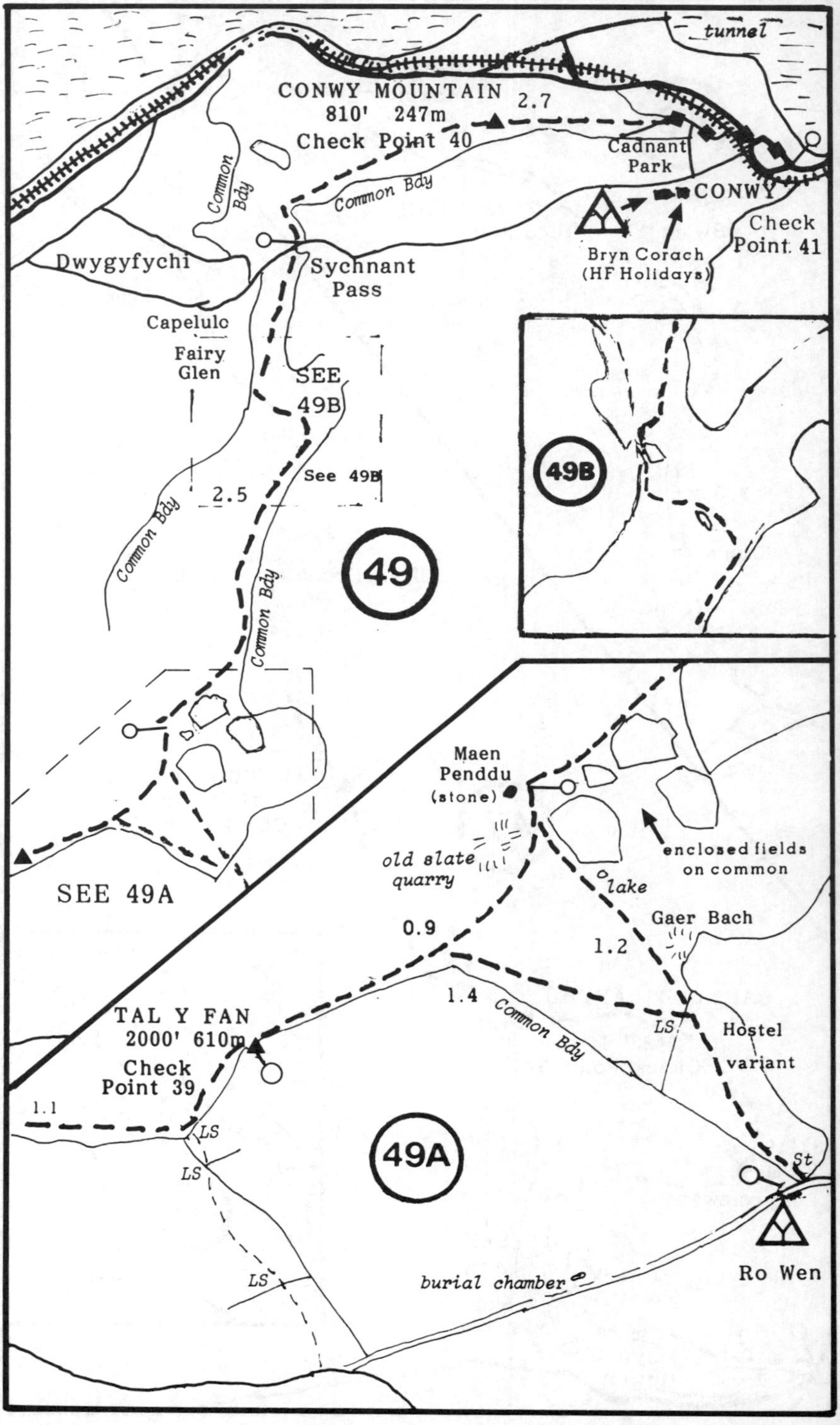
tunnel
CONWY MOUNTAIN
810' 247m
Check Point 40
2.7
Cadnant
Park
Common Bdy
Common Bdy
CONWY
Check
Point 41
Bryn Corach
(HF Holidays)
Dwygyfychi
Sychnant
Pass
Capelulo
Fairy
Glen
SEE
49B
See 49B
2.5
Common Bdy
Common Bdy
49
49B
SEE 49A
Maen
Penddu
(stone)
old slate
quarry
enclosed fields
on common
lake
Gaer Bach
0.9
1.2
1.4
Common Bdy
LS
Hostel
variant
TAL Y FAN
2000' 610m
Check
Point 39
1.1
LS
LS
LS
49A
St
burial chamber
Ro Wen

holiday and time does not permit an extra day discretion may be the better part of valour. On the other hand, navigation is not as difficult over the Carneddau as many parts of the Cambrian Way which may have already been traversed in cloud.

The whole way from Ogwen to Conwy is either National Trust land with unrestricted access (Ogwen to beyond Drum) or is over common land in former urban districts, some of it also crown common, and therefore with public right of access for air and exercise. Once over the stile at Ogwen there are no more stiles or gates to negotiate on the main route until Conwy.

Just over the road bridge at Ogwen go over the slate stile in the wall. This was put up in memory of Alfred Embleton, a Youth Hostel pioneer and for many years hon. treasurer of the Ramblers Association. The obvious route onto the Carneddau is straight up Penyrole-wen, average gradient 1 in 2½, but the frightful erosion, although partly repaired, still makes it an unpleasant and dangerous route, and is not recommended. Instead a longer and more pleasant way starts along the north side of Llyn Ogwen. The public footpath becomes undefined near Tal-y-llyn Ogwen Farm. Turn left before the river at the farm and proceed up, parallel to the river. Those who have stayed the night east of Llyn Ogwen can join the route here by the public footpath and permissive diversion at Talyllyn Ogwen Farm, (see map 47A). In order to discourage use of the eroded direct approach to Penyrole-wen the bridge north of the farm is a checkpoint. Note that the crossing of the Afon Lloer shown on the black dashed line on the Ordnance maps is not recommended . Head for a ladder stile and then when due east of the prominent crags on the left make for an obvious gully where an easy scramble leads up to the east ridge of Penyrole-wen. This can be difficult to find in cloud.

Most of the way along the Carneddau is on reasonably firm ground -no floundering in bog to get to a summit such as the Cheviot. Along the main ridge the way is usually visible on the ground though at places like north-west of Craig Llugwy the rocky ground does not reveal any path, and the drop on the left needs to be kept in view. The ridge is mostly broad north of Carnedd Llewelyn and it is easy to get off course. A sharp turn at Garnedd Uchaf for no apparent reason on open plateau needs to be watched for. Once a fence looms up on the right about half a mile before Foel Fras navigational worries should be over for the next five miles as one follows the west side of the fence all the way to beyond Tal-y-fan.

If making a detour to the delightful small hostel at Rowen, there are three options as to where to turn off the main route but one should bear in mind that- Tal-y-fan is a check point. The hostel variant leads down to a stile onto the steep road,then up 150metres to the hostel.

From Tal-y-fan (just 2000 feet) the way is across open common, mostly on rights of way, but the most spectacular section is a nondefinitive traverse path on an ex urban district common leading to Sychnant Pass. The road crossing was once the main coast road before tunnels were made in the cliff at Penmaen-bach Point. Those tunnels have been replaced with wider tunnels and since 1991 the Conwy estuary itself has been tunnelled under to preserve Conwy's character as a fine walled town.

Positively the last climb is over Conwy Mountain, a fine vantage point overlooking the sea and the north Wales coastline, as well as back to the Carneddau. Gorse and heather in late summer make this much path covered hill a most pleasant spot.

The castle at Conwy makes a fitting terminus for our long walk. The author hopes you have enjoyed it - you certainly won't forget it and his guess is that you will return to explore more of Wales you didn't know. You will find, as the author has done that the Welsh mountains grow on you. You will also wonder what all the fuss was about in the opposition to the Cambrian Way.

Improvements to this guide are largely dependent on comments sent in by walkers The author collects not only picture postcards of Conwy Castle from successful Cambrian Way Connoisseurs but more particularly detailed accounts of problems and comments good, bad and indifferent on the accommodation or camping spots.

STAGE PLANNING

This section seeks to assist in planning to walk the Cambrian Way. It will be noted that heights of ascent are given against all distances. This must be taken very seriously into account in estimating the time required for each daily section.

Naismith's formula of three miles per hour plus half an hour per thousand feet is reduced to about two and a half miles an hour plus three quarters of an hour per thousand feet for those carrying heavy, packs . Slower walkers and leaders of parties would be wiser to work on under 2 miles per hour and over an hour per 1000ft

Plan to finish well before sunset to allow for mistakes in navigation, fatigue and accidents, but as a precaution ensure that every member of a party has a torch that works, if only to read a map by when it is still possible to see one's way.

Distances in the chart below are derived from map measurements and are shown in miles, together with the feet of ascent, on lines in between the place name lines. The Y.H.A. and other variant columns show relevant distances and heights between dashes level with the places concerned..

The stages shown are not necessarily all suggested as daily sections and in some cases two or more sections may be covered in a day. More detailed distances are shown between flagged points on the maps in this guide.

Cambrian Way is planned as a northbound excursion working up to a climax in Snowdonia. Do not be tempted to omit the Cardiff to Abergavenny section and then regret later on that the whole path has not been walked. It is well worth walking but do not try to "knock it off" in two days unless you are already very fit and are sure you can do it. **Most people try to do too much in the early days of a long distance walk.**

STAGE PLANNER - SOUTHERN SECTION

Main Route Cumul Miles	Stage Miles Main Route	Feet of Ascent North-bound	Staging Points Main Route	Staging Points Variants	YHA Variants Miles	YHA Variants Asc.	*Other* Variants Miles	*Other* Variants Asc.
0			Cardiff Castle					
	5.4	125						
5.4			Tongwynlais					
	8.3	875						
13.7			Machen					
	3	1022						
16.7			Risca					
	8.2	1504						
24.9			Pontypool					
	11.3	1691						
36.2			Abergavenny		-			
							10.7	*2885*
	13.1	3443		*Llanthony*				
49.3			Capel y ffin		14.2	3913		
				Capel y f.YH	-		*11.6*	*2144*
	16.0	2652		*Pengenfordd*	15.5	2347		
							10.2	*2338*
65.3			Crickhowell		-			
							13.9	*1808*
	20.0	4896		Aber (Talybont)				
							10.7	*3865*
85.3			Storey Arms		-		-	
					1.5	90		
				Llwyn y c.YH -	-			
					7.3	1150	12.1	1470
	8.1	2183		Ystadfellte YH	-			
				Glyntawe	16.0	3000	-	
93.4			A4067 Bwlch Bryn-rhudd		17.3	4000		
	7.2	1940		Llanddeusant YH -	-			
100.6			Llanddeusant/Trecastle rd.					
	3.8	359						
104.4			Myddfai		9.4	1017		
	3.5	473						
107.9			Llandovery		-			
	107.9	**21163**	Southern Section Sub Totals					

STAGE PLANNER - CENTRAL SECTION

Main Route Cumul Miles	Stage Miles Main Route	Feet of Ascent North-bound	Staging Points Main Route	Staging Points Variants	YHA Variants Miles	YHA Variants Asc.	Other Variants Miles	Other Variants Asc.
107.5			Llandovery					
	6.6	1033						
114.1			Rhandirmwyn		-			
					8.6	864		
	12.0	1579		Tyncornel YH	-			
					3.1	550		
126.1			Nant y maen junc.		-		-	
					4.3	400		
	6.6	946		Blaencaron YH	-		6.8	926
				Pontrhydfendigaid	5.4	1106	-	
132.7			Strata Florida		–			
	9.1	1408					10.5	1438
141.8			Cwmystwyth				-	
	5.0	590						
146.8			Devil's Bridge					
	6.8	1340						
153.6			Dyffryn Castell					
	11.4	2560						
165.0			Dylife					
	8.6	750						
173.6			Commins Coch					
	13.0	2460						
186.6			Dinas Mawddwy					
	79.1	**12666**	**Central Section Sub Totals**					

STAGE PLANNER - NORTHERN (SNOWDONIA) SECTION

Main Route Cumul Miles	Stage Miles Main Route	Feet of Ascent North-bound	Staging Points Main Route	Staging Points Variants	YHA Variants Miles	YHA Variants Asc.	Other Variants Miles	Other Variants Asc.
186.6			Dinas Mawddwy		-		-	
	8.6	2883					10.8	2883
195.2			Bwlch Llyn Bach A487		15.0	5096		
				Minffordd			-	
	11.3	2643		Kings YH	-		11.0	3048
					5.6	700		
206.5			Barmouth		-		-	
							10.8	3434
	10.5	4118		Cwm Nantcol Tel.			-	
217.0			Bwlch Drws Ardudwy					
	3.5	1416		Cwm Na.(Maes y garnedd)			-	
							5.5	1836
220.5			Cwm Bychan				-	
	8.5	2394						
228.4			Maentwrog		-			
	12.8	3617			12.0	3457		
241.8			Beddgelert					
	10.0	3590		Bryn Gwynant YH	-			
					7.8	3360		
251.8			Pen y Pass	YH	-			
	4.8	2353			4.8	2353		
256.6			Ogwen	Idwal Cott.YH	-			
					13.5	4388		
	18.3	4697		Rowen YH	-			
					6.4	9-09		
274.9			Conwy Castle		-			
	88.3	**27711**	**Northern Section Sub Totals**					

	275.3	**61540**	**GRAND TOTAL CAMBRIAN WAY**

MAPS FOR CAMBRIAN WAY

Maps are **absolutely essential** for navigation on the Cambrian Way., Much of the way is undefined on the ground and those used to the Pennine Way and most other long distance paths will find they have to be good map readers and that time must be allowed for frequent looks at the maps.

The maps in this guidebook are designed to be read in conjunction with the Ordnance Survey maps and **are not intended to be used on their own.**

Map reading ability is essential to avoid unnecessary trespass and aggravation of farmers. Just a few bad map readers can incur the quite justifiable wrath of farmers if they climb over walls and fences where they have no right to go.

General Map. For planning purposes, sorting out one's travel to and from the area, and worth taking for identifying distant views is the Ordnance Survey's 1:250,000 Travelmaster map, sheet 7, "Wales and West Midlands", price £4.25 (1999).This map shows the mountain ranges clearly and marks railways and youth hostels.

1:25,000 and 1:50,000 Maps. The situation with maps for the Cambrian Way has changed dramatically for the better during 1999 with the publication by Ordnance Survey of the Explorer series at 1:25,000 (about 2½" to mile). The two national parks have been covered for some time by the Outdoor Leisure maps at that scale but now the bits in between have similar maps which are usually double sided, and covering 4½ times as much ground as the former Pathfinder series (for not much more cost). If one scale only is to be acquired the author strongly advises purchase of the 5 Outdoor Leisure maps plus 4 Explorer maps. (see key map pages 16 & 17). Turning these maps over even in only a moderate wind is a problem and inside a car almost impossible. Plan the turnover points carefully. The Foel Grach shelter on the Carneddau comes at a convenient spot.

The recommendation in previous editions was to at least have the 1:50,000 Landranger maps (1¼" to mile), especially as the basic maps in this guide are at that scale. They do give a broader picture and are sometimes more helpful especially for contour reading in mountains. They do not however show field boundaries and one must stress that more reliance on map reading is necessary on the Cambrian Way because it is not waymarked and often undefined on the ground. Seven maps are required. Both scales now show ORPAs (see page 13).

Costs and Weights Prices in 1999 were Outdoor Leisure £6.50, Explorer £5.50, Landranger £5.25. Thus outlay at 25K would be £54.50 and at 50k £36.75.

The nine 25K maps plus the all Wales map weigh about 2¾lb,/1.2kg. The seven 50k maps plus Wales map weigh 1¾/0.8kg. Covers can be removed or maps cut down to reduce weight but note that flat maps which can be ordered through shops cost the same as folded maps.

The Maps in this guide are of three kinds:-

1. **Key maps** - (a) South and (b) North, showing layout of the 1:50,000 strip maps and to the 1:25,000 and1:50,000 Ordnance Survey maps . See pages 16 and 17.

2 . **1: 50,000 strip maps** covering the whole route, derived from out of copyright Ordnance Survey one inch to mile (1:63,360) maps of the 1920s, together with observed amendments, and enlarged to 1: 50,000 for convenience of readers' comparison with the current O.S. maps of that scale. They are serial numbered from the south end. North is at the top of each map unless otherwise marked.

3. **Inset maps** covering parts of the route, usually at 1:25,000 scale but some at six inch to mile (1:10,560) or other scales. These are derived from out of copyright six inch to the mile Ordnance Survey maps of about 1905 . The scale has been contracted to 1:25,000 as being a scale familiar to walkers and one at which one can conveniently show field boundaries . Again all maps have north at the top unless otherwise marked.The maps are numbered with a letter following the number of the 1:50,000 map of which they are an enlargement.Thus 25B is the second inset map to map 25.

Map Carrying Particular attention needs to be paid to the problems of how to frequently refer to both the Ordnance maps and to the maps and text in this guide book. Misnavigation is usually due to not looking at the maps often enough and this in turn is usually due to the physical difficulties of viewing them easily. It may be easy enough to refer to them if the weather is fine or if the user has large cagoule pockets, but what if it is raining or blowing a gale? If it is too hot to wear a cagoule or jacket will the maps go in the pockets of one's lower garment?

Ideally one needs an arrangement whereby the two maps and the text can be viewed through the transparent plastic of a bag that can be folded up and the whole affair slipped into a hip pocket when not in use. This ideal is well nigh impossible without some compromise. Map cases are usually about ten inches square and will take an O.S. map bent over, as it is not meant to be, to show two segments each side. Most map cases are too rigid to go in a pocket and have a cord so that they can be suspended round the neck. The author of this guide is one who detests such flapping cases but these can be tamed by being put under the waste strap of the rucksack. A large plastic bag that is pliable enough to fold with the map and go in a pocket is another solution. Whatever method is adopted a recent trend towards the use of two walking poles, to take 30% weight off the feet and give the arms something useful to do, all makes map reading more difficult.

A compromise that can be made is to reduce the bulk of both the O.S. map and the guide book. For a start the covers of the maps can be removed (or buy flat maps) and the maps cut in size. As regards this guide book, it has been arranged that the pages of route description and maps are in the centre of the book so that they can be removed by opening the staples. Thus only the map and description in use need be in the map carrier.

Pockets for maps can also be a problem. Walking and climbing breeches usually have good deep pockets with zip or button fastening but jeans, shorts and trousers generally have uselessly small pockets. Cutting the teeth out of zips of hip pockets and adding to pocket length is one way the author has enabled OS maps to be carried comfortably and safely in a hip pocket.

WEATHER FORECASTS

Commercial weather services can be obtained in various forms. The expensive way is by telephone though to avoid putting coins in slots acquire a BT Chargecard and dial from any number with charge to your home account.

"Weathercall" 7 day forecast at 60p per minute Telephone 09068 500 4 plus area number, S.Wales 09, Central Wales 14 and North Wales 15. For FAX service at £1.50 per minute 09065 300 1 plus 30 for Wales.

"Mountaincall" for Snowdonia, 0891 500 449 gives cloud heights, and mountain conditions, followed by longer term forecast for Wales.

"WeatherGen" website www.weathergens.co-m- Put the cursor on area required for local forecast

METRIC/IMPERIAL CONVERSION SLIDE RULE

Miles (times 10)

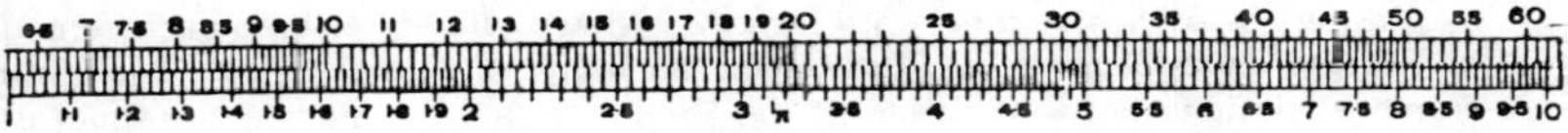

Kilometres

Miles 0.621 1 1.609 Kilometres

Metres

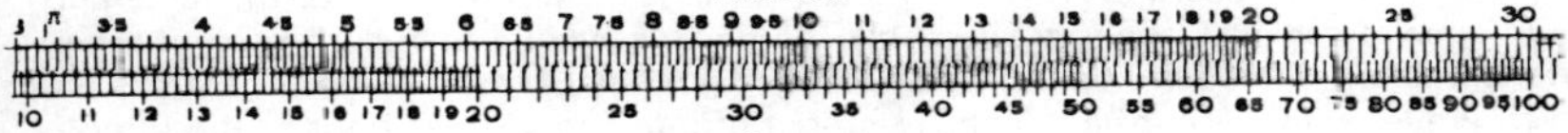

Feet

Feet 3.281 1 0.305 metres

YOUTH HOSTEL SECTION

The Cambrian Way is blessed with a chain of Youth Hostels which is more complete than was available on the Pennine Way when that trail was opened. Those who desire a roof over their heads at night will find it is almost essential to use hostels in some of the central Wales sections, and even in the heart of Snowdonia, there is only Youth Hostel accommodation at Pen-y-pass and Ogwen. At about half the price of bed and breakfast establishments they provide at least basic needs and in some cases almost luxurious facilities, together with a friendly atmosphere and understanding of walkers' needs. The facility to make a meal quite late at night, and early in the morning gives hostellers much greater flexibility than staying in commercial accommodation. Older walkers who hostelled in their earlier years will be amazed, and even horrified, to find how standards have been improved and how the higher grade and larger hostels have much greater facilities and comfort, They may, however, find the smaller simpler hostels in Central Wales more to their liking. The simple hostels of South Wales are renowned for being "what hostelling is all about", They are much underused and will go if not better patronised. School parties are only likely to be found at some of the larger hostels but not in school holidays and half terms.

Membership of YHA is necessary. 2000 fees are senior £12.00, Under 18 £6. (including accommodation guide) Membership fees can be paid at any hostel, or at YHA shops such as Cardiff, or to Head Office.

Overnight fees vary according to the scale rate for the hostel. 2000 fees on the Cambrian Way hostels vary from £6.65 at the simple hostels up to £11.90 for Conwy. Under 18 members pay about two-thirds of senior rate. Booking in advance is normally direct to the warden but a centralised booking system has been imminent for several years. There is a central number for booking at some of the smaller hostels such as Tyncornel, Dolgoch, Blaencaron and Llanddeusant (up to 7 days in advance) There is currently no booking bureau arrangement for the Cambrian Way hostels but most Hostels operate a Book a Bed Ahead system, using fax booking. Firm bookings by telephone can be made using Access or Visa cards, except for most of the smaller hostels. Reservations less than seven days in advance, without payment, can only be held until 6pm. Telephone calls to wardens should only be made during hostel opening hours and preferably not during meal times. All hostels can be full in holiday periods but larger meals provided hostels can also get booked up in May, June and early July with school parties. Note particularly that Pen-y-Pass Hostel is not open for ordinary walkers for most of May, June and July except weekends and half term. Be particularly watchful of weekly closing nights for wardens' day off and periods such as September when some hostels, such as Llanddeusant and Kings are only available for exclusive use by parties under the Rent a Hostel scheme. Very few small hostels are open in the winter months, though some, may be willing to open for parties of walkers. The smallest hostels are wardened on a voluntary basis by members who come for a week at a time. Information about openings below are generalised and liable to vary considerably from year to year.

At the hostels where meals are provided, these will either be a set evening meal at £4.80 (2000), usually at 7pm, or increasingly hostels are going over to a more flexible arrangement with "Dish of the Day", (or a vegetarian alternative) at £4.15. Starters and sweets are optional extras. Members may bring their own alcoholic drinks to the table and some hostels(e.g. Cardiff) have table licences. (bet that shook some readers !). All this is meant to tempt you not to eat at the local pub. Two sizes of packed lunches are available. All hostels have a members kitchen where utensils are provided for preparing and cooking meals. Most have refrigerators and microwave ovens. Most hostels have stores of basic food to sell but at the remoter hostels too much reliance should not be placed on them - see notes under individual hostels. Fresh milk and bread should be ordered in advance but are often available on arrival.

Camping is allowed at five of the hostels listed below at half the senior bednight fee regardless of age. Campers can use the hostel facilities but must not take hostel bedding or utensils to their tents.

Booking into hostels can be up to 10.30p.m. Hostellers are expected to be in by 11 and lights out is usually at 11.30 p.m. Many long distance walkers will find it frustrating to wait until 8.0 or even 8.30 for the hostel breakfast and prefer to get their own. Tell the warden if you want to make an early getaway. Times are generally more flexible at the smaller more remote hostels . Eighteen hostels are listed below. Some are too close together to be used by all except very slow walkers but the average keen hosteller is likely to use about thirteen. Very regrettably several hostels on or near the Way have closed down in recent years. These were Crickhowell, Bryn Poeth Uchaf, Ystumtuen, Dinas Mawddwy, Harlech, Gerddi Bluog (near Harlech), Ffestiniog, Penmaenmawr, and Colwyn Bay. Conwy is the only new hostel.

Y.H.A. OFFICES AND SHOP

Youth Hostels Association (England & Wales) , National Office, Trevelyan House, 8 St. Stephens Hill, St. Albans, Herts, AL1 2DY. Customer Services ☎.0870.870 8808. For membership & accommodation guide.

Wales Regional Office , 4th Floor, 1 Cathedral Rd., Cardiff , CF1 9HA . ☎029 20 396766 for hostel enquiries.

YHA Adventure Shop, 13 Castle St. (opposite the Castle), Cardiff, ☎029 20 399178. Open Mon-Sat. 9.30 to 5.30 (Sat. 9 - 6,Sun.11-5). For enrolments and large selection of walking and camping equipment. *YHA members get 10% discount.*

Blacks Camping & Leisure is at 17 Castle St.

YHA Website www.yha.org.uk

HOSTELS BY OR NEAR THE CAMBRIAN WAY (2000 information)

For full postal addresses see YHA Guide

Cardiff at ST184789, 2 Wedal Rd, Roath Park, Cardiff, ☎029 2046 2303. 68 beds. This hostel is very popular with the internationals, so booking can be important. EM 6 - 7pm Table licence. No closing night. Two miles from start of Cambrian Way (bus services). Open all day.

Capel-y-ffin, Black Mountains, at SO250328, 40 beds plus limited camping, ☎01873 890650 . No closing night May - Aug (see handbook), resident warden. This homely and magnificently situated hostel is in a former farmhouse converted from King George VI Memorial Fund. It is popular for pony trekking and Offa's Dyke path walkers, so booking is important. Evening meal at 7.30.

Llwyn-y-celyn (pronounced "thlcoinakellin"), Brecon Beacons, at SN973225, 40 beds, ☎01874 624261. No closing night mid April to Aug.(see handbook). Like Capel-y-ffin, this hostel was once the highest farm in its valley. Attractive surroundings with scattered natural woodland around and nature reserve nearby. Note new access from old road.

Ystradfellte (pronounced "Ustradvethta"), south of Brecon Beacons at SN925127, 28 beds, simple, ☎01639 720301. Closed Wed. & Thur. except mid-July to end of August. (Check handbook) No meals provided. No hostel shop. Shop 1 mile south. Pub meals at 930134 (check availability). Common room and one dormitory in house across the road.

Llanddeusant (pronounced "Thlandysant") at SN776245, 28 beds, simple, camping, ☎01550 740218. Bookings up to 7 days before ☎01629 581399. No closing night. No meals provided. Hot shower. Central heating. Hostel was once the Old Red Lion Inn, though it is difficult to imagine how this tiny hamlet supported a pub. No hostel shop. No bread or milk. Closed for Rent-a-Hostel up to late April and from early September.(Complain to YHA, with copy to author, if you would have used hostel during R a H period). Nearest shop 1½ miles away. Stock up at Llwyn-y-celyn or Ystradfellte or even Crickhowell.

Tyncornel, at SN751534, 16 beds, simple, no telephone. Bookings as Llanddeusant. No meals provided. No closing night. Road access is only from Llanddewi Brefi by 7 mile narrow road (rough for the last mile). Usually open mid April to early September. No hostel shop so stock up at the post office at Rhandirmwyn (next shop at Pontrhydfendigaid unless detour is made to Tregaron). Hostel is the most remote in Wales. Former farmhouse with gas lighting. Drying facilities if you light the fire. Hot shower. Wardens at this hostel are volunteers who come for a week at a time.

Dolgoch, at SN806561, 22 beds, simple, some way off the main route. ☎ 01974 298680. Bookings as Llanddeusant. No meals provided . No closing night. Volunteer warden. Gas lighting. Hot shower, small store. Payphone. Car access by very rough track. (Not through a forest as implied by 2000 handbook)

Blaencaron at SN713608, 16 beds, simple, Only open July and August. Volunteer warden. Once a primitive hostel in an old school but now much updated. No closing night. No meals provided. No hostel store. ☎01974 298199. Bookings as Llanddeusant.

Corris at SH753080, 48 beds, simple, ☎01654 761686. Privately run hostel providing meals. Small store at hostel and PO/shop in village (ECD Wed./Sat) . Another former school but with central heating. Green Tourism Award winner. No closing night. A family room is sometimes available. Showers. Corris is a former slate quarrying village in spectacular wooded surroundings. It has a railway museum and a craft centre, and 3 miles to the south is the Centre for Alternative Technology. Divergence from the main route can be made at Mynydd Ceiswyn, thence via Cwm Ratgoed and Aberllefenni making 11.3 miles from Dinas Mawddwy. Corris to Cader Idris involves a minimum of 1.2 miles of the A487 and distances are 9.1 miles to Kings (plus 2933' of ascent) and 14 miles to Barmouth.

Kings, Dolgellau, at SH683161, 56 beds, ☎01341 422392. No closing night May to Aug, but closed for Rent a Hostel from early September. Complain to Wales YHA, with copy to author, if you would have used this hostel during R a H period. House in idyllic wooded valley setting with river running through grounds. Some dormitories in outbuilding, (Check on access into house and kitchen if leaving early in morning). Members' kitchen can get congested. Strategically awkwardly placed for next night's stop unless camping on the Rhinogs (suggest easy day to Barmouth!)

Llanbedr at SH585267, 47 beds, family room, ☎01341 241287. No closing night Apr - Aug, but closed Sun & Mon Sept & Oct.. House by main road where it crosses river Artro.

Bryn Gwynant at SH641513, 67 beds, family rooms, camping, ☎01766 890251. Good drying room. Open Mar-Oct, no closing night. Magnificently situated former mansion in 40 acres of grounds overlooking Llyn Gwynant. Access from public footpath at SH643511 by courtesy path for hostellers only, waymarked by the author with white arrows. Two nights can be spent here, using the Sherpa bus service for return from Pen-y-pass, thus enabling light load over Snowdon

Pen-y-pass at SH647556, 84 beds, inc.2 and 4 bedded rooms, open all day. ☎01286 870428. Formerly a famous climbers' pub on the pass, converted and added to at great expense to become the largest hostel in Snowdonia. Mainly a school party hostel, this important staging point on the Cambrian Way is only available to ordinary hostellers Fridays, Saturdays, and bank holiday weeks April to late July, then open to end of September. Complain to YHA, with copy to author, if you would have stayed in the school party period.

Llanberis SH 574597 60 beds. ☎01286 870280, Sherpa bus from Pen-y-pass. hostel ½mile from town centre.

Idwal Cottage, Ogwen, at SH648603, 44 beds, camping, ☎01248 600225. Being converted to ideal walkers self catering hostel. Super members' kitchen. No school parties. Mountain rescue post Well situated at focal point of wild and popular mountain area. Grand scenery. Closed exc Fri. & Sat. from early September.

Capel Curig at SH726579, 52 beds, ☎01690 720225, No closing night. Useful if Idwal Cottage is full. Sherpa bus service can be used to and from Ogwen.

Rowen, North Carneddau, at SH747721, 24 beds, simple, ☎01492 650089 . A gem set half way up side of Tal-y-Fan, in an old farmhouse. Enables the long trek across the Carneddau to be broken up, leaving a half day on to the finish at Conwy. Wardens are volunteers on weekly basis. No meals provided. Open late April to August. No closing night Closed for Rent a Hostel exclusive usage from September. Complain to YHA,with copy to author, if you would have stayed there. No stores, bread or milk. Shop is 1½ miles away and 700ft below .

Conwy, at SH775773, 80 beds. ☎01492 593571. Open all day. Wales YHA's flagship hostel, previously a convalescent home, Spacious, well appointed. and with panoramic views. Half mile from castle and railway station.

TRANSPORT TO AND FROM THE CAMBRIAN WAY

RAIL

Points on Cambrian Way marked in italics.

Cardiff, main lines from London, Midlands and the North.

Conwy, on main line - London, Crewe , Chester, Holyhead.

Heart of Wales line, - Shrewsbury *Llandovery*, Llanelli, Swansea , *Cardiff.*

Cambrian Coast line, - Shrewsbury, Newtown, Machynlleth, Dovey Junc., *Barmouth*, Llanbedr, Harlech, Portmadoc, (for Ffestiniog line), Pwllheli, .also Dovey Junction, Aberystwyth, (for *Devils Bridge* line).

Llandudno Junction, (1 mile from *Conwy*), to Blaenau Ffestiniog (2m off Way).

Ffestiniog line. Portmadoc, *Dualit*, Blaenau Ffestiniog. ☎01766 512340.

Note possible return route Conwy to Barmouth via Blaenau F. and Portmadoc.

COACH and BUS

National Express,- London, Shrewsbury, *Ponterwyd*, Aberystwyth (Check re limited stops) Enquiries ☎0990 808080

National Express 390/545 London, *Conwy*, Bangor, Caernarfon, Pwllheli.

Trawscambria, - *Cardiff*, Swansea, Aberystwyth, Machynlleth, *Corris*, Cross Foxes, Dolgellau, Trawsfynydd, *Maentwrog*, Caernarfon, Bangor, Holyhead. Operated by Arriva, ☎01248 750444 (Check re limited stops).

Machynlleth to Dinas Mawddwy, Arriva No 518, Wed. and schooldays. Last bus about 15.45..

Sherpa bus services, Snowdon area - Timetable from Snowdonia N.P.(page 95)

ACCOMMODATION & SERVICES

This section includes principally bed and breakfast addresses, small hotels and camp sites, but also includes some inns providing meals, cafes, food shops, village post offices and a taxi service. Youth Hostels are listed without full detail, as they are more comprehensively covered on pages 82 to 85.

No fee or inducement has been accepted for any entry. This list is provided purely as a service to Cambrian Way walkers. Entry is entirely at the discretion of the author. Almost all have been personally visited by the author and over half have actually been used for overnight accommodation. ***Whilst every effort has been made to secure accuracy of the information provided nevertheless the author accepts no responsibity for errors or for the standards of accommodation or other services provided.***

Place names are given in capital letters followed by the postal address, and the telephone dialling code, e.g. **CAPEL-Y-FFIN,** Abergavenny, Mon. ☎ 01873

Grid References are given thus:- SO123456. A full explanation of how to read a grid reference is given on all Ordnance Survey Landranger, Outdoor Leisure, and Explorer maps.

Rooms - number of rooms in each category are given as D=double bed, T=twin beds, F= family rooms, (usually a double and one or more single beds) S=single bed. ES = en suite, i.e private toilet with bath or shower or both. Absence of ES does not mean such facilities are not available.

Prices are normally the basic bed and breakfast price per person. S before a price is for single room. The figure in brackets after the price indicates the year for which prices were last checked by the author, e.g. ('99 = 1999). Prices are liable to rise, apart from inflation, not least because of improvements such as the provision of en suite facilities.

Meals - EM means evening meal provided, EMO means to order only. It is always wise not to expect a meal if arriving without booking. The price if given is only a rough guide at the date obtained. SB = bar snacks in a pub, "Restaurant" usually means a separate dining room.

Amendment sheets to the information that follows will be issued from time to time and attached to the inside back cover, For latest information ring the author, or send a stamped addressed envelope, & 2 X 26p stamps to the address on page1.

The Cambrian Way Walkers Association is an informal group of bed and breakfast operators who provide transport to and from the Cambrian Way to enable their guests to have the same base for several nights. An information pack and logbook can be obtained from the organiser, Nick Bointon, (see under Rhandirmwyn, page 89). The Association is not a national trail membership organisation like the Offa's Dyke or South-West Way associations. **Guided walks** for strong walkers along Cambrian Way, 6 days Cader to Ogwen, then Deiniolen. are provided by **High Trek,Snowdonia,** Tal y Waen, Deiniolen, Gwynedd LL55 3NA, ☎01286 871232 . Costs for 2000 £425. **HF Holidays,** once a year, provide guided walks for (a) week on Black Mts & Brecon Beacons based on their Brecon house, and (b) for Snowdonia section based on Conwy.(see page 93)

Stilwell's National Trail Guide, (£9.95 -1999), published annually, has a 12 page section on the Cambrian Way. Its usefulness increases with time within each edition of this book.

CARDIFF, South Glamorgan. ☎029

Booking bureau, Cardiff Marketing Ltd, ☎20227281.

Youth Hostel, ST184789, 68 beds, - see separate list.

Bon Maison, 39 Plasturton Gardens, (parallel to Cathedral Rd.) CF1 9HG, ST170769, Mrs.M.A.George, ☎20383660, T2 D2 F1 £19- S£26. ('99), EMO, breakfast from 7.30.

Rambler Court Hotel, 188 Cathedral Rd, ST167773, Wendy Oxley, CF1 9JE, ☎20221187, D4 T4 F4 S3,

Cardiff Backpacker, 98 Neville St, ST175762, CF! 8LS, ☎20345577, 80 beds, B&B inc light breakfast.£12.50 (dormitory), £18 private room.

There are several hotels in Cathedral Rd area, around ST171770.

TONGWYNLAIS, Cardiff.

Three pubs and a fish and chip shop,ST133822.

CAERPHILLY, Mid Glamorgan. ☎029

Tourist Information / Visitor Centre, Twyn Square, ST157870, ☎20880011.

Lugano, Hillside, off Mountain Rd, ST155863, Mrs.M.Dowson, CF83 1HN, ☎20852672, D1 T2, S1, £22 ('99).

Yfron Guest House, Mountain View, Pwllypant, ST152888, Mrs J Morgan, CF83 3HW ☎20882896, T3 F4 £22 ('99), EM,Transport to & from Machen or Risca. by arrangement.

Travellers Rest Inn, ST158843, ☎20886894, SB, No accommodation.

RUDRY, Caerphilly, Mid Glamorgan. ☎029

Maenllwyd Inn, ST201866, SB, No accommodation.

The Coach House, 2 Twyn Sych, Rudry, ST187870, G, & E Davies, ☎20884772, D2 T3 S3. £15 - £17.50 ('99)

MACHEN, Newport, Mon. ☎ 01633

The Forge, Lower Machen, ST226879, Mrs J.M.Jones, NP1 8UU, ☎440226, D1 T1 F1, £16.50, S£18 ('99). NoEM (pub at Draethen)

NEWPORT, Mon (bus stop for Risca at Oakfield Rd, ST302879.) ☎01633

Caerleon House Hotel, Caerau Rd, ST304878, Judy Grundy & Jeff Shepherd, ☎264869, 7 rooms £20 -S£25

RISCA, Newport, Mon..

Westwood Villa Guest H'se, 59 Risca Rd, Crosskeys, ST223917, Bob & Maureen Evans, NP1 7BT, ☎ 01495 270336, S1 D3 F2 £18 - £22, S£24 EMO(lic)(99)

Darren Inn, ST234915 Gary Cook, ☎01633 612414, D1 T1 F2 £17.50 -£22 ('99) SB.

Cwmcarn Forest Drive Camp Site, (Islwyn Borough Council), ST230935, ☎01495 272001, tent £5,

CWMBRAN, Newport, Mon. ☎01633

Cwrt Henllys Country Inn & Restaurant, Henllys Village Rd, ST267940, NF44 6HX, ☎484697, D4 (ES), room £38, Br.£5.50 ('98), also SB at Dorallt Inn nearby. except Sun Ev.

PONTYPOOL,. Torfaen. ☎ 01495

Lamb Inn, ST282991, SB.

Ty Shon Jacob Farm, Coch-y-North Lane, Tranch, SO267009, Altitude 340m(1100ft), panoramic views. Mrs.A.Harris, NP4 6BP ☎757536, D1 T2 £15 to £18 including transport to and from Pontypool.

Ty'r Ywen, Mamhilad, SO 296046, Mrs Susan Armitage, ☎785200, D3 T1 ES £20, £28 with jacuzzi, ('99), EM £7. website with Cambrian Way.

Hen Felin (Mill Farm), Cwmavon, SO272052, fascinating 15th cent.farmhouse, heated indoor pool, Mr & Mrs C.Jayne, NP4 8XJ ☎774588, D2 T1 S1 £20-£25, EMO, also self catering kitchen. Exit common at SO279050.

Goose & Cuckoo Inn, SO291073, SB, rough camping, ☎ 01873 880277.

ABERGAVENNY, Mon. ☎01873

Tourist Information & National Park Centre, Monmouth Rd, SO301140, ☎857588, for accommodation lists and bookings.

Belchamps Guest House, 1 Holywell Rd, SO302139, Tom & Charlotte Moodie, NP7 5LP, ☎853204, D2 F2 S1 £18('98)

Park Guest House, 36 Hereford Rd, SO 303146, Julie Herring, ☎853715, D3 T2 F1 S1 £14 ('98), EMO 6.30pm £11.

Tyn-y-Bryn, Deriside, SO300166, Mrs Sandra Belcham, NP7 7HT,☎856682, F1(ES),T1, £20 -21,S£22-25 ('99) EMO

Ty'r Morwydd House Environment Study Centre, Pen y Pound, SO297146, ☎855959, NP7 5UD, Accom for 72, T18, S31, from £14.60 ('98)

Smithy's Bunkhouse, Lower House Farm, Pantgelli, SO304178, Neil Smith, ☎853432, sleeps 24 (2X12), bed £7, self catering, SB at pub.

Pysgodlyn Farm, SO261155, Camping. Mr.K.T.Davies, ☎853271.

PARTISHOW and LLANTHONY, Abergavenny,Mon. ☎01873

New Inn Farm, SO287217, Judy & Adrian Bull, NP7 7LT, ☎890466,D1 T1,F1 £19 ('98), EM £12.

Half Moon Inn, Llanthony, SO286279, NP7 7NN, Christine Smith, ☎890611, D4 T2 F1 - £20 S1 £22 Bunk room,4 beds £16 ('99) SB.

CAPEL Y FFIN, Abergavenny.Mon. ☎01873

Youth Hostel, SO250328, 38 beds, see separate list.

Grange Pony Trekking Centre, SO251315, Mrs.Griffiths, NP7 7NP, ☎890215, T2 F3, £22.50 ('99), EMO £12, camping.

Chapel Farm, SO254315, rough camping

PENGENFORDD, Talgarth, Powys ☎01874

Castle Inn, SO174296., Paul Mountjoy, LD3 0EP, ☎711353, D2 T1 F1 S1 £19 -22 ('99), bunkhouse B&B £12, SB, camping

CRICKHOWELL, Powys. ☎01873

Dragon Hotel, High St., NP8 1BE, SO217183, Alan & Christine Thomas, ☎810362, 17rooms (9ES),D3 T8 F3 S3, £26 - £40 ('99), Minibus transport arranged to and from Cambrian Way for stages between Cardiff and Brecon Beacons,

2 Greenhill Villas, Beaufort St., NP8 1AL, SO220182, Ian & Lona Morgan, ☎811177, D2 F1, £15 ,S £18, ('99)

Riverside Caravan & Camping Park, New Rd, SO215184, ☎810397,

TALYBONT ON USK, / ABER, Brecon,Powys. ☎01874
Abercynafon Lodge, SO 080175, Mrs J.Carr, LD3 7YT ☎676342, D1 T1 S1, £18 -£23 ('99), EMO. Access from Pen rhiw calch, SO101176, and river at SO 082173. FB awaiting replacement as at 8/99,river deep to ford after rain
Talybont, SB and B&B at.3 pubs plus hotel .
Camp site (National Park), SO105209, small basic site with water and toilets.

STOREY ARMS / LIBANUS, Brecon,Powys. ☎01874
Youth Hostel, Llwyn-y-celyn, SO973225, 46 beds, see separate list.
Tai'r Bull Inn,SN995260, L & E Williams, Libanus,LD3 8EL, ☎625849, D3 F2 £40 room, ('99) SB, restaurant.
Berth y Beili Farm, SN 002263, LD3 8ND, Mrs.R.Harris,☎623614, Accom 6 inc self cater flat, £12.50 -£15 ('99) Possible transport to Storey Arms.

YSTRADFELLTE, Aberdare, Mid Glamorgan. ☎01639
Youth Hostel, SO925127, 28 beds,see separate list.
Ty-y-Berllan, SN930134, Mrs.L.Barry, ☎722242, D3 £15 ('99), No EM,?trans.
Maes-y-ronnen,SN929135,Mrs Morgan,☎722343, D1 T1,£16.50-19('99)EMO
Food shop at Rhos filling station. Robert Tay, SN917108, ☎ 720547

GLYNTAWE, Pen-y-cae, Abercrave, Swansea, West Glamorgan. ☎01639
Dderi Farm, SN851174, Mrs.Jennifer Williams, ☎730458, F1ES £16-17 ('99)
Cooper Beech Inn, Abercrave, SN824129, SA9 1XS, ☎ 730269, £18, S21 ,SB ,Transport to and from Cambrian Way
Gwyn Arms, SN846165 ☎730310, Restaurant,
Tafarn-y-garreg Inn, SN849171, ☎ 730267 SB
Blaen Tywni Farm,SN852173, ☎730664, camping. Mrs.E.Benham.
Dan-yr-Ogof Caves camp site, SN843163, SA9, 1GF, ☎730284

LLANDDEUSANT, Llangadog,Dyfed.
Youth Hostel, SN776245, 28 beds, see separate list.
Cross Inn, SN773258, SB, camping, caravans, shop.

MYDDFAI, Llandovery, Dyfed. ☎01550
Plough Inn, SN772301,SA20 0NZ, ☎720643, D1 T1 S1 £18 ('99),SB
Erwlas, SN768307, SA20 0JB, Margaret & John Holloway, ☎720797, D1 T1 £13.50 ('99) EMO .

LLANDOVERY, Dyfed. ☎01550
Tourist Nat. Pk. Information Centre SN767343, ☎720693.
Llwyncelyn Guest House, Chainbridge, SN761347, SA20 0EP, , Mrs. Griffiths, ☎720566, D1 T3 F1 S1, £18('99), S£20, EM £11.50 (7pm).
Ash Grove, Llangadog Rd., SN761336, SA20 0DJ, Mrs Theresa Hay, ☎720136, D1 T1 F1 S1 £18 ('99)
Drovers, 9 Market Square, SN767343, Jill & Michael Blud, ☎721115, D2 T1 £18 ('99)
Erwlon Caravan Park,Brecon Rd, SN779343, Mr.& Mrs.C.R. Rees, ☎720332 camping and possibility of caravan for 1 night, all facilities.

RHANDIRMWYN, Llandovery,Dyfed. ☎01550
Royal Oak Inn, SN785437,SA20 0NY,☎760201,D1 T1 F1 S2, £22.50('98)SB
Nantybai Mill, SN774445, Anthea Jones, ☎760211, D1 T1 S1 £16 ('99) EMO
Mia'r Nant, SN786436, Mrs Price, ☎760219, D1 T1 £15 ('99).
Llanerchindda Farm, Cynghordy, SN807427, SA20 0NB, Nick & Irene Bointon, ☎750274, Capacity 24 inc D4 T4 F1 S1, ES, £24('99) EM£12, Minibus transport provided for Cambrian Way walkers to and from stages from Brecon Beacons to Strata Florida, plus mobile phone. See note page 86.
Bwlch-y-Ffin (near Llyn Brianne dam), SN795481, SA20 0PG, Bryan & Pat Williams, ☎ 760311, D1 T2 £16, EMO.('99),Transport to and from Camb.W. website - bppaw@aol..comm

Continued

Pen Rhiw Fach, SN782417, Mrs Waddon,☎760234, D1 £16 ('99), 6 berth caravan (super view), £20.for 2 + £5 per person. Transport to Royal Oak.
Camp site (Camping and Caravanning Club), SN779436, ☎05506 257,
Post Office stores,SN785437, 9am-8pm, 7days (summer), last provisions before Tregaron or Pontrhydfendigaid.`

DOETHIE & UPPER TWYI (TOWY) VALLEYS.
Tyncornel Youth Hostel, SN751534, 18 beds, see separate list.
Dolgoch Youth Hostel, SN806561, 20 beds, see separate list.

TREGARON, Dyfed ☎01974
Blaencaron Youth Hostel, SN713608, 18 beds, see separate list.
Luest Guest House, SN677597, Lampeter Rd. SY25 6HG Mrs Bull ☎298936, D2 T1 S1 £19.50 ES('99)

PONTRHYDFENDIGAID, Ystrad Meurig, Dyfed. ☎01974
Red Lion (Llew Coch), SN730665, S.Earey, ☎831232 D1 T1 F2 all ES £18.50 ('98), camping £4.
Black Lion,SN731666, P Dark, SY25 6BE ☎831550 D1 T4 ES £17.50 ('98)SB
Berthgoed, SN767653, Fillimore, SY25 6ET, ☎ 831565, selfcater fam.flat£25
Claerddu, N. of Teifi Pools, SN792687, isolated ex farmhouse renovated by Elan Valley Trust as camping barn, minimal facilities. Enquiries to Di Owen ☎ 831663 or 01597 810880

CWMYSTWYTH, Aberystwyth, Dyfed. ☎01974
Tainewyddion Uchaf, SN791750, Peg & Red Liford, (Wales Wildlife Holidays), ☎282672, T2 S2 £13 ('98)
Hafod Lodge, SN784742, SY23 4AD, J.Davis,☎282247, D2 T1 ES, £18 ('98), transport to EM.(eg Miners Arms, Pontrhydygroes)

DEVIL'S BRIDGE, Aberystwyth, Dyfed. ☎01970
Mount Pleasant, SN736769, SY23 3LB, Mike & Judith Connell ☎890219, D2 T2 S1, £21 ('98) EM £9.50, WTB 3*
Llysamaeth, SN736770, Mrs Davies,SY23 3JS, ☎890219, F1 (4 beds), kitchen, £17.50 ('99).
Erwbarfe Farm, SN749784, SY23 3JR, Mrs.Lewis,☎890251, D1 F1 £16, EM
Woodlands Camp site, SN746773, Mr R.P.Davis, ☎890233 . Tent £5.
Post Office Stores and cafe, SN738769, Mr.Birchell, ☎890228 Mon-Sat

PONTERWYD, Aberystwyth,Dyfed. ☎01970
George Borrow Hotel, SN746805, John & Jill Wall, ☎890230. 10 rooms, £22,('99) SB, and restaurant. Transport to and from Camb.W stages between Cwmystwyth and Dylife. See page 86)
Bryn-Rheidol, SN751806, Mrs A.Lloyd, SY23 3JS, ☎890212, D1 T2 £17('99)
Dyffryn Castell Hotel, SN774817, SY23 3LB Anne & Merwyn Bunton ☎890237, D2 T1 F5 S1, £22.50 ES ('98), SB .
Filling Station & shop on A44, SN748807. Next shop Commins Coch or Mallwyd., also Post Office / stores, SN750808, Mrs Hewson, No ECD.

DYLIFE, STAYLITTLE, BONT DOLGADFAN Llanbrynmair,Powys. ☎01650
Star Inn, Dylife, SN863940. SY19 7BW, Tony & Susan Banks, ☎521345, S2 D2 T2 F1, £17/18 ('99), SB. EM, Residents' lounge.
Maesmedrisiol Farm, Staylittle, SN884945, SY19 7BN, Mrs Paula .Anwyl, ☎521494, F2 , £15 ('98), EMO.£8,

continued

Cyfeiliog Guest House, Bont Dolgadfan, SN886003, SY19 7BB, Liz & Andrew Fox, ☎521231, D1 T1 F1 £18 ('98), EMO £7.50, transport to/fr CW

COMMINS COCH, CEMMAES & CEMMAES ROAD, Machynlleth,Powys. ☎01650

Gwalia, SH853048, SY20 9PU, Harry & Olivia Chandler,☎511377, D1 T1 F1, £15, EM £8 (vegetarian only), ('98), limited camping.

Cefn Goch Uchaf, SH835032, Cemmaes Road, Ian & Eirlys Harris, ☎511552, D2 T1 ES £14 EM £7 ('95), Altitude 221m, panoramic views, path from Darowen road at SH842033. Road access from Cemmaes Road.

Penrhos Arms Hotel, Cemmaes, SH839061, SY20 9PR, T.Liggett ☎511243, D3 S1, £25, S£35. SB

PO stores,Commins Coch, SH844032.Mrs Thomas, ☎ 511233, ECD Thur.

Filling station/shop, Cemmaes Road, SH820043, ☎511841, Open 8 to 8.

DINAS MAWDDWY & MALLWYD, Machynlleth, Powys. ☎01650

Tremynfa, SH857148, Mrs.D.E.Rees, ☎531240, D2 T1, £15 ('99).

Buckley Pines Hotel, SH859140, SY20 9LP, G & L Wilson, ☎531261, D4 T2 F1 S1, £20-26 ('99), SB, restaurant.

Red Lion Inn, (Llew Coch), SH859148, Mrs Jenkins, ☎531247, D2,T1 F1, £17.50 - 19 ('98), SB, restaurant.

Brigands Inn, Mallwyd, SH863125, ☎531208, D3 T4 F2 S2 £23 S£28 restaurant licence

Celyn Brithion camp site, SH861137, L.Rees, ☎531344.

Filling station / food shop / cafe, Mallwyd, SH863125

CORRIS, Machynlleth,Powys. ☎01654

Youth Hostel, SH753080, 42 beds, see separate list.

Bronwydd, Bridge St, SH755077, SY20 9SS, Sue Darbyshire-Robert, ☎761381 D1 T1 F1 , £16, EMO ('99), kitchen available .

MINFFORDD / DOLFFANOG, Talyllyn, Tywyn, Gwynedd. ☎01654

Dolffanog Fach, SH729105, LL36 9AJ, Mrs.Meirwen Pughe, ☎761235, D1,F2, S1, £22, S£25, EM £13 ('99).

Dol Einion Camp Site, SH729113, Mrs.M.Rees, ☎ 0654 761312, showers.

Cwmrhwyddfor Farm, Minffordd, SH737120, ☎761286/380, Camp site & B&B.

DOLGELLAU, Gwynedd. ☎01341

Tourist Information Centre, Eldon Sq. SH728178, ☎422888

Ivy House, Finsbury Sq. SH728177, Mr.Bamford, ☎422535, LL40 1RF, D3 T2 F1 ES £18.50 to £24.50 (ES), ('99), Restaurant.

ISLAW'R DREF, Dolgellau,Gwynedd. ☎ 01341

Kings Youth Hostel, SH683160, 56 beds, see separate list.

Tyddynmawr SH703154, Mrs Olwen Evans, ☎422331, D2 £22, S£30 ('99), WTB 4 star farmhouse, super view, transport to recommended EM.

Gwernan Lake Hotel, SH704159, ☎422488, D6 S5, £22.50('99) EM

Cader Bunkhouse, SH682169, Mr.Rhys ☎423178 or 01248 600478, Sleeps 19, £6 ('99)

ARTHOG, Dolgellau, Gwynedd. ☎01341

Graig Wen House, SH655158, LL39 1BQ, T & E Ameson, ☎250482 or 250900, D3 F1 T2 S1, £18.50 - £23, ('99), EM, (Oriental speciality), Camping park.

Garthyfog Camp Site, SH636139, quiet farm site, estuary views.

BARMOUTH,Gwynedd. ☎01341

Tourist Information Office, Old Library, Station Rd, ☎280787

Bay View, 6 Porkington Terrace LL42 1LY, SH619156, Colin & Vera Portman, ☎ 280284, D1 T2 F1 £16 ('99). EMO.

Lawrenny Lodge Hotel, SH620156, LL42 1DQ, Mr.&Mrs K.Barber,☎280466 about 8 rooms, £22('99), restaurant.

Marine Parade, SH610159, numbers 4, 5, 7 etc

CWM NANTCOL, Llanbedr,Gwynedd. ☎01341

Maes-y-Garnedd, SH642269, Mrs.Ann Evans, LL45 2PL, ☎ 241342, D1 £16, ('99), EMO.

Cefn Uchaf Farm (Cefncwmerau Uchaf on OS), SH611274, Mrs.E.O.Jones, LL45 2PL, ☎241209, D1 F1 £15 S£20,('99), No EM but transport to Llanbedr.

Craig Isaf, SH635259, Mr Jones, ☎241341, camping.

LLANBEDR & HARLECH, Gwynedd. ☎01341

TAXI service (e.g. from phone box in Cwm Nantcol at SH623262 to Llanbedr etc), D.Griffiths, Bryn Coch, Dyffryn Ardudwy, LL44 2DN, ☎247741 or mobile 07899 791919. Prior notice day before of intention to ring advisable.

Youth Hostel, Llanbedr, SH585267, 47 beds, see separate list.

Tourist Information Office, Harlech, SH581310, ☎780658

Glanwern, Llanbedr SH584270,LL45 2HL, M.& R. Fuller, ☎241292, D1 T1 F1 S1 £14, EM £4 ('99)

Byrdir Hotel, High St, Harlech, SH582310, LL46 2YA, Pat & Ken Elford ☎780316, T&D12 S3 £16 - £20 ('99) EM

The Mill, Llanbedr, SH589268, Mrs Roberts, camp site, caravans to let.

CWM BYCHAN, Llanbedr,Gwynedd.

Camping, SH646315, basic, toilets.

TRAWSFYNYDD,Gwynedd. ☎01766

Bryn Dedwydd Guest House, SH708354, B.& L.Collins, LL41 4SW, ☎540681, D1 T2 some ES, £18.50 - £19.50 ('98), EM £10.75.

FFESTINIOG, Blaenau Ffestiniog,Gwynedd. ☎01766

Tourist Information Centre, Blaenau Ffestiniog, ☎830360

Moranedd Guest House, SH704423, LL41 4LGG, Brian & Gwen Maddison ☎762734, D2 T1 S1, £19 -21 ('99) EMO.

MAENTWROG,& **GELLILYDAN** , Blaenau Ffestiniog, Gwynedd. ☎01766

Bron-y-wern, Maentwrog, SH665405, LL41 4HN,, Mrs.E.Jackson, ☎590210, D1 T1 S1, £14 ('98)

Grapes Hotel, SH665406, LL41 4HN, ☎590208, D3 S3, £25, Restaurant.

Plas Tan-y-Bwlch, (Snowdonia National Park Study Centre), SH655406, ☎590324, £21 ('99), EM £13. Availability dependant on courses.

Llechrwd camp site, SH678413, by A496, Mrs Edwards. showers.

Bryn Arms, Gellilydan, SH684396. SB, basic camping.

Pen-y-Bont stores, Gellilydan, SH687397

BEDDGELERT Gwynedd. ☎01766

Plas Colwyn, SH589482, LL55 4UY, Lynda Osmond, ☎890458, D2 T1 F2 S1 £18-20 ('99), EM restaurant, Transport for guests to and from Cambrian Way for stages between Maentwrog and Ogwen, (see page 86)

Gwesty Plas Tan-y-Graig, SH591482, LL55 4LT, John & Rae Duffield, ☎890310, F6, £15 - £22.50 ('99) EM £12.50.

Camp site, entrance over bridge (not on OS), off A498 at SH594485. spacious.

NANT GWYNANT, Caernarfon, Gwynedd. ☎01766

Bryn Gwynant Youth Hostel, 67 beds, SH641513. See separate list.

Glan Gwynant Country Guest House, SH639514, Ken Cattrell,, ☎890440 D2 T1 F1 £15 - £25 (99), EM £10. Lic.

Bryn Dinas, LL55 4NH, SH625503, Vince & Annette Webb, ☎890234. Bunk beds for 23 in house £7.95 ('99), accom for 27 in timber cabins £6.50. Sleeping bags and pillow cases provided. Kitchen in house, also in separate bunkhouse.

PEN-Y-PASS & PEN-Y-GWRYD, Nant Gwynant, Gwynedd. ☎01286

Pen-y-Pass Youth Hostel, 84 beds, SH647556, see separate list.

Pen-y-Gwryd Hotel, SH660558, LL55 4NT, Briggs/Pullee, ☎870211 & 870768, £22 - 27('99), dinner £16, Breakfast 9am.

LLANBERIS ☎01286

Accessible by Sherpa bus from Pen-y-pass (see page 85)

Tourist Information Centre, ☎870765.

Youth Hostel, SH870280, see separate list.

Snowdon Cottage, Pentre Castell, Mr. & Mrs.Cobb, SH585596. LL55 4UB, ☎872015, D1 T1 S1, £16, ('99) EMO £14 (five course) or eat in Llanberis.

OGWEN, Bethesda, Gwynedd.

Idwal Cottage Youth Hostel, SH648603, 56 beds,see separate list.

Gwern Gof Uchaf, camp site SH673603,

Gwern Gof Isaf camp site, SH685601. D & E Williams, ☎01690 720276 bunkhouse for 6 (Williams Barn), £5, camping barn for 16 £4 ('99).

CAPEL CURIG, Betws-y-Coed, ☎01690

By Sherpa bus from Ogwen to A5/A4086 junc. (some go on to Bettws -y-coed

Youth Hostel, SH726579, 60 beds, see separate list.

Bron Eryri, SH733573, LL24 0EE, Jane & Richard Salter, ☎ 720240, D3 T1 F1 ES, EM at Cobdens or Tyn-y-coed hotels nearby

ROEWEN, Conwy, ☎01492

Youth Hostel, 27 beds, self catering, SH747721, see separate list.

CONWY, ☎01492

Tourist Information Centre, Castle St, ☎592248.

Youth Hostel, SH775773, 80 beds, see separate list.

15 Cadnant Park, SH776777, LL32 8PR, Mrs.N.M.Hughes, ☎592319, D2 T1 F2 £15 ('99). Also 13 and 25 Cadnant Park and Llys Gwilym, 3 Mountain Rd

Bryn Corach, HF Holidays, Sychnant Pass Rd, SH775774, 84 beds. Bookings ☎0181 905 9558 or at short notice ☎01492 596339. Used as base for 6 days on Cambrian Way from Barmouth. (Usually in June)

GLOSSARY OF WELSH WORDS AND PLACE NAMES ON THE CAMBRIAN WAY

ABER rivermouth
ADAR bird
AFON river
AGEN ALLWEDD keyhole cave
ALLT wooded hill
BACH & FACH small
BEDDGELERT grave of Gelert
BLAEN valley head
BRYN hill
BUGEILYN sheep pasture
BWLCH mountain pass
CADAIR IDRIS Idris's chair
CAER fort
CAPEL-Y-FFIN chapel on the border
CASEG mare
CASTELL castle
CARN & GARN cairn, heap of stones
CARNEDDAU cairns
CEMAIS bend in river
CNEWR meandering stream
CNICHT knight
COCH red
COED wood
COMMINS COCH red commons
CRAIG crag cliff
CROCBEN gallows
DAU & DWY two
DU black
DDUALLT black hillside
DIAL GARREG stone of revenge
DIFFWYS wilderness,precipice
DINAS hill,fortress
DOLGELLAU meadow of the monks'- cells
DOMEN & TOMEN mound
DRUM ridge
DRWS narrow pass
DWYRYD two fords or streams
DWYGYFYLCHI two round forts
DYFFRYN CASTELL valley of the river Castell
DYLIFE floods
EGLWYS church
ESGAIR ridge
FAEN stone
FAN peak
FAWR & MAWR large
FFORDD ford
FOEL & MOEL bare hill
GABALFA ferry
GALLT slope
GARN GRON round cairn
GELLI grove
GLAN riverbank
GLAS blue/green
HAFOD summer dwelling
HARLECH beautiful rock
HENDRE winter dwelling
IS below
ISAF lower
LIBANUS Lebanon
LLAN church
LLANDDEUSANTchurch of two saints
LLETHYR slope
LLUEST TY MAWR hill farm of big - house
LLWYN-Y-CELYN holly grove.
LLWYN ONN ash grove
LLYN lake
LLYWERNOG place of foxes
MAES meadow
MAESTEG fair meadow
MAEN stone
MAENTWROG stone of Twrog
MALLWYD grey field
MINFFORDD edge of road
MOEL,MOELFRE bare hill
MYDDFAI meadow of the round hollow
MYNYDD mountain
NANT brook
NEWYDD new
NEUADD mansion
OER cold
OGOF cave
OLEU light
PANT hollow
PANTYFEDWEN hollow of birch trees
PEN peak or top.
PENMAENMAWR head of large rock
PENNANT head of stream or valley
PENGENFFORDD head of ridge road
PEN-Y-FAN top of the peak
PENYGWRYD-GWRYD length of outstretched arm
PLAS mansion
PUMLUMON (Plynlimon) five peaks
POETH hot
PONT & BONT bridge
PONTERWYD bridge of poles
PONTARFRYNACH bridge over the river MYNACH(monk),(Devils Bridge)
PONTRHYDFENDIGAID bridge of the blessed ones
PONTSTICILL bridge of the stile
PWLL pit, pool
PYSGOTWR fishermen
RHANDIRMWYN land of minerals
RHIW hillside
RHOS moorland
RHYD ford
RO-WEN white pebbles
SARN paved way
SCWD waterfall
SYCHNANT stream that dries up
TAL end
TALWRN rocky place
TALYLLYN end of the lake
TORPANTAU break in the hollows
TRAWSFYNYDD across the m'tain
TRYFAN high pointed mountain
TWYMYN feverish
TY house
TY BACH little house (toilet)
TYNCORNEL house in the corner
WAUN moorland , meadow
WAUN OER cold moorland
WEN white
YSTRAD wide valley bottom
YSTRADFELLTE valley of the MELLTE(swift)
YSGYFARNOGOD bare hill of hares
YR WYDDFA(Snowdon summit) grave

THE CHECK POINTS

To have walked the Cambrian Way route described in this guidebook it is not necessary to follow the exact route prescribed, in fact individuality is to be encouraged, provided it does not involve trespass. However, to give some yardstick of achievement the following check points must have been visited on a continuous walk, though the walk need not necessarily have been on consecutive days.

1	ST	180765	Cardiff Castle	22	SH	833136	Bwlch Siglen
2	ST	131827	Castell Coch	23	SH	711130	Cader Idris
3	ST	224900	Mynydd Machen	24	SH	620155	Barmouth Bridge
4	ST	242926	Twmbarlwm	25	SH	661258	Y Llethyr
5	SO	270119	Blorenge	26	SH	665270	Rhinog Fach
6	SO	272188	Sugar Loaf	27	SH	657290	Rhinog Fawr
7	SO	255315	Capel-y-ffin	28	SH	659347	Moel Ysgyfarnogod
8	SO	225351	Tumpa	29	SH	683359	Moelfryn
9	SO	216290	Waun Fach	30	SH	658449	Moelwyn Mawr
10	SO	207243	Pen Allt Mawr	31	SH	648467	Cnicht
11	SO	192157	Eglwys Faen	32a	SH	594462	Pont Aberglaslyn or
12	SO	012216	Pen-y-fan	32b	SH	641513	Bryn Gwynant YH
13a	SN	881191	Fan Gihirych or	33	SH	610544	Snowdon
13b	SN	408144	Blaen Nedd Isaf.junc	34	SH	643579	Glyder Fawr
14	SN	825218	Bannau Brycheiniog	35	SH	656583	Glyder Fach
15	SN	767447	Towy Bridge	36	SH	666608	Tal-y-llyn Ogwen
16	SN	740610	Garn Gron	37	SH	663631	Carnedd Dafydd
17	SN	809720	Domen Milwyn	38	SH	684645	Carnedd Llewelyn
18	SN	727782	Pontbren Plwca	39	SH	729727	Tal-y-fan
19	SN	790869	Plynlimon	40	SH	760778	Conwy Mountain
20	SN	861940	Dylife	41	SH	783775	Conwy Castle
21	SH	859149	Dinas Mawddwy				

USEFUL ADDRESSES

Ramblers Association. Central Office, 1/5 Wandsworth Rd., London SW8 2XX, 0171 339 8500. For membership details and postal sales of this book. *Welsh Office,* Ty'r Cerddwyr, High St, Gresford, Wrexham, Clwyd LL12 8PT, 01978 855148.

Offa's Dyke Association. Offa's Dyke Centre, West St., Knighton, Powys, LD7 IEN, 01547 528753. Send s.a.e. for information on Offa's Dyke Path, Glyndwr's Way, and postal sales of this book.

Snowdonia National Park Authority. Penrhyndeudraeth, Gwynedd, LL48 6LF, 01766 770274.(Sherpa bus times leaflet and Gwynedd public transport maps and timetables)

Snowdonia Society. Ty Hyll (The Ugly House) (SH 757575), Capel Curig, Betws-y-coed, Gwynedd, LL24 ODS, 01690 720287.

Brecon Beacons National Park Authority, 7 Glamorgan St. Brecon, LD3 7DP. 01874 624437

Brecon Beacons Park Society, Carn y Crochan Farm, Pontneddfechan, Glyn Neath, SA11 5UP. 01639 722461

Campaign for the Protection of Rural Wales Ty Gwyn , 31 High St, Welshpool, Powys, SY21 7JP, 01938 552525

Long Distance Walkers Association, Sec B.Smith, 10 Temple Park Close, Leeds, W.Yorks, LS15 OJJ,

Welsh Tourist Board, Brunel House, 2 Fitzalan Rd, Cardiff CF2 1UY, 01222 499909.

ABBREVIATIONS

B&B	bed and breakfast	NT	National Trust
bdy	boundary	OS	Ordnance Survey
BG	bridle gate	otw	old tramway
Br	bracken	P	car park
Bn	barn	p	limited parking
BTCV	British Trust for Conservation Volunteers	pa	path-
		PC	public convenience, toilets
Ca	cairn		
ECD	early closing day(shops)	PH	public house,inn,pub
En	enclosed	PO	post office and shop
ES	En Suite,i.e. private toilet & bath and/or shower	RA	Ramblers Association
		Qu	quarry
F	fence	Rd	road
FB	footbridge	Res	reservoir
F&C	fish and chips	Rp	road used as public path
FC	Forestry Commission	RSPB	Royal Society for the Protection of Birds
FE	Forest Enterprise(FC)		
FG	fieldgate	Ru	ruined building
Fm	farm	Sh	shop selling food
FmRd	farm road	Sn	stone
FoRd	forest road	SP	signpost
GL	green lane	Sta	railway station
HG	hunting gate (about metre wide)	Tr	track
		T	telephone call box
i	information /tourist office	Und	undefined route
ind	indistinct route	Urd	untarred road
int	intermittent path	Wm	waymarked path
KG	kissing gate	YHA	Youth Hostels Association
LS	double ladder stile	YH	Youth Hostel
MeF	square mesh fence		

KEY TO STRIP MAPS

Recommended Cambrian Way route, including Hostel and major variants

on paths or undefined **on roads**

Roads major minor

Selected other paths and side routes

Railways and stations buildings

Field boundaries, where shown camp sites

Rivers streams lakes, sea

Boundaries of inset maps on 1: 50, 000 maps

Trees deciduous coniferous

Summits churches, chapels Youth Hostels

Scales - maps with numbers only - 1: 50,000 (including 17A)

maps with numbers and letters - 1:25,000 unless otherwise stated

North is at the top of the maps unless otherwise stated

Mileage points Electric power lines

CAMBRIAN WAY The Mountain Connoisseur's Walk

5th Edition 2nd AMENDMENT SHEET January 2001

This cumulative amendment sheet is supplied free with the book as a service to Cambrian Way walkers. For information as to later amendment sheets ring the author (see page 1) or E mail to tony.drake@lineone.net. Copies of the latest sheet will be sent on receipt of an s.a.e plus 54p (2 X 27p stamps accepted as payment.)

ACCESS TO OPEN COUNTRY ! The Countryside and Rights of Way Act 2000 will open up much of the Welsh hills and mountains to walkers though not just yet. As far as Cambrian Way is concerned it should not make a lot of difference as so much is already legal or permissive access, but the de facto access enjoyed for many years on the commons and other stretches of open country will be legalised, though maybe with restrictions The devil will be in the detail and meanwhile it must be appreciated that the act will not in any case apply to cultivated land or lower fields. Cambrian Way walkers must undersstand that there is hostility in some farming circles to the right of access conception, despite the support of the Welsh Assembly. Much tact and diplomacy will be needed for walkers to get what the act intends. The act is a triumph for the devotion and persistence of the Ramblers Association since its formation but particularly over the recent years. It deserves your support. It has a new address at Camelford House, Albert Embankment, London SE1 2TW, 020 7339 8500. E mail ramblers@London.ramblers.org.uk, website www.ramblers.org.uk.

CAPEL Y FFIN. Add Pen y maes, SO 251318, Alice Field, ☎ 890477, D2 F1 £19 EM £8 Youth Hostel. Apr/June & Sept/Oct closed Wed and Thur. EM 7pm

TALYBONT ON USK Abercynafon. FB replacement may be in 2001/2

LLANDDEUSANT, Youth Hostel, delete booking number

RHANDIRMWYN Page 46 lower right corner - delete Y symbol and "SEE 21C"

Tyncornel Youth Hostel - bookings to 01629 592707
Dolgoch Youth Hostel - bookings up to 7 days before 01629 592707
Blaencaron Youth Hostel, Bookings up to 7 days as Dolgoch.

PONTRHYDFENDIGAID Delete Black Lion
Add Bryn y gors Holiday Park, SN728658, D.Sykes, tent £4, ☎831675
Add Glanbeauno (small shop) SN 730663

DEVILS BRIDGE Former PO now food shop, B&B, & day café, SN738769, D & J.Birchell, 890228, D1 S2 £17.50 (00). EM at Hafod Hotel SN 741770

PONTERWYD Delete Bryn Rheidol

Kings Youth Hostel - self catering except for groups Apl-July. Advance booking through Llanbedr Youth Hostel
Rowen Youth Hostel - book through Conwy Youth Hostel